Sibling Loss

Joanna H. Fanos
National Center for Human
Genome Research,
National Institutes of Health

LEA LAWRENCE ERLBAUM ASSOCIATES, PUBLISHERS
1996 Mahwah, New Jersey

Lawrence Erlbaum Associates, Inc., Publishers
10 Industrial Avenue
Mahwah, New Jersey 07430

Cover design by Gail Silverman

Library of Congress Cataloging-in-Publication Data

Fanos, Joanna H.
    Sibling loss / Joanna H. Fanos.
        p.   cm. —
    Includes bibliographical references and index.
    ISBN 0-8058-1777-8 (c : alk. paper). — ISBN 0-8058-
1778-6 (p : alk. paper)
    1. Death—Psychological aspects. 2. Brothers and
sisters—Death—Psychological aspects. 3. Children—Death. 4. Bereavement—Psychological aspects.
5. Terminally ill children—Family relationships.   6.
Parents of terminally ill children—Psychology. I. Title.

BF789.D4F36 1996
155.9 ‘ 37 ‘ 0855—dc20   95-49698
                                                    CIP

Books published by Lawrence Erlbaum Associates are printed
on acid-free paper, and their bindings are chosen for strength
and durability.

Printed in the United States of America
10 9 8 7 6 5 4 3 2 1

*To my Father and Mother
and to my sister Judy (1939–1960)*

Contents

Foreword

This is a superb book. It is based on extensive interviews, careful and complete mastery of existing literature, and the research of others. It is a significant contribution to our understanding of mourning, childhood and adolescent psychology, and of specific diseases, particularly cystic fibrosis. Dr. Fanos extends this research to study siblings of HIV-infected children and now into other genetic and genetically influenced disorders. She synthesizes many ideas from different fields and addresses this complexity in a meaningful way without being simplistic or reductionist.

It was a privilege to meet Dr. Fanos, discuss her ideas with her, and appreciate her earlier and her ongoing contributions. Her research has been "hands on"; for example, she went to visit her respondents in various parts of the country. Her tact and empathy, together with her excellent scientific approach, comes through not only in her writings but also in her face-to-face discussions.

There are many areas covered—trauma, loss, coping, and development, as well as research methodology, her samples, contacts, procedures, interview guide, her rating scales, and the statistical quantitative treatment of her data.

This volume, already a classic before publication, will serve many purposes. It is recommended to all mental health researchers and clinicians.

—*George H. Pollock, MD, PhD*

Preface

We understand that a parent's loss of a child is one of the most devastating experiences that one can confront. What is overlooked, however, is that when a child dies, siblings experience a unique loss of their own, with little societal recognition of the impact. We know very little about what it is like for these siblings. Unstudied by researchers, unseen by medical caregivers, unnoticed by grieving parents, these siblings represent the invisible part of the drama when there is a seriously ill child in a family.

The emerging incidence of chronic illness in youngsters poses serious psychosocial challenges. Many different chronic and/or fatal illnesses afflict young people, with resultant effects on their families, including their well brothers and sisters. Technological advances, pharmaceutical treatments, and earlier diagnoses have allowed children with serious illnesses to live into their teens and beyond. An appreciation of the enormity of the impact on the family and the well siblings has not kept pace with such remarkable medical breakthroughs. Although the severity of the impact on siblings is beginning to be acknowledged in the literature, there has been little understanding of exactly how exposure to chronic illness and death of a sibling generates subsequent difficulties.

The disease I selected to investigate in the mid-1980s was cystic fibrosis (CF), for the following reasons: (a) It is often fatal and frequently chronic, (b) it profoundly shapes family functioning over a long period of time, and (c) it is the most common fatal inherited disorder of Caucasian children today, affecting approximately 30,000 children and young adults (Cystic Fibrosis Foundation, 1995). I hoped that this disease—as it was in the 1980s—could be a useful model for the impact of sibling loss to illness, and would illuminate both the impact of having a chronically ill child on siblings as well as the impact of the inevitable loss itself. Because I wanted to understand the long-term effects, and how the well siblings' experience had shaped their lives as adults, I decided to talk to people who had lost a sibling many years ago. In the past 10 years since this study began, the disease itself has changed and presents a much more hopeful picture. With more sophisticated medical treatments available, the average life span of an individual with CF is currently 29 years, and increases each year. But for the families in this study, a diagnosis was dreaded news, as the child was not expected to live beyond his or her teen years.

When I began the process of obtaining permission from human protection committees and funding for the study, reactions were guarded. Hospital committees were uncertain. They worried that asking siblings to talk about their experience would cause further trauma. One granting agency predicted that I would not find enough individuals who would be willing to talk. Friends were concerned that it would be too depressing for me to deal with day after day.

My experience was just the opposite. In 1984, I was able to locate and interview 75 adults who, during childhood, adolescence, or adulthood, had lost a sibling to CF. During the 1960s and 1970s, the ill children had been treated at Children's Hospital, Boston; Children's Hospital, Oakland; and the University of California, San Francisco. The 75 participants, whose names have been changed to preserve confidentiality, represent more than twice the number of individuals I anticipated being able to interview. The willingness, indeed the eagerness, on the part of these individuals to talk about their experience was extraordinary. I was moved by the generosity of spirit of these adults, some of whom had lost two or three siblings to this devastating illness.

Many could not travel the long distances from their home to the Boston clinic, so I went to them. I took trains and buses and drove thousands of miles around California, Maine, New Hampshire, Massachusetts, Vermont, Connecticut, Rhode Island, and New York. I spoke with lawyers in the city and dairy farmers in the Berkshires. I talked with mill workers along the rivers in Massachusetts and veal farmers in the gracious countryside of Connecticut.

The enormity of psychological and somatic problems that I encountered in this population of young adults was very disturbing. I was not able in this study to explore the myriad of problems besetting the young adults I came across who are themselves afflicted with CF and who have already watched their sisters and brothers succumb to this disease, nor study the seemingly unrelenting pain of the parents who have to live on after spending 20 years watching their child die, the frustration of the physicians, and the loneliness of the young children who died alone because no one could face speaking with them of their dying.

A few siblings came through this very difficult experience stronger and more resilient. In those families in which there seemed to have been good emotional support for the surviving child (both during the long illness and following the death), there was an ability to help the child mourn and to contain the illness experience to the sick child. In short, surviving siblings seemed able to mourn the loss and get on with their lives. However, most families faltered in one or more ways, and siblings were still struggling, 15 and 20 years later, with the loss. Difficulties included interpersonal prob-lems, problems in school, alcoholism and drug abuse, automobile accidents, severe nightmares, hypochondriasis, depression, and chronic guilt, to name only a few.

In 1989, the CF gene was identified. The identification of the CF gene (Rommens et al., 1989) allows for direct genetic testing in most CF-affected families and possibly in the general population. The ramifications are only now being felt as people are faced with decisions about whether or not to be tested (Fanos & Johnson, 1993, 1994, 1995a, 1995b). Parents are uncertain about whether or when to have their well children tested for CF carrier status (Wertz, Fanos, & Reilly, 1994). In early 1993, the first experimental gene therapy treatment was given to a patient with CF, and currently gene therapy studies are underway. But for the individuals in this book, siblings had no way of finding out whether or not they were carriers of the gene for CF.

CONTENTS OF THIS VOLUME

Chapter 1 sets the problem in theoretical context. I review the literature on the effects on the parents of having a fatally ill child, the impact of parental mourning on surviving children, children's reactions to the loss of a parent, and children's reactions to the loss of a sibling.

Chapter 2 places the sibling in the family setting and describes the economic and emotional impact of having a chronically ill child on their parents. Frequent parental responses to the strain imposed by the illness are illustrated and their impact on the sibling discussed.

Chapter 3 discusses the ways in which the illness experience of the child alters the sibling relationship. For some siblings, jealousy over the attention the sick child received created distances between them, for others the attachment bond was forged deeper. Many different roles were lost when the sibling died—a best friend, a vital link, a surrogate parent, a role model, and the irreplaceable role of "sibling."

Chapter 4 discusses the ways in which communication around the illness and possibility of early death were handled within the family. Developmental levels in the ability to understand the illness, with their important ramifications, are explored. The communication in most families was very veiled and siblings grew up with a family secret, which paved the way for the death to be shocking and traumatic.

Chapter 5 traces the impact of the actual death of the individual on the sibling. The death was a devastating experience for almost all the siblings

I interviewed. In fact, it bore all the earmarks of a traumatic event in the lives of these individuals, giving rise to many of the sequelae associated with posttraumatic stress disorders. Although reactions among siblings bore similarities, there were concerns and responses that appeared to be related to developmental capacities.

Chapter 6 discusses typical responses on the part of the parents to the loss of the child and their impact on the surviving siblings. Idealization, substitution, memorialization, and refocusing on the surviving child are seen as ways of defending against the work of mourning. Fathers and mothers tended to cope differently, causing problems within the relationship. Parental redirection of anger and blame onto surviving siblings is discussed.

Chapter 7 recounts the ordeal of the ensuing weeks and months following the death of the sibling. Although many concerns were shared by all siblings, some issues were emphasized depending on the individual's developmental stage at the time the loss occurred.

Chapter 8 explores the high degree of chronic anxiety that survivor siblings demonstrated. Van der Kolk (1987) pointed out that traumatized individuals have difficulty controlling anxious and aggressive feelings. Unavoidable traumatic memories seek expression in various forms, including nightmares and somatic disturbances.

Chapter 9 examines dissociative processes that seem to have been set in motion in survivor siblings due to the death. Eth and Pynoos (1985) stressed that traumatized individuals cannot mourn until the traumatic elements have been resolved. Individuals in my sample show very little evidence of having completed the necessary grief work. The role of parents, locked in their own inability to relinquish the lost child, is examined; defenses against experiencing guilt are explored.

Chapter 10 explores the complex issue of guilt experienced by survivor siblings. Issues related to a global sense of guilt, guilt over handling of illness and death, and survival guilt are examined; defenses erected against experiencing guilt are explored.

Chapter 11 discusses some positive aspects for growth on the part of survivor siblings. Creative solutions—with varying degrees of success—to work through and master the loss through occupational choice and relationships are illustrated by case examples.

Chapter 12 explores the role of the health professional; the reasons why the medical system fails siblings are discussed. Preventive measures within pediatric health care settings are recommended, including suggestions made by the siblings themselves, and treatment methods suggested.

The appendix discusses the sample, the contact procedures, the interview guide, the rating scales that were developed, and the quantitative treatment of the data. A smaller sample of 25 siblings was drawn from the complete sample in order to avoid confounding of variables for statistical analyses, and the the sampling criteria are described. Results from statistical analyses are presented.

ACKNOWLEDGMENTS

This study was made possible through the compassion and enthusiasm of many people. Anna Freud and Erik Erikson gave me encouragement when I most needed it, right at the beginning. The faculty of the Human Development Program, especially Irving Rosow, director, gave support throughout the work and provided much appreciated office space. I would like to thank the members of my dissertation committee: Norman Livson, for being such a constant mentor and friend; Robert Wallerstein, for protecting and furthering the work and for accepting his role as ego ideal of psychoanalytic researcher with such elegance and grace; and most of all Morton Lieberman, chairman, for encouraging, supporting, and skillfully guiding the work throughout, and for instilling a deep respect for a highly cautious and critical approach to one's data. Funding was provided by an Officer's Discretionary Award from the William T. Grant Foundation, a Mary Singleton Sigourney Award for Psychoanalytic Research through the Department of Psychiatry, University of California, San Francisco (UCSF), and a Children's Hospital Foundation Award through the Cystic Fibrosis Clinic at Children's Hospital, Oakland. A Chancellor's Fellowship for Excellence in Research gave me the freedom to concentrate on the task at hand. More recently, a grant from the Ethical, Legal, and Social Implications Branch, National Center for Human Genome Research, National Institutes of Health, provided financial support, while emotional support was provided by Dr. Kenneth Cox, Dr. Robert Hales, and David Fielder at California Pacific Medical Center, San Francisco. Finally, a Visiting Investigator Award to the National Center for Human Genome Research, National Institutes of Health, in the Medical Genetics Branch, gave me time to put the finishing touches on the manuscript.

So many others have helped: Charles Binger, Frank Johnson, Harvey Peskin, George Pollock, George Silberschatz, Albert Solnit, Philip Spielman, Dennis Weiss, Robert Weiss, and Peter Wolff all gave enthusiastic support. Theoretical conversations with Calvin Settlage were always a delight. Nancy Bliwise's generosity with time and statistical advice can never be repaid. Phyllis Olsen and Leslie Delehanty dispensed practical and emotional support in timely measures. Alison Cormak made what could have been an arduous task of rating enjoyable. Judi Amsel, Kathy Dolan, and Robin Weisberg, at Lawrence Erlbaum Associates, ably steered the manuscript through its final phases, and Maggi Mackintosh and Rachel Spiegel provided greatly appreciated help with the final editing. Cover artist, Gail Silverman, captured in form the essence of the book.

Deep thanks to the caring and dedicated physicians who generously gave their time, resources, and memories: Louise Yeazell and Christopher Newth of UCSF, Bruce Nickerson, John McQuitty, Herm Lipow, John Whalen, and Alan Mitchell of Children's Hospital, Oakland, and Harry Shwachman of Children's Hospital, Boston. Special thanks go to Bruce Nickerson for providing a nest for the first trimester of developing scales and for providing enthusiastic support throughout. The late Dr. and Mrs. Shwachman were models of dedication, inspiring in placing themselves squarely and steadfastly in the midst of human suffering.

I would like to thank, above all, the courageous siblings themselves, who invited me into their homes and into their lives, who wanted so much to understand themselves and to help others.

—*Joanna H. Fanos*

Chapter 1

The Problem

Two charming little sisters were brought to me,
one very sick.

—Harry Schwachman, MD (1950)

This book explores the long-term consequences on adult adjustment of chronic illness followed by the death of a sibling. The illness and loss of the child will have a direct impact on the siblings, depending on their own capacity to give meaning to its occurrence and to mourn the loss effectively. In addition, the well sibling's world is inexorably shaped by the parents' handling of the illness and loss.

The death of a child has generally been considered to be one of the most stressful events encountered by families in our society (Futterman & Hoffman, 1973). The chronicity of illnesses such as cystic fibrosis (CF) is in a sense new, an outgrowth of recent advances in medical treatment that have considerably extended the lives of children stricken with leukemia, CF, diabetes, and the like.

The psychological literature is largely descriptive, focusing on the reactions of mothers, a captive research pool as they brought their children to the clinic for medical treatment. Much less is known of the impact on fathers, and even less on healthy siblings. Although there is a vast psychoanalytic literature on the childhood loss of a parent (see Miller, 1971, for an excellent review), the psychoanalytic literature on the effects of a child's death is very limited. This is particularly surprising because there have been implications of sibling death in the etiology of schizophrenia (Blum & Rosenzweig, 1944; Rosenzweig, 1943). As Cain, Fast, and Erikson (1964) complained:

We have barely progressed beyond the time when lengthy, intensive psychiatric case studies could note in a passing sentence that "one of the patient's

1

siblings died when he was four" and omit any further reference to the event's meaning to the patient. Similarly, current studies showing a sharp awareness of the complex reactions of parents to the death of a child may omit any mention of the impact of the death upon other family members. (pp. 741–742)

In the psychoanalytic literature on sibling death, rivalry-bred guilt has been the exclusive focus of theoretical interest since Freud (e.g., Berman, 1978). Although this theory may well explain Freud's own reactions to the death of his younger brother Julius when Freud was 19 months old (Pollock, 1972), it remains mute before the myriad complex and longlasting psychological difficulties found by investigators such as Cain et al. (1964). As they pointed out at that time:

Our growing case material soon served to demonstrate the limitations of perhaps the one notion of any currency about the import of sibling death, namely, the concept that the primary if not exclusive pathological impact of a sibling's death upon the surviving child is one of guilt over rivalry-bred hostile wishes which, through the early omnipotence of thought, are seen as having been fulfilled by and responsible for the sibling's death. (p. 742)

Our focus on the loss of a chronically ill sibling offers us a unique and fertile opportunity for observation. We can begin, as it were, at the beginning, and gain some understanding into those effects that arise from the chronic strain of illness of the child apart from those that arise from failures at negotiating the task of mourning. Do the demands of living with a sick child set into motion processes that hinder adaptation to the new situational demands that arise following the death of the child? Are the pathological effects observed in some children related to the bereavement itself or to the prolonged absence of a depressed or overwhelmed parent from certain critical roles? Does the actual loss of the sibling represent only the loss of a competitive figure, or does it signify the loss of other possible roles as well?

STATEMENT OF THE PROBLEM

The aim of the study reported here is to examine the consequences on adults of growing up with a sibling who was chronically ill and ultimately died before adulthood. Although the severity of the impact has been noted in the literature (Cain et al., 1964), there has been little understanding of how exposure to chronic illness and death of a sibling generates these effects.

Some problems, I expect, would arise from the impact of the death itself. Effects would arise in two ways: directly, through the sibling's own understanding of the nature of the death, largely dependent on his or her developmental level and capacity to interpret its cause and to mourn its occurrence; and indirectly, in that the capacity of the parents to mourn effectively and completely will dictate the ability of the parents to provide a healthy, nurturing environment for survivor siblings.

I would expect other problem areas to arise from the necessity of dealing with the chronic illness of the child. Although the death of the sibling may be traumatic for the surviving children, the reorganization that takes place within the family as it struggles to cope with the long years of the illness may be equally serious. I view the disease as initiating responses in advance of the ultimate death, particularly on the part of the parents, that create a developmental environment for the children that is far from a normal one. The withdrawal of emotional resources from the well sibling may have serious and adverse effects on adaptation.

THE DISEASE

Cystic fibrosis is the most common fatal genetic disease in the United States today. It is an inherited disease that affects the exocrine glands of the body. In CF, the mucus-producing glands secrete a thick, sticky mucus that tends to clog and block ducts, interfering with vital functions such as breathing and digestion. The basic defect in CF cells is faulty transport of sodium and chloride within epithelial cells, which line organs such as the lungs and pancreas, to their outer surfaces. In the United States in the mid-1990s, approximately 30,000 children and young adults are afflicted with the disease. About 1,300 new cases are diagnosed each year, generally by the time the child reaches age 3. Equally common among males and females, CF was long considered a disease fatal in childhood; however, research accomplishments have increased the life expectancy for a person with CF to 29 years old.

Affecting 1 in every 2,500 live-born White newborns, CF is the most common lethal genetic disease among White children; Blacks are affected less frequently, and the disease is rare among Asians. Recognized as a distinct disease only since 1938, CF is now being diagnosed with increasing frequency throughout the world. The diagnostic test for CF is the sweat test, which measures the amount of salt in the sweat. Although carriers can pass this trait on to their children, they themselves are symptom free. Treatment for CF is expensive and time consuming and depends on the stage of the disease. The regimen consists of a variety of antibiotics to combat lung infections, supplemented by physical therapy and inhalation therapy or postural drainage methods to help remove mucus from the lungs (Cystic Fibrosis Foundation, 1995).

THEORETICAL BACKGROUND

This section briefly reviews the literature on the effects on parents of having a child who is seriously ill, the impact of parental mourning on the surviving children, children's reactions to loss of a parent, and children's reactions to loss of a sibling.

The Parent–Child Relationship

The experience of having a fatally ill child represents perhaps the enactment of the worst fear of any parent. Even researchers, working with families with dying children, make their way through bouts of depression and visits to therapists (Binger, personal communication, February 20, 1981).

One of the earliest studies of leukemia, perhaps the most researched disease in psychosocial studies of this area, was undertaken by Bozeman, Orbach, and Sutherland (1955) to determine how mothers adapt to the threatened loss of their children from leukemia. Intensive focused interviews of 20 mothers of afflicted children showed maternal reactions to the threatened loss of their children to be severe, with much expressed guilt. Natterson and Knudson (1960) studied the mothers of 33 children diagnosed with cancer, leukemia, or blood disease. During the end phase of their children's illnesses, almost half the mothers were tense or had a strong tendency to weep and cling to hope; when the children actually died, these mothers reacted hysterically. Binger et al. (1969) undertook a retrospective study of parents of 20 children who had died from leukemia between 1964 and 1966. In half the families, one or more members had emotional disturbances that were sufficiently severe to require psychiatric help, although none had required such help before; in other families, milder disturbances occurred. Fathers, a group neglected in most studies in this area, were coping by various ways of absenting themselves from involvement with their families, with profound ramifications for their wives and children. Futterman and Hoffman (1973) conducted extensive open-ended interviews with 23 sets of parents of children with leukemia during various points during the course of the illness and after the death. They described a number of dilemmas confronting parents in adapting to the fatal illness of their children. Parents must work out a balance between conflicting tasks such as attending to immediate needs of the child and planning for the future; cherishing the child and allowing him or her to separate; and caring for the child while preparing for his or her death through gradual detachment. If it seems extremely difficult to achieve these kinds of delicate balances for a relatively short interval of time, the difficulties arising when the length of time is far greater such as is the case with CF, can be imagined. A child with CF frequently lives until early adulthood.

Although far less investigated than leukemia, the literature on the impact of CF is much more pessimistic. Turk (1964), in a study of 28 parents from 25 families with a child afflicted with CF, described the difficulties for families as they struggle to care for their ill child. Lawler, Nakiekny, and Wright (1966), in an intensive psychiatric study of 11 families of patients with CF, found 8 of the 11 mothers showed symptoms in interviews of being clinically depressed, and the majority said they felt that they were "living in the shadow of death" (p. 1044). The fathers showed unusual incidence of psychopathology; many had ulcers. Tropauer, Franz, and Dilgard (1970) studied 20 children with CF and 23 mothers and confirmed the high degree of maladaptation in mothers. Leiken and Hassakis (1973), selecting 4 parents from a CF clinic for clinical discussion, pointed out how the adaptive balance is necessary once again. The "doing defense" (p. 55) can be helpful, but if overdone, the parents rarely see each other and are not available to give each other support. The commonly used defense of suppression also can be problematic. These parents must maintain an ability to suppress freely and frequently. Families must think of the death of their child very rarely. They must suppress or even deny, at times, that the future is filled with uncertainty. However, massive suppression or denial can be only ineffective in coping with anxiety and also can cause interference with medical care.

More recent studies of families coping with a child with CF have reported similar difficult stresses. Phillips, Bohannon, Gayton, and Friedman (1985) found 10% to 15% of the parents described major problems related to their marital relationship, feeling guilt about not doing more for their child with CF, and concerns for their other children. Quittner, Di Girolamo, Michel, and Eigen (1992) found that mothers reported greater strain than fathers in managing their caregiving role and reported higher levels of depression. Bluebond-Langner (1991a) identified the various strategies that families use in order to contain the intrusion that the disease makes into the life of the family. Patterson, Budd, Goetz, and Warwick (1993) stressed the importance of encouraging families to balance their resources between the child's needs and the needs of the family.

Families adjust to the serious illness of a child in a variety of ways. Two main coping mechanisms would appear to be normalizing as much as possible and restricting perspective.

Normalize as Much as Possible.   There is a social stigma inevitably associated with having hereditary disorders (Gordon & Kutner, 1965), and this must be managed as effectively as possible (Birenbaum, 1970). Most families attempt to achieve a balance between using other afflicted families as a reference group and maintaining themselves as part of normal society. Within the family, the sick child is treated as normally as possible within the confines of his or her illness, and with objective losses minimized. Necessary restrictions on activities are generally placed for all children alike, preparation of medication becomes a game, and so forth, in an attempt to make this routine.

The increased caretaking burden on the mother initially falls within the rubric of her natural role as mother. The family attempts to retain impressions of normality within the community as far as possible, and friends may be dropped if they do not demonstrate a careful "inattention" to certain facts about the family (Birenbaum, 1971). As the child ages, however, this becomes more problematic. The central goal of the conventional parent–child relationship is one of greater independence of the child. As the sick child grows older, however, the parent's role becomes increasingly discrepant from parental roles in "normal" society. In conventional families, change in relationship is constant, as parents look forward to seeing their children establish their own households, and as they themselves look forward to becoming grandparents, perhaps anticipating some degree of dependence on their children when they reach old age. The continued use of the early parent–child relationship when the ill child is in adolescence or early adulthood conveys the impression noted by Birenbaum (1971) of "forever crystallized relationships" (p. 64).

Through the desire to spare the feelings of the sick child as well as to normalize the experience within the family, restrictions that are necessary for the survival of the sick child may be applied to all the children alike, so the healthy siblings may be treated as though they, too, were sick, and they may end up believing they are. Due to the confusion surrounding the illness, siblings grow up with distorted concepts of illness, death, and the relationship between the two. Siblings have learned firsthand that rare things are not so rare, that statistical odds are meaningless experientially, and that if something bad can happen, it will. Their own survival may be perceived as by capricious luck rather than by any mastery on their part, similar to the perception of survival by the concentration camp survivor (Benner, Roskies, & Lazarus, 1980).

Restrict Perspective. The capacity to change the environment is severely limited; thus individuals are forced to rely on intrapsychic modes of coping that are essentially palliative in function. Heavily used defenses such as suppression and denial wrap the entire family in the chronic "web of silence" described by Turk (1964). Unfortunately, what this can mean for the children is a learning experience of denial and suppression to problems rather than an experience in meeting difficulties head on and mastering them.

Suppression of the ultimate outcome is necessary on a continued daily basis. The goals become keeping death at bay a little longer, increasing the value in living for the moment (Futterman & Hoffman, 1973), and centering achievement on survival. Fathers who, prior to learning the prognosis, had been considering vocational changes postponed any decisions, mothers found it impossible to make decisions about future pregnancies, and so on (Bozeman et al., 1955). The contraction of the future corresponds to a gradual curtailment of hope. If in the beginning of the illness there is hope for a cure, toward the end, as Friedman, Chodoff, Mason, and Hamburg (1963) pointed out, there is only hope for one more remission or one more good day. Such essential coping strategies as contraction of the future and curtailment of hope rearrange priorities for the sick child, for whom achievement is defined as survival, and living for the moment becomes less a hedonistic creed than the most reasonable *modus operandi* available.

Because the reason underlying this massive restructuring of expectations is not explicit (through suppression, denial, desire to spare the feelings of the sick child, and attempts to appear as normal as possible) this orientation generally spills over onto the entire family, including healthy siblings, and especially younger ones, who have had no previous exposure to a healthy upbringing. If the healthy sibling understands that he or she is indeed healthy, he or she may wish to be sick in order to gain parental attention. Illness has come to be seen as the only route to the inaccessible mother (Tropauer et al., 1970). Because the future is rarely discussed in the family, growing up is inextricably associated with dying and parenting is seen as problematic at best, there is little socialization into future adult roles within the nuclear family. At the same time, there may be inadvertent socialization into a sick role.

We are reminded of Parsons and Fox's (1952) conceptualization of illness as both a psychological disturbance and a deviant social role. The deviant unit, set in the middle of an isolated nuclear family, might be expected to have widespread ramifications. Deviance is usually controlled within the social structure by a complex system of mechanics, as Parsons (1951) elucidated:

> Very broadly these may be divided into the three classes of a) those which tend to "nip in the bud" tendencies to development of compulsively deviant motivation before they reach the vicious circle stage, b) those which insulate the bearers of such motivation from influence on others, and c) the "secondary defenses" which are able, to varying degrees, to reverse the vicious circle processes. (p. 321)

In the situation of chronic illness, the sick child (a) is not responsible for his or her deviance; (b) is cared for primarily within the family unit itself, and is therefore not at all isolated from influencing others; and (c) sets a machinery of defenses in motion that serve psychological needs, not control of deviance. Because the child will never get well, he or she is under no role obligation to "recover," allowing for the "contamination" elaborated by Parsons and Fox (1952). Here, deviance is allowed to set the norm, and change may follow. The situation tends to grow worse as the child becomes more ill. Parents feel increasingly excluded from the normal community (Gordon & Kutner, 1965); friends drop by less and less (Turk, 1964); fathers absent themselves from their families in order to hide their pain (Binger et al., 1969); communication between husband and wife flounders as blame is shifted back and forth (Gordon & Kutner, 1965); and family integration, seriously endangered, frequently breaks down (Crain, Sussman, & Weil, 1966).

Researchers have investigated the impact of different communication styles within families that have children suffering from various diseases, including cancer (Spinetta & Maloney, 1978), CF (Fanos, 1987), and HIV (Hardy, Armstrong, Routh, Albrecht, & Davis, 1994). An open communication style, which is characterized by parents being available and honest with children if they wish to talk about their illness, has been found to enhance the coping strategies of both children suffering from pediatric cancer and their parents (Koocher & O'Malley, 1981). In addition, better overall psychological adjustment in the family has been related both to an open communication style and to emotional expression (Koch, 1985; Spinetta & Maloney, 1978). Providing information about a child's illness and treatment program to the healthy siblings of patients with cancer has also been related to better coping (Kramer, 1984). Unfortunately, in most families with chronically ill children, communication about the disease and its implications tends to be closed (Mellins & Ehrhardt, 1993; Turk, 1964). For example, researchers studying both CF (Fanos, 1987) and pediatric HIV (Mellins & Erhardt, 1993) found that most parents do not talk about the child's illness with the affected child. Hardy et al. (1994) found that only 20% of their sample of HIV-infected children had been informed of their diagnosis. This lack of communication impacts not only the adaptation of individual family members but also affects the relationships between members. Tasker (1992) explored the complexities of disclosure in pediatric HIV. Fanos and Wiener (1994) discussed how this enforced silence negatively impacts both the parent–child and sibling relationships, and may even threaten healthy development for healthy siblings.

Mourning in Children and Adolescents

The actual death, no matter how well prepared for, always comes, in some measure, unexpectedly. Although some anticipatory mourning operates, over long years parents report that they stopped believing their child would die, a suspension of belief aided by friends and relatives who do not allow the parents to give up hope (Friedman et al., 1963). To the healthy siblings, both those who know and those who do not know that the child is dying, death can come as an enormous surprise.

Freud (1917) pointed out that there is a psychological process normally exhibited by individuals who experience the loss of an emotionally important person: "Each single one of the memories and expectations in which the libido is bound to the object is brought up and hypercathected, and detachment of the libido is accomplished in respect of it. ... When the work of mourning is completed the ego becomes free and uninhibited again"(p. 245). Later (1926) he explained that the work of mourning is the appropriate response to a situation in which the individual is forever lost:

> Mourning occurs under the influence of reality-testing; for the latter function demands categorically from the bereaved person that he should separate himself from the object, since it no longer exists. Mourning is entrusted with the task of carrying out this retreat from the object in all those situations in which it was the recipient of a high degree of cathexis. (p. 172)

Writers following Freud have conceptualized mourning as a regular sequential process occurring in more or less distinct stages: the initial stage of shock, the grief reaction, and the separation reaction in which the inner representation of the object is clearly restructured from a representation of a reality to one of a memory (Bowlby, 1961a, 1961b; Engel, 1961; Pollock, 1961).

Freud (1918, 1927), Abraham (1924), Klein (1940), Lindemann (1944), Bergler (1948), Loewald (1962), and Moriarty (1967) observed significant deviations from the "normal" process of mourning. The response of children to the death of an important other is seen as very similar to pathological forms of mourning as they occur.

A number of investigators attempted to conceptualize the mourning process within a systematic developmental framework. An issue of major concern has involved the age or developmental stage at which human beings are capable of a mourning process. Exponents of this view hold that the process of mourning, involving as it does the tolerance of powerful painful affects and repeated demands for reality testing in opposition to strong wishes, requires the operation of ego functions to which the child does not yet have firmly established access. Mourning, according to this view, does not occur in children of preadolescent age (Deutsch, 1937; Fleming & Altschul, 1963; Rochlin, 1965; Wolfenstein, 1966, 1969). Although the primary function of the mourning process is to detach the survivor's memories and hopes from the dead, the reactions to object loss in children are seen as having an equally precise but contrary aim, namely to avoid the acceptance of the reality and emotional meaning of the death and to maintain in some internal form the relationship that has been ended in external reality (Miller, 1971).

Writers in this area have based their conclusions on clinical experience with children and adults who have suffered the childhood loss of parents through death. Wolfenstein (1966) presented the most complete exposition of the consensus psychoanalytic view on children's reactions to the death of a parent. She reported clinical data on 42 children, ranging in age from early latency to adolescence, who had lost parents to death.

Mourning, as described by Freud, did not occur in these children. At the time of the loss, sad feelings were curtailed and there was little weeping. Immersion in the activities of everyday life continued, with no withdrawal into preoccupation with thoughts of the lost parent, such as is observed in mourning adults. The children seemed to be denying the finality of the loss. The painful necessary withdrawal of emotional involvement with the lost parent was avoided, permitting more or less conscious expectation of return. When depressed moods occurred in the children, especially in adolescence, they were not connected with thoughts of the death of the parent, to which reality testing had not yet been applied. The internal representation of the lost parent was not decreased in its emotional significance for the child but rather became invested with intensified importance. Good moods observed in these children were frequently the counterpart to denial rather than a normal feeling of well-being. Development of hostile feelings toward the surviving parent, together with the idealization of the one who had died, represented an attempt to undo previous hostile feelings toward the dead parent through displacement onto the survivor. Identification with the dead parent was frequent, with resulting positive or negative consequences. Whereas good qualities of the parent could become a part of the growing ego of the child, frequently identification rather took the form of identification with the parent as experienced in final stages of the illness.

This view of the nature of children's reactions to the death of a parent is further supported by the reports of other investigators who conducted a clinical study (Altschul, 1968; Fleming, 1963; Fleming & Altschul, 1963). The participants were psychoanalytic patients who had lost a parent by death in childhood or adolescence. The consensus position is that a particular set of responses tend to occur in children who experience the death of a parent. These include unconscious and sometimes conscious denial of the reality of the parent's death; rigid screening out of all affective responses connected with the parent's death; marked increase in identification with and idealization of the dead parent; decrease in self-esteem; feelings of guilt; and persistent unconscious fantasies of ongoing relationship or reunion with the dead parent. These responses are viewed as being directed toward avoiding the acceptance of the parent's death and the consequent necessity to make the radical reorganization in object attachments that such an acceptance would require.

More recently, Gray (1987) studied 50 adolescents whose parents had died and found a higher level of depression than in nonbereaved high school students. Serious difficulties in adjustment were confirmed by Murphy (1986–1987) and Berlinsky and Biller (1982). Silverman and Worden (1992) cautioned that the death of a parent should not be viewed as a single stressful event but as a series of events that occurred before and after the death. Many pointed out that children need to remain connected to the deceased and that this need seems to be a necessary part of the bereavement process (Klass, 1988; Rubin, 1985; Silverman, Nickman, & Worden, 1992).

Eth and Pynoos (1985) stressed that traumatized individuals cannot mourn until the traumatic elements of the loss have been resolved. Many traumatized individuals have difficulty controlling their anxious and aggressive feelings (Van der Kolk, 1987). The hallmarks of posttraumatic disorder—amnesia, detachment, obsessive thoughts, reliving the trauma—surface in other cases of sibling loss such as with CF. In addition, as with pediatric AIDS, the child may be facing not just one loss but many, as several children in a family may be afflicted with CF (Fanos & Wiener, 1994).

There seem to be developmental variations in the capacity to conceptualize death. Nagy (1948), for example, reported that in children from 3 to 5 years old, death is denied; the change is seen as not permanent, but is perceived only as a temporary absence. From ages 5 to 9, children generally personify death. By age 7 or 8, children have the capacity to begin to understand the finality of death, and by age 10 or 11, causes of death may be understood (Siegel & Gorey, 1994).

Bereaved children need a setting in which they can communicate thoughts and feelings openly. Children's adjustment to death of a parent is less difficult when families tolerate open expressions of anger, guilt, depression, and shared feelings (Black & Urbanowicz, 1987; Bowlby 1980; Kliman, 1973).

Ritual Handling of the Death

Important and related questions are the following: Do the rituals that have evolved to assist adults in our society to handle loss also serve children, or do they themselves cause further trauma? Does a viewing of the body, for example, interfere with the child's need to deny the death? If the identification process is affected by the final stages of the illness, how will it be altered further with reconciliation of the experience with the dead body itself?

The difficulty with which Americans as a whole handle the experience of bereavement has generated much psychiatric interest (Volkart & Michael, 1976). It becomes important to ask whether there is something about the cultural handling of grief that is not functioning well enough. Or, to put the question in another way, do mourning customs in the United States provide sufficient assistance to the bereaved?

What are the functions of mourning customs for a culture? To quote Wallace (1966):

> The departed soul and the survivors must be released from each other; otherwise, the living will remain miserable in their frustrated devotion and the departed soul will be unhappy. Once again, the goal of ritual is to separate effectively the living from the dead, to accomplish the transition, to bring about the incorporation of the dead into its proper place in the hereafter, and to reconstitute the mourners with each other and with the community. (p. 129)

Each of these functions are discussed here.

Separate the Living From the Dead.   To assist in the necessary emotional separation of the dead from the survivors, there are various potential tie-breaking customs that societies can institutionalize: giving away or putting aside for some amount of time personal property of the deceased, destruction of property of the deceased, temporarily or permanently abandoning the dwelling of the deceased, temporarily or permanently abandoning the community in which the survivors lived with the deceased, and the practice of a temporary or permanent taboo on the name of the deceased (Rosenblatt, Walsh, & Jackson, 1976). Although Americans may give away personal possessions of the dead (e.g., clothes), they rarely change dwelling or community as part of the bereavement process, and there is certainly no culturally sanctioned or enforced taboo on the name of the deceased.

There is another way in which a culture can aid in the necessary separation process, and that is to allow the dying to be an active participant. In the late Middle Ages and Renaissance, for example, a man was considered to be the master of his own death, and the circumstances under which it took place. In fact, he was expected to preside over it (Aries, 1975). In modern society, death has been relegated for the most part to the hospital and the family to the waiting room. This can have severe consequences for the surviving siblings in the case of a dying child, as they frequently are left at home when the sick child becomes terminally ill. Hospital rules tend to exclude children under the age of 12 from entrance to wards at any time, due to risk of infection of seriously ill patients by common childhood diseases.

If modern man is denied mastery of his own death, survivors are denied direct expression of their own grief. Mourning was until recently the highest form of grief, and it was right and necessary to express it. Although its demonstration was either culturally prescribed or allowed to assert itself spontaneously, grief over the centuries was the most violent expression of feelings. The paroxysm of grief of earlier centuries has largely been succeeded by its prohibition (Gorer, 1965).

Grief is not the only emotion experienced by the bereaved; many have noted that anger is generally intertwined with it (Durkheim, 1961; Freud, 1917, among others). Just as many cultures allow for violent expression of grief, most likewise allow for direct expression of aggression—mourners may inflict pain and disfigurement on their own bodies, and so on (Rosenblatt et al., 1976). Socialization for the suppression of anger is dangerous, because self-suppression can lead to prolonged depression or to redirection of hostility onto survivor children.

To Accomplish the Transition. A death empties social roles and creates a need for redistribution of responsibilities and obligations onto the rest of society (Mandelbaum, 1976). In the case of a child dying, hopes for narcissistic fulfillment on the part of the parents, stifled during the many years while the dying child is part of the family, assert themselves full force on survivor children, with much pressure on them to carry forth formerly thwarted ambitions. Although social roles can be replaced, damage to identity formation notwithstanding, individual personalities cannot. Family structure in the United States is such that individual members are very vulnerable to loss (Volkart & Michael, 1976). Americans grow up in small nuclear families with strong and lifelong attachments to particular people. Emotional attachments to particular family members are fostered, with individuals dependent on unique personalities in addition to the roles they fulfill. In U.S. families, a major role embedded in individuals is frequently a psychological one. The death of a child may have a major impact on remaining siblings by disrupting the internal balance of interrelated emotional roles in the family structure, which requires shifts in dynamics. The unmet psychological needs can be transferred to survivor siblings, sometimes with disastrous consequences (Cain et al., 1964).

To Bring the Dead to the Hereafter. A counterpart of the need to push the dead away is the need to keep them alive. The latter is acknowledged in much symbolic ritual action, of which religion plays a major part. To quote Malinowski (1948):

> The ceremonial of death which ties the survivors to the body and rivets them to the place of death, the beliefs in the existence of the spirit, in its beneficent influences or malevolent intentions, in the duties of a series of commemorative or sacrificial ceremonies—in all this religion counteracts the centrifugal forces of fear, dismay, demoralization, and provides the most powerful means of reintegration of the group's shaken solidarity and of the re-establishment of its morale. (p. 53)

With the decline of belief in an afterlife, the bereaved can no longer comfort themselves with the thought that something lives on after death. Even the cemetery, a visual symbol that the individual lives on as long as he or she continues in someone's memory, is no longer centrally located in the community, beside the church (Warner, 1976). If death can end everything, can completely obliterate the person, then death must be denied. If death is indeed to be denied, as many have noted it to be in the United States (e.g., Becker, 1973), then the deceased must be shown not to be dead. Thus we have the wake. Not dead but "asleep," the body peacefully rests in a "slumber room," stretched out in a casket selected by the bereaved for the comfort of the loved one. Stage director *par excellence*, the funeral director takes pride in his or her artful production of a "pleasant memory picture" (Mitford, 1978). Whether this visual image is actually helpful or, rather, traumatic, has not been investigated.

Reconstitute Mourners With Each Other and With the Community. Ceremonies following a death may reinforce ties through the shared work and coordination required (Rosenblatt et al., 1976). From colonial days through the 19th century, the American funeral was almost exclusively a family affair. Family and friends performed most of the duties in connection with the dead body; they washed and laid it out, ordered the coffin from the local carpenter, carried the coffin on foot from the home to the church and then to the graveyard, and frequently, unless the church sexton was available, dug the grave (Mitford, 1978). Where this kind of interdependence is essential, the support serves to obligate the bereaved to those providing the support, so there is a greater possibility of reciprocation when the latter are themselves in need of help; required support thus helps to bind people to each other (Rosenblatt et al., 1976). With the rise in the role of the funeral director at the turn of the century, all of these services fell into the hands of a specialist, with only the emotional needs of the bereaved remaining. Even these are increasingly falling into the role of the funeral director, who is now seen as a grief counselor as well (Mitford, 1978).

In our society, local ties are attenuated by frequent change of residence, work diversity, and even by the desire for somewhat anonymous neighbors that can be found in many urban areas; the lack of *gemeinshaft* and the growth of individualism create a withdrawal from each others' problems (Goody, 1975). The fact that family and friends may gather together to pay a visit to the deceased at the wake or funeral can be problematic in itself. Family may come from miles, not having seen each other for years; neighbors may not know work associates or even each other. People in contemporary society juggle complicated and far-reaching divergent ties, not adequately understood as territorial relationships. People are reminded through the ritual that the bonds they are strengthening through the dramatic enactment are no longer the real bonds that actually hold them together, which can cause deep uneasiness. As Geertz (1957) warned us, ritual fails when people are pressed into an intimacy they would prefer to avoid or where there is incongruity between the social assumptions of the ritual (we are all culturally homogeneous) and what is the case (we are all different). Having evolved from a predominantly rural society, the cultural framework of meaning surrounding the gathering together of people at death ceremonies no longer fits the actual pattern of social relationships (Goody, 1975).

In order to mark the official end of the mourning period and the need for reintegration into the group, there is in many societies a final ceremony for the dead person, which may include reburial of the corpse, and the like (Rosenblatt et al., 1976). Final ceremonies may occur some weeks, months, or years after the death, and serve two very useful functions—to let the survivors know that they have mourned long enough and to signal to community members that they may properly initiate social invitations to the bereaved without ambiguity or uncertainty. Americans have no final ceremonies, and many experience such omissions as personal anniversary reactions and so forth. This lack may contribute to the severity of bereavement disorders in this country, because mourning can go on indefinitely, with no ritual to signal its proper termination.

Impact of Parental Mourning on Children

Parental accessibility for the support of the surviving sibling is vital to the adjustment process (Rosen, 1985). Parents' preoccupation with their own grief can have consequences for survivor children. Sigal (1971), for example, referred to "maternal preoccupation" to describe the way in which energy is bound up with prior stress to the detriment of the present. Horowitz (1986) also found that survivors are unable to cope effectively with the present because they are busy trying to assimilate the past. Pound (1982) found the depressed mother to be considerably impaired in her role. Siegel and Gorey (1994) discussed parental mourning in detail.

Recent data on responses of parents grieving the loss of their child suggest that parents grieve for much longer periods of time than was formerly assumed, and that well-adjusted parents do not necessarily go through typical stages of mourning (Wortman & Silver, 1989). In sibling survivors of an individual with CF, there was much anger expressed about the parental handling of their own mourning. Some siblings were furious that their parents had memorialized or idealized the deceased child, making it impossible for them to live up to fantastic images of perfection. Some siblings resented that, following the death, a parent suddenly focused all his or her attention on the surviving sibling, perhaps dealing with the loss through substitution. Some mothers were perceived as having become overprotective of their remaining children well into their adulthood (Fanos, 1987). Bank and Kahn (1982) believe that most parents communicate their own fear of further loss by attempting to stifle the child's advances toward independence.

Although the emphasis in attachment research initially has been on the effects of the physical separation of the child from the mother in the early years, theorists increasingly have turned their attention to emotional availability of the parent as a vital consideration in the developmental history of the child. Investigators support the increasing sense that attachment behavior is in some way related to the communicative ability of the mother and therefore the sense of mastery the child learns to expect from his environment. Spitz and Woolff (1946) traced the origins of the infant's first tie to the mother and stressed the necessity for the mother's sufficient involvement with the child through satisfying handling. Mahler, Pine, and Bergman (1975) explored the complexities of the separation–individuation phase in the second year of life, the necessity for the prior establishment of basic trust in order to allow for separation from the mother without distress. Ainsworth, Blehar, Waters, and Wall (1978) explored the difference between the securely and insecurely attached child, finding the difference related to the mother's sensitivity to the signs and communications of her infant.

Increasingly, attachment behavior has been viewed in relation to maternal depression, which is seen as a serious impediment to the development of the child. The depressed mother is found to be considerably impaired in her role and either overconcerned, guilty, and helpless or overtly hostile. She finds it difficult to be involved in her children's lives, to communicate with them, and to show affection to them. Those most vulnerable to her negative mood and impaired capacity for relating are her children, who depend on her for their survival and who cannot escape her presence no matter how distressing it becomes (Pound, 1982).

Some of the unusual features of the relationship between the mother and child can be seen arising from reversals of the balance of power that normally prevails between the two. Instead of the mother's holding the child in her concerned attention, as the normal mother would, the child of a depressed mother watches the child, ready to respond to his or her need as it arises. Although the healthy mother sees herself as responsible for the child's survival, in a depressed mother, the child comes to feel responsible for the mother. In some cases the child perceives him or herself as keeping the mother alive when there seems nothing else for her to live for:

> In short, the child of a depressed mother is forced into a precocious maturity and has to become an attachment figure before he has had sufficient experience of being attached. ... He is precipitated into what Winnicott (1958, p.

206) calls the "stage of concern" before he has fully completed using and sometimes misusing the attachment figure to establish his own sense of identity. (Pound, 1982, pp. 126–127)

The presence of a chronically grieving, depressed, and withdrawn mother can lead to the inhibition of aggression, and the mother can appear to the child as either too fragile to withstand the expression of a normal amount of assertiveness or as already damaged by it. This perception, coupled with the lack of understanding about whether the child's aggression is implicated in the death of the sibling, can contribute to a number of developmental complications: inhibitions in drive expression, an overly harsh superego, separation–individuation problems, and disturbances in the formation of a normally assertive, autonomous self (Levine, 1982).

It is interesting to note that survivor siblings are not only survivors themselves but are the children of survivors as well. The relationship between both groups of children and their parents are remarkably similar. Concentration camp survivor parents are described by their children and by investigators as depressed (Barocas & Barocas, 1979), overprotective (Trossman, 1968), suspicious (Laufer, 1973), and overvaluing of their children (Krell, 1979). They expect their children to function as a source of nurture (Phillips, 1978), fulfillment (Trossman, 1968), and to vindicate their suffering (Trossman, 1968). They have difficulty in letting their children separate from the family (Lipkowitz, 1973; Russell, 1974), often making the child feel that it would be disloyal to do so (Barocas & Barocas, 1979).

In the concentration camps in which children witnessed the degradation of their parents and lost their trust in them, many transferred their belief in parental omnipotence onto the persecutors, whom they put in the role of powerful, avenging, punitive parents (Kestenberg, 1980). This is not unlike the situation of families with a fatally ill child, in which children witness their parents as powerless before the onslaught of the disease of their sibling, and in which the parents, ignorant before the vast medical establishment that they must repeatedly encounter, are too frequently infantalized by the doctor (Nathanson, personal communication, March 1, 1984). Does the physician absorb the omnipotent role for the child?

In normal development, through the mechanism of parental identification, the child comes to see him or herself as a confident and adequate person in the world; part of this confidence is borrowed magically from his or her parents by identification with their perceived adequacy and strength. This sense of benign omnipotence is almost completely extinguished when the parents have prematurely been perceived as inadequate (Wahl, 1976). What happens when siblings, confronting a world with more than their share of hidden fears and terrors, bring their anxiety to parents already overwhelmed with their own?

The lack of capacity to perceive parents as omnipotent at the proper developmental time could have grave consequences for the child's capacity to move away from the parents. Adolescence, for example, is normally seen as a time at which an individual must make a psychical renunciation and suffer the loss of childhood aims and objects (Root, 1957). In normal development the individual would experience and come to understand the parents with increased clarity as whole people in their own right, a complex combination of strengths and weaknesses. In a situation in which the omnipotent childhood object resides outside the family, the child does not have the opportunity for repeated observation and checking of increasingly accurate and realistic perceptions of this figure. Where this normal process has been interfered with too early, the individual may continuously search for an all-powerful other. (Kohut, 1971, 1977). An individual whose earliest attachment was insecure may have difficulty throughout life handling change, as Parkes (1982) noted. The individual may have greater difficulty dealing with stress because his or her self-esteem and mastery, two of the most useful devices against it (Pearlin & Schooler, 1978), have both been rendered problematic.

Processes of adjustment to later loss seem related to the security–anxiety dimension of early attachments. Individuals whose earlier relationships are secure tend, after a period of mourning, to be able to resume normal lives and find new attachment bonds; those whose early relationships were anxious are more likely to manifest pathological variations of the mourning process and to find it more difficult to resume intimate relationships with others later on (Bowlby, 1969, 1973, 1979, 1980).

The death of a parent might be expected to be more traumatic for these individuals as well. The death of the mother, for example, could be more difficult for a number of reasons. First, one might expect to find increased guilt because the person had functioned in the role of savior of the depressed mother. Second, there may have been lessened ability to separate from the mother and move on to other intimate relationships. Third, in adolescence the normal mourning process of the loss of omnipotent parental figures, in which the mother would be perceived more realistically, may not have occurred. The concomitant loss of the ill sibling would have removed—in the case of a family in which only one healthy sibling survives—the use of siblings as an aid to modifying perceptions of the parents throughout the life cycle.

Loss of a Sibling

An early study of children's reactions to the death of their sibling is Cain et al.'s (1964) study of 58 children ages 2½ to 14 seen at outpatient and inpatient psychiatric settings; all were psychiatric patients. In about half of the cases, guilt was directly present 5 years or more after the sibling's death. The children considered themselves responsible for the death, insisted that it was their fault, felt that they should have died too, or that they should have died instead of the sibling. The guilt was handled in individual ways: depressive withdrawal, accident-prone behavior, punishment-seeking, testing, projection of superego accusations, and so forth. Alternately, family members blamed themselves, each other, and often, in order to maintain self-esteem and family relationships, tried not to blame each other.

Cain et al. related that the siblings often had confused, distorted concepts of illness, death, and the relationship between the two. Having been told that only old people die, they struggled with the contradiction manifested by the death of their sibling, and their confidence in adults was seriously undermined. Some solved it by believing they would die at the same age as their sibling. The children often assumed that symptoms such as coughs or fever led to death; death was the enemy, constantly to be warded off. Parental admonitions as to eating vegetables or dressing warmly and so forth, led to confusions about the cause of death—"he didn't eat his vegetables" (p. 746). In most children, fears of doctors were greatly increased. Doctors were perceived at best as impotent in the face of illness and at worst as closely associated with illness and death. Hospitals were even more frightening to the children, for to them going into a hospital for a routine operation meant they would die. Benevolent images of God were undermined; many children needed continuous reassurance that God didn't want to hurt people.

An intense fear of death was present in almost all the children studied by Cain et al. They were convinced that they would die too, either at exactly the same age, as just mentioned, or from the same disease. They acutely felt that death could strike other siblings, parents, or themselves at any moment, and the parents' potential as protectors was destroyed. These children were generally passive–dependent and fearful, feeling small and vulnerable in a frighteningly dangerous world.

The identity formation of the siblings was often seriously endangered. The parents often looked to them as replacements or even substitutes, and based their expectations on the idealized image of the dead child. Because the children were aware that they could not possibly replace the dead child, they resented the implicit demand, and were aware of the subtle message that they, and not their sibling, should have died. Some children were conceived specifically to replace a child, which resulted in severe problems; in a few extraordinary cases, parents even changed the living child's name to that of the dead child.

These findings, emerging from a psychiatric clinic population, can point us to those areas in which we might expect to encounter difficulties in a community sample. The literature that has included comments on sibling reactions would seem to suggest the seriousness of possible difficulties. Binger et al. (1969), for example, found that in approximately half of the 20 families studied, one or more previously well siblings showed behavioral problems following a sibling's diagnosis.

Since the 1970s, there has been a growing body of research on sibling adaptation. Some researchers have found adjustment problems in children whose siblings suffered from chronic illnesses such as CF and diabetes and physical disabilities such as cleft palate (see Howe, 1993, for review). Problems included lowered self-concepts, personality problems, higher levels of anxiety, depression and guilt, social withdrawal, and academic problems (Balk 1990; Ferrari, 1987; Lavigne & Ryan, 1979; Tritt & Esses, 1988; Vance, Fazan, Satterwhite, & Pless, 1980).

Breslau and Prabucki (1987), in a study of siblings of children who suffered from CF and various congenital handicaps, found that siblings were at increased risk of depressive symptoms and social isolation, as well as increased general symptom levels, which included both internalizing and externalizing behaviors. Longitudinal follow-ups found that the symptom levels of siblings of physically disabled and chronically ill children remained stable or increased across the 5 years of the study, whereas symptom levels for healthy siblings decreased. Davies (1983, 1988), studying sibling bereavement, found significantly higher internalizing behavior problems (anxiety, depression, guilt), as well as significantly lower social competency scores.

Other researchers have found no differences between siblings of chronically ill children and normative samples or control groups of healthy siblings (Cowen et al., 1986; Farkas, 1974; Ferrari, 1984; Gayton, Friedman, Tavormena, & Tucker, 1977; Lavigne, Traisman, Marr, & Chasnoff, 1982; Tritt & Esses, 1988). In fact, Drotar et al. (1981), in a study of siblings of patients with CF and asthma, found that the siblings were rated as more highly adjusted than a normative sample based on a parent-behavior checklist. Gayton et al. (1977) also found that siblings of individuals with CF reported higher self-concept scores than norms predicted.

Many studies have found that only certain subsets of children are at increased risk for adjustment problems (Caudman, Boyle, & Offord, 1988; Cowen et al., 1986; Ferrari, 1987; Lavigne & Ryan, 1979). Caudman et al. (1988) found that siblings of children with various physical disabilities and chronic illnesses were at a significantly increased risk of developing problems getting along with their peers. However, the researchers found no differences in ratings of social competency or isolation, particularly relating to the children's leisure and recreational activities. Cowen et al. (1986), in a study of children with CF, found that only preschoolers were at an increased risk for exhibiting behavioral problems, whereas older children were not.

Other researchers have investigated positive outcomes of sibling loss (Martinson & Campos, 1991; Oltjenbruns, 1991). In a longitudinal follow-up of individuals who were adolescents when their siblings died of cancer, Martinson and Campos (1991) found that almost 50% of the participants reported a positive legacy of the experiences associated with their sibling's death. Oltjenbruns (1991) reported that 96% of her sample who had lost a family member or close friend during adolescence identified at least one positive outcome of the death, such as having a deeper appreciation of life, showing greater caring for loved ones, strengthened emotional bonds with others, and the development of emotional strength.

Recently, researchers have begun to study factors that influence the adaptation to the loss of a sibling (Balk, 1991; Breslau, 1982; Breslau, Wietzman, & Messenger, 1981; Dyson, 1989; Ferrari, 1984, 1987; Gruszk, 1988; Hoare, 1984; Kazak & Clark, 1986; Lavigne & Ryan, 1979): Gender, age, sibling constellation factors such as age-spacing and birth order, chronicity of the disease, and the interaction of these factors have all been found to influence sibling adaptation (see Lobato, 1990, for a review of research). Breslau (1982), in a study of siblings of children with congenital disabilities, found that only younger male and older female siblings were at increased risk for aggressive behavior and symptoms of depression and anxiety. Dyson (1989) found that adjustment problems were related to both the number of children in a family and the age-spacing among siblings. As the number of children in the family and the difference in ages between the healthy and sick sibling increased, better adjustment was reported.

Resilience

Recent research has begun to explore resilience factors accounting for variation in adjustment. Families differ greatly in the extent to which they allow the sick child to become the focus of reorganization. Does this happen more frequently, for example, when the sick child has been the favorite one before the diagnosis? When the genders of the children are the same, is the impact worse because of greater identification? If the father is seen as powerless, does this interfere with sexual identification for the surviving male siblings but not for the females?

Siblings at risk will also differ greatly in ability throughout their lives to overcome their experience of early loss. There is some suggestion that men may be able to recover from early deprivation better than women (Lowenthal, Thurnher, Chiriboga, & Associates, 1975). Marriage, at least for men (Chodorow, 1978), or parenthood, for women (Benedek, 1959), may afford opportunities to replace in some way the lost attachment relationship. There may be various ways of handling the loss through substitution.

Others may move to attempt to master the experience directly, perhaps years later. A good example is the heart surgeon Christian Barnard (1970), who developed the very operation that could have saved his little brother's life.

A third alternative to handling loss is to move away from the source of distress toward alternative sources of gratification. Pearlin (1980) discussed "selective commitment" to roles in our society in which individuals frequently move roles that are painful to the periphery of importance and make more central those that are less conflict-ridden. Offspring of a depressed and withdrawn mother may, for example, move away from the importance of a family life to sources of fulfillment such as school or occupation. It may be the unusually talented who possess the flexibility to move into alternate areas of gratification in this way.

Originally, the psychoanalytic understanding of talent and creativity borrowed heavily from our understanding of pathological personality development. Increasingly, exceptional abilities are seen as having origins separate from, although at times inextricably intertwined with, pathological structures (Oremland, 1989). Kris (1952) earlier emphasized the relationship between exceptional ability and flexibility rather than pathology in psychic organization. Greenacre (1957) stressed the importance of innate sensorimotor conceptual endowment with its potential toward development of a different order of object relatedness, the "collective alternates" strikingly similar to Winnicott's (1953) concept of transitional space. Kohut (1971) elaborated the use of creativity in some artists as the creation of a self by completing it with the artistic product as self-object. An illustrative example is Virginia Woolf, whose mother died when the girl was an early adolescent. The mother had always been perceived by the young girl as unempathic and distant. Woolf was obsessed by her mother's memory daily until, at the age of 44, she began to work on her autobiographical novel *To the Lighthouse.* When it was completed she ceased to be obsessed with her mother and could no longer see her nor hear her voice (Wolf & Wolf, 1979). Turning to a nonhuman environment as a consequence of having serious difficulties in a human area, however, does not allow for the mutual enrichment that is possible in relationships (Searles, 1960). This may help us to understand Woolf's ultimate suicide despite her artistic talent. Pollock (1977, 1978) explored the relationship between early loss and creativity and more recently (1989) traced the mourning-liberation process through the lives of creative geniuses.

The more we become familiar with the specific unhealthy ingredients of a parent's personality, the developmental stage of the surviving sibling at the time of the loss, and any unique talents and inborn predispositions, the more we will be able to understand individual variations in capacity to move away from or to master despair, or, rather, to become engulfed by it.

Chapter 2

The Family Setting

We shall not cease from exploration
And the end of all our exploring
Will be to arrive where we started
And know the place for the first time.
Through the unknown, remembered gate
When the last of earth left to discover
Is that which was the beginning ...
—T.S. Eliot (*Four Quartets*, 1962)

Coming to understand the psychological forces at work in the families I studied meant exploring the way in which the surviving siblings thought about and remembered their lives as children. Therefore, the interviews began with a very open-ended question, "Can you tell me a little about your childhood?" The ease with which siblings recalled their young years, the family members who were mentioned or who were absent in their recounting, provided a great deal of information.

Most siblings began the recital of their story with a quick statement that growing up in their family had been "just normal." To some extent, this reflected the attempt on the part of the parents to maintain as normal a family life as possible. At times it seemed a somewhat defensive stance, keeping constant cherished family illusions that all was well despite stubborn evidence to the contrary. It also seemed to demonstrate the children's tendency to regard whatever they saw in their own home as usual and ordinary. One young man, 10 years old when his brother died, recalled that his brother sometimes slept in a mist tent in order to improve his breathing but that it never seemed odd; after all, he said, "some people go to bed with mud packs on their face." When asked to recount their earliest memories, however, a different story emerged. Siblings eloquently described the beauty of the mountains where they grew up, the backyard of their house, or their favorite pet. Parental figures were rarely mentioned in an active way, but rather, themes of parental absence were frequent. One young woman, whose mother worked nights while her father worked days, said her earliest memory is of trying in vain to reach the light so she could find the bathroom in the night darkness. One young man's earliest memory was when his mother's car had a flat tire at the beach, and his mother repeatedly called his father but to no avail. Occasionally, the portrait of a parent is one of longing and poignant nostalgia. Jenny, 14 years old when her older sister died, recalled when she and her sister were very young, her father would be sitting in the chair reading the paper. "We'd just sit there and comb his hair and put little bows in his hair. Me and my sister just loved that."

The lost sibling was often mentioned in the early memories. For some respondents, themes of deprivation in relation to the illness of the sibling with CF appeared. Frequently they appeared as screen memories, with a discrete illness of a healthy sibling the cause of the deprivation, rather than CF. Common themes were anxiety concerning illness and disability, again not directly linked to the sibling but displaced from the chronic illness of their sibling. Peter, 10 years old when his sister died, recalled seeing a woman in a wheelchair, and having nightmares all that night. Predominant themes were of trauma to the self. One young woman remembered "the abrupt beginning in life." Joan, 7 years old when her older brother died, remembered "trauma themes," like cutting a piece of cardboard as she was going up the stairs and sticking the scissors in her throat. Many individuals remembered situations of danger to themselves that they survived. One sibling reported falling in a fish pond when he was about 3 years old. One young woman recalled falling into a snow bank when she was 5 years old. Another young man remembered a near-drowning episode when he was 5 years old, one in which, interestingly enough, he was saved not by a parent but by the kindness of a stranger. Some siblings remembered a hospital stay for a minor operation, or having had an accident requiring medical intervention. One young man recalled that a candy counter fell on him when he was 3 years old. He remembered being in the car with blood on his face and doctors stitching his eye. Another young man recalled cutting his thumb, being taken to the hospital for stitches, and being convinced that he was going to die.

It was very difficult for some respondents to elaborate on their early memories. They seemed to be trying to assure the interviewer that their childhood had been normal, because it was less threatening than trying to remember what had really happened. Some siblings quickly stated that their childhood was pretty much a blank. One young man, 18 years old when his sister died, reported, "I don't have good memories of childhood. That might be an interesting fact for you. I don't have vivid memories. Some of my friends have much more vivid memories than I do." Another young man could not recall much of his childhood at all, stating that he does not like to "dwell on those kinds of thoughts." Another sibling, 13 years old when her sister died, reported that she never really thinks back to her childhood, and that it is "like ghosts sometimes." Amnesia as a response to early trauma has been discussed by many clinicians, including Van der Kolk (1987).

Where are the missing parents? What are the memories that are warded off? In response to further probing, parental portraits began to emerge. Mothers were generally seen as trying to be available but struggling to take care of the ill child. In the statistical sample, 15 of the 25 mothers were coded as available, 8 mothers were reported as unpredictable, and only 2 as unavailable. The sheer amount of physical involvement that one or both of the parents must have on a daily basis with the affected child is demanding, because CF can be an extremely time-consuming illness. The child is placed on a complex regime of pancreatic enzymes, antibiotics, bronchodilators, vitamins, and other nutritional supplements, some to be taken with meals, others between meals. Postural drainage, in which the chest is pounded in order to loosen mucus from the lungs, must be done for about an hour several times a day. During more acute phases of the illness, aerosol treatments must be provided. In some families, siblings shared the tasks, and the care of the child was embraced by the whole family. Some descriptions of care of the ill child were almost idyllic in families in which, despite the fact that several children had CF, caretaking was incorporated within the family schedule. One young woman, who had already lost three of her siblings to the illness before she was 10 years old, described the way she and her family took care of the three children who had CF: "In the morning we'd have their pills ready for them. When we first started doing the therapy all we had was a board, like a big ironing board that we sat up and tilted and they would lay on it and we'd thump them. It was the hardest when we had to bring them to the hospital because we always knew they weren't going to come back."

In most families, however, the task of respiratory therapy fell to mothers, who tried to meet the needs of the sick child and have something left over for their other children. Some siblings were able to understand why there was little time for them. Jenny remembered how much time her mother had to spend doing therapy with her sister, often 4 hours a day. "I'd go up to her and say, 'Mommy, come play a game with me,' and she'd say, 'I'm sorry, I can't.'" Mothers were generally seen as bearing the brunt of the caretaking even during periods of crisis. This lack of paternal availability dismayed siblings. Rick recalled his father's absence during a frightening episode at home when his sister suddenly vomited blood: "Something inside went wrong. Something burst and she passed out and threw up blood. I distinctly remember my mother. She was near hysteria trying to talk on the phone with the doctor. I don't know where my father was, but it was my mother who was doing all of the action."

It seemed typical for families to redirect emotional resources around the sick child. Unfortunately, most survivor siblings perceived the inequality of time and attention, but did not understand the link between this redistribution of emotional resources and the demands of the illness. Kathy, 13 years old when her younger sister died, reported that she does not remember much about her early childhood: "What I remember most is the last few years. It was hard, mostly because I more or less resented it. I never remember feelings. I only remember things. I wish I had a good memory. I think I just block things out, it's easier."

Some respondents who were older than their sick sibling recalled a dramatic change in their relationship when their brother or sister was diagnosed with CF. One young man, who was 5 years old when his brother was born and diagnosed, noticed a significant change in his relationship with his father at that point, "not only because there was another child in the family, but also because a lot of the attention had to be focused on him because of his illness. He was in and out of the hospital weekly." Some individuals recalled their childhood had been permeated by the sickness of their sibling. One young woman remembered an autumn when she was excited about the new school year because it signaled new clothes and books. This particular year, however, her younger brother was very sick, so there was no time to go shopping. A young man recalled that his family had only one bedroom for the children. Because he was the healthy one, he was always the one having to "rough it"— to sleep up in the attic or out in the storeroom, a converted turkey house. "So out to the storeroom I went," he reported.

Many respondents felt they were different from everybody else because they had a sibling who was obviously sick. The child with CF often had teeth stained yellow from the antibiotics, was generally thin, and coughed frequently. Several individuals recalled concerned mothers pulling their children away in an attempt to protect their own children from what they assumed was a contagious illness. It was not at all unusual for unknowing peers to taunt the sick child, and siblings struggled with feelings of resentment that their brother or sister was different, guilt for their "selfish" feelings, and desire to protect the sibling. Adolescence was a particularly difficult time for many, when peer approval was most important. One young woman remembered that she and her siblings were made fun of because of their sister. "Growing up was really hard because she used to cough. They used to cough behind her back and behind ours, and they'd make up names. It was really tough growing up. It was really tough. I wouldn't want to do it again."

For some young children, when the sibling was very sick and frequent hospitalizations became necessary, there was a long period of disorientation. One sibling, only 5 years old when his brother died, remembered that he was constantly shifted around to stay with relatives during his brother's hospital stays when his parents were away. Very attached to his mother, the youngster experienced her leaving every weekend to go to the hospital as the worst part of the whole ordeal. He recalled that his mother once told him that, when he was young, he had told someone that his mother was dead because she was so rarely home. Youngsters were often separated from each other, one child being taken in by one relative, another by a different relative or friend or neighbor. Confused and bewildered, siblings struggled to make sense of what was happening. Even very young children were called upon by distracted parents to be "little adults." Thrust into such an improbable role so early, anxieties ran rampant. Simon, 10 years old when his older brother died, remembered one dream he used to have when his parents were away at the hospital visiting his brother:

I was at my grandmother's house. I think it was quite a while before he died. It came back to me every time I would close my eyes. Things were constantly after me, and it didn't matter where I was. There was music too, like it was a jungle setting. I can remember alligators and things like that and just being really scared.

Even if parents did not stay at the hospital, as the illness progressed, there was less time and energy for the well sibling. One young woman remembered that during her brother's acute episodes she would try to sit very quietly in the corner, playing with her dolls. Parents, preoccupied with their own fears concerning the illness, were often the last place siblings felt they could bring their concerns. The well siblings sensed that they were not to complicate the situation. One young man recalled that he felt his job was to keep his family's world as simple as possible because it was already difficult enough. His reaction was, "So just don't raise any dust. Don't make any more trouble than there already is."

With parents so overwhelmed with the sick child, siblings were often left in the care of even slightly older siblings. The responsibility for other siblings fell more frequently upon females than males. Sally recalled that when her brother was in the hospital, her mother would visit him every day and not return until 9 or 10 o'clock at night, "Then a lot of the responsibility fell on me to take care of things, and get dinner on the table." Male children were sometimes expected to help with the family finances. One young man recalled that when he was 11 years old, he worked at a golf course, and all the money he earned had to be turned over to his father. With parental attention elsewhere, siblings' own developmental needs were overlooked. For some children, receiving help with homework from exhausted parents became a luxury, and their school motivation and performance suffered as a consequence. One young woman, who lost her older brother when she was 14 and her older sister when she was 16, felt that she never learned good study habits:

> When I came home from school, being home alone, there were much more interesting things going on—watching TV, going over to a friend's house—than sitting down and studying. I never remember my mother sitting down with me in first or second grade to help me read, like I sit with my daughter and read her stories. I never remember any of that.

If young children were not able to get help with their homework, similarly, adolescents often received no help planning a career. For some families, the future represented a threatening concept in which, for one member, there might be none. In addition, siblings were distracted by dealing with the unrelenting demands and crises of the illness at a time when their young peers were able to concentrate fully on their goals. One young man remembered that his family spent a lot of time with his brother when he had serious medical episodes, "Going through the '70s, it seemed like we were always down at Children's Hospital. He needed somebody around, so we all shared that part. I was kind of floating along. I look at that period as pretty scrambled." Worrying about the condition of their affected siblings distracted many individuals from focusing on their own lives. One young woman, 25 years old when her younger sister died, remembered overhearing her mother talking to a neighbor about the difficulty of having a very sick child. That conversation started years of worrying about her sister. As a high school senior, she chose CF as her topic for a research paper. Learning the facts of the disease only made her fears worse, "After that, I can remember staying up a lot of nights listening to her cough, and looking at her. I became really obsessed. I'd stay awake nights and listen down the hall to make sure she was breathing." When another young woman was in junior high school and her brother was home sick, she reported that she used to call home twice a day to check on him. Other individuals struggled alone with the question of why this serious illness happened to their sibling. One young man recalled that throughout his childhood he was distracted by guilty ruminations about why his brother was sick, "It took up a lot of people's time. Emotional energy is what it is. If you want to talk about standing and having any clear, comfortable, free thinking time it was always a constant thought, why is it, why him and not me? Trading places would have been easier."

Many siblings felt the need to be less of a strain on their parents, and tried to be, as Jane stated, "independent, intelligent, rational, and supportive" for them. Seeing their parents, particularly their mothers, so worried and unhappy, they chose to contain normal adolescent rebellions. Danelle, 15 years old when her younger sister died, recalled how she could see her mother's hurt and tried to be as good as possible:

> I think I never went through a rebellious period. I didn't do this consciously. It was a subconscious thing. But I saw through my mother. I saw such pain in her eyes all the time. I couldn't stand it. I didn't want to do anything to hurt anyone. I wanted everything to be okay. So I would try to be a model child.

Some siblings obeyed the rules of the home without question, concerned that they would cause their parents more anxiety than they already had: "I always felt like if I had to be in by 12, I'd better be in by 12. I wouldn't want them to think something happened to me, 'cause I felt they had gone through enough."

For some young adults, career choices were directly influenced by concern about parents. Frank, 24 years old when his younger sister died, had spent some time in South America and could not stop worrying about how his mother was doing back at home. He decided to return home shortly after the following dream:

> I was running up and down these streets looking for my sister. I got further and further out from the city. I had this feeling of urgency and I rode out and out into the mountains. Then I jumped down this mountainside and there were all these crevices, and I kept jumping over the crevices while looking for my sister. In one of the crevices there was some sort of a creature threatening my mother. This creature may have been death or the burden that my sister's illness placed on her, and I jumped down there and helped rescue my mother. It was really apparent that I felt the urgency that I just couldn't run off to the other side of the world. I had to be there to help pull her through.

A major issue for mothers seemed to be how to handle their anxiety. Concerns related to having a seriously ill child altered previously calm personalities. The experience of having a fatally ill child shattered former illusions of a safe and sane world. Several mothers had nervous break-downs while the siblings were young. One young woman reported that her mother had felt that she had to be in control of the situation all the time, and she couldn't be, and that's what "put her over the edge at one time." Another sibling complained that her mother became fanatical about sched-uling, and compulsive about cleaning. Everything had to be done at the right time and done to perfection, in order to keep some semblance of being in control of things. Some mothers became extremely overprotective of their well children. Leslie recalled that her mother did not want anything to happen to her because, "there was already something wrong with the other two. I was the only healthy one. So you know, 'Don't get near my daughter, don't touch her, she has to stay the way she is.'" The anxiety of the mothers in some instances directly spilled over to their children. One unfortunate lesson that siblings learned from parents was that the world was a scary place. Sally, 18 years old when her sibling died, reported: "My mother is a very anxious person and I know that from the time I was very young, one of the biggest things I learned from her were her anxieties." Some respondents reported that their mothers turned to alcohol. One individual's mother had watched her own mother die and could not do anything about it. Now she was watching her own son die and again was helpless: "She began drinking a lot, which was hard for us to see, because we weren't used to seeing things like that. I talked to her about it and she said, 'Well, I just can't deal with it. It's an escape for me. For an hour or so a day, I just don't feel any pain.'" As one empathic sibling suggested, to lose a child is to lose the future, one's own chance for a better life:

> I don't think a parent can really ever be happy when they know their child won't grow up to be healthy. To me, when your kids grow up and they're healthy and happy then you can be truly satisfied. Even if your own life has been sort of a miserable failure, at least you know then that you made it possible for somebody else to have a better life. But when your children grow up to be sickly and they can never be well, I think that kills you just a little bit every day inside.

Fathers were frequently seen as unavailable. In the statistical sample of 25 respondents, one fourth of the fathers were coded as unavailable. Almost half of the statistical sample were described as unpredictable, preoccupied with their role as providers. Seen either as remote and shadowy, or as angry with short tempers, they were frequently recalled with dismay. Bruce, 16 years old when his younger brother died, had only vague recollections of his father, because they did not see him much: "When I did see him, he was ripping telephones out of the walls, or beating my mother. Yelling, screaming at her. We used to hide." Even during times of medical crises, there seemed to be little help forthcoming from fathers, often to the puzzled amazement and annoyance of the siblings. One young woman stated that her mother still tells them about times when she needed to go to the hospital and her father was too busy with something else. "You can't understand why he just didn't drop it and go too, it really was kind of ridiculous." Fathers often felt considerable economic strain of the illness. Medical insurance was not always available, and if it was, covered the cost of the illness only for a short time. One sibling remembered a comment that over half of the family income went to medicine alone. Fathers often worked two or three jobs, and it was not unusual for some mothers to have to work outside the home as well. Dennie, 10 years old when her older brother Mark died, reported how she would try very hard to see her mother for a few moments.

"Mom was always working. She worked 3 to 11 when I was small and Dad worked during the day. I'd run home from school because I'd get home just in time to talk to her while she took a shower and then see her off to work. But I remember missing her a lot. And she was with Mark a lot." Some insurance plans covered hospitalizations but not medications, which were very expensive. It was common to exceed covered benefits if the child's hospital stay went on for months. Only a lucky few siblings, who had fathers whose jobs kept them at home, were able to retain a protected sphere in which they could enjoy their relationship. One young man, who grew up on a ranch in the country, reported that his father would take him with him whenever he could: "When I was real small he'd take me in the pickup. Then when I was about 6 or 7 and I was able to ride a horse, I'd go with him working cattle horseback out in the mountains just like I was a regular cowboy, except he'd keep a little closer eye on me. We had a great time." But most fathers did not work at home. Some regularly worked overtime all of the sick child's life. Vacations were foregone. When fathers were at home, financial and emotional concerns occupied their attention, and fathers were lost to their children. One young man recalled that until he was 5 years old, when his two brothers were diagnosed with CF, he and his father were very close:

> I really felt like my father started out with a lot of energy and potential for being a very great person as a dad, and that the burden, the responsibility of having two children with CF just wiped it out right off the bat. I don't know to this day what went on inside him, what decisions he made, how he handled it all up here, but he really pretty much checked out as a sharing person.

Siblings speculated about the reason why their fathers appeared to be in psychological distress. One young woman believed that her father, who had been "top banana and everything, top athlete, top of the class," could not accept that he "had produced something that wasn't perfect." Some individuals felt that their fathers had withdrawn into their work not only because of the economic exigencies but because it was an escape from an emotional ordeal they could not face. Rick attributed his father's withdrawal from the family as linked to his difficulty in handling the illness:

> I love my father and did then. He was good to us I suppose. But he was very much involved in his existence as an artist, he had his own world and he remained within it. He couldn't stand the thought of anybody being sick. That repulsed him. He refrained, kept his hands off, was on the periphery of it, wouldn't dig in, I think not particularly because he's a weak man in that respect but because he loved her a great deal, and he could not tolerate seeing, thinking, conceiving of her as sick or dealing with that sickness.

Many siblings recalled that anger and arguments were "just generally in the air" and a familiar part of family life. Many men attacked their wives simply because they were easy targets, close at hand. Sally explained how her parents handled their anger: "It's got to go somewhere, and for someone who's ill-equipped, they're going to hang it on the person they used to love." Physicians have noted that no matter how hard they try to explain the shared genetic responsibility of CF to the parents, men tend to blame their wives—after all, it was the woman's job to have a healthy baby (Nathanson, personal communication, March 1, 1984). Conflict between preferred male and female coping styles also seemed to generate much anger, with wives wanting to talk about their feelings and men wishing to withdraw and not dwell on them. Accommodations were made generally by the wife, sometimes at great personal cost. One sibling stated that her mother began drinking because her father could not stand to see his wife cry. When she drank, she could get some temporary relief without upsetting him. Wives absorbed their husbands' anger, trying to keep peace as much as possible. One young man recalled the distressing family atmosphere in his home and his mother's attempt to keep it as pleasant as she could:

> My early years were pretty tumultuous. I can remember my parents being upset enormously, almost constantly, especially my father. My mother's role in my early years was more a consoler, a protector, from my father and his upset. I think he bore the brunt of the responsibility of raising all of us. My mother's world was the realm of the known. The home, providing food, keeping the children clean.

Because CF is a recessive genetic disease in which both parents have to be carriers, some siblings speculated that the marriage itself was called into question. One young man believed that although his parents would not admit it, the hostility that they had toward each other may have been brought on by the thought, "Well, if I'd have married somebody else, I might not have had a child with CF." Others felt that only those marriages with previous difficulties became problematic. One young man, 19 years old when his old brother died, explained how a diagnosis of CF in a child could be the last straw in a troubled marriage: "I think they had problems to start with. When they had the CF thing, it was almost like a slap in the face. Not only do you two have to live together, but I'm going to give you these two kids that require so much care that you're not gonna know what hit you."

Unfortunately, it seemed that anger and guilt were frequently displaced onto the well siblings. One young woman, 15 years old when her older sister died, looked back on her tumultuous childhood years and gave one poignant example of her father shouting at her for blocking her sister's reading light:

I was standing looking at my fish one day. I'll never forget that. My sister was sitting there on the couch, and my father comes in. Nobody said anything to him; he just flew off the handle, and yelled at me for standing there in her light. She never said a word, I wasn't even in her way. He just flips out on things like that. Goes crazy. Every time I walk in the house, that's all he ever tells me, "you're nothing but a jackass." That's all he ever told me, from the day I was born, "you're nothing but a jackass."

One perceptive sibling suggested that his father covered up his sadness with anger. Some individuals were able to look beyond the rage and see that their fathers were in great emotional pain. One young woman, 13 years old when her older sister died, explained how she felt watching her father cry:

You could see it in his eyes. That's what would break me down. If my sister would come home from the hospital and the doctor had something else to say to my father, he would take off into another room. I'd peek in or something and see him crying. For a man to cry really hurts me, because they've got to be strong.

Some fathers had to pass up job advancements because they were restricted to living in an area near the hospital. Others were advised by physicians to refuse job offers that were located in climates thought congenial to the disease. For a few men, having a fatally ill child was just another unfortunate blow in a life worn down by prior adversity. One young woman understood her father's difficulty in accepting that his child had CF, because his sister had been retarded, and everything had focused on her throughout his childhood. Another young woman recalled a conversation between her father and their parish priest when her father said there would not be another hell, because he had already come through it. She feels that every time her father had tried to make a positive move for himself, he had been thwarted. She sadly described her father's early family life:

His father died at an early age of cancer of the colon. His brother had spina bifida and died at the age of 19, and my father was the one who would cart him around in the wagon because he couldn't walk. And then to have a son who he knew was going to die at an early age, I think it just ripped him apart.

What is unfortunate is that siblings were unable to connect parental unhappiness to the difficult situation. Instead, they too often concluded that, because the parent was unavailable to them, they must be unlovable.

Chapter 3

The Sibling Relationship

Once I had a brother
Born to my sweet mother ...
—Brother Blue, Storyteller, Cambridge, Massachusetts

Since the 1980s, the sibling relationship has received increasing amounts of research and theoretical attention (Bank & Kahn, 1982; Dunn, 1985; Rosen, 1985). Investigators have begun to explore reactions to serious illness and the death of a sibling to various illnesses (Armstrong-Dailey & Goltzer, 1993; Balk 1983; Bearison & Mulhern, 1994; Bluebond-Langner, 1991b; Fanos & Nickerson, 1991; Fanos & Wiener, 1994; Koch-Hattem 1986; Krell & Rabkin, 1979; Lobato, 1990; Martinson & Campos, 1991; Pollock 1986; Spinetta, 1981). The complex sibling bond as it changes and evolves over the entire life span has only begun to be explored (Boer & Dunn, 1992; Hetherington, Reiss, & Plomin, 1993; Lamb & Sutton-Smith, 1982).

In the families that I studied, it was clear that the sibling was generally of great importance to the survivor, although individuals expressed differing degrees of actual involvement while growing up. In the statistical sample, 20% of the siblings were coded as having idealized the individual with CF, 36% expressed warmth, and 44% expressed slight attachment. Factors that seemed to have influenced the intensity of the bond were closeness in age, sharing a room, or having similar personalities or shared interests. But for other individuals, the sibling bond seemed to have been altered in subtle ways by the illness experience.

DISTANCES

For some of the siblings, there had been a loss in emotional relationship with the afflicted sibling before the death. Out of a desire to protect the sick child, parents warned their other children not to hit him or her, not to play roughly, and so forth, often with no explanation offered. One young man, 18 years old when his sister died, could never understand why he could not play with his sister as other children could. He recalled the day when he was playing football and had set up his sister as the tackling dummy. His parents came out and ordered him to stop, and the intensity of their response bewildered him.

Because the child with CF was often not feeling well, his or her sibling resorted to playing almost exclusively with peers outside the family. As one young man stated, "I guess I had my own friends. Timmy was in the oxygen tent or going through therapy." As the disease progressed, some sick children would spend increasing periods of time in the hospital, and hospital rules discouraged the well children from visiting. It was extremely rare for siblings to talk with each other about the illness or the possibility of dying. With such an important secret wedged between them, relationships suffered. In families where one child had already died from CF, some well siblings detached themselves from affected brothers or sisters out of a desire to protect themselves from the inevitable hurt. One young man explained that when his younger brother died, he comforted his other brother who had CF, but the following thought ran through his mind, "I don't want to get close to him, because he's gonna die on me." One young woman reported that when she was 15 years old, her brother was diagnosed. She never let herself get as attached to him as she did to her other siblings. Andy recalled that when he was 9 years old and the first of his siblings died, he detached himself from his CF-affected twin Bill: "I just kind of kept my distance. I mean we were close in one way and distant in another." Andy continued: "And then it made me not hate Bill, but I was scared of him. I knew he was next. I knew he was going to be the next one, and when it was going to strike, I didn't know. I was afraid to get close. And God, he was my brother, and I was more distant than if he was a stranger." Ralph, deeply moved at 10 years old by the death of his older brother, distanced himself from his younger well sibling to protect himself from the possibility of being hurt again. He told himself that it would make him stronger to grow up independent, reasoning that "when you get so you depend on somebody, if that person's not there, you don't know what to do. You get lost." He felt this independence was also something that his younger brother should have, and actively tried to develop this quality in him: "I just had a feeling that I should try to do that. For his own good."

In other families it seemed that it was the sick child who distanced him or herself from the well sibling. For some individuals, this may have been a response to not feeling well. One young man, 10 years old when his older brother died, can remember looking forward to visiting him in the hospital. However, the sick child was grouchy or abrupt, because he was not feeling well. His parents would explain to the healthy child that he should not feel hurt, because his brother was trying to protect him from seeing him so sick. For other children afflicted with CF, their distancing may have arisen from their own difficulty in talking to anyone about their illness or their desire to shield friends from sharing an experience that would be difficult to understand, and, frequently, friends were shocked by the death. Regarding one of her brother's friends, Anna said, "She was one of the very few outsiders that got close to him, as close as you could get to Sammy." She continued: "I don't think he was *withdrawn* withdrawn. He just decided he wasn't going to get involved with outside people. At school he would start setting up friendships—like there was this one guy he used to walk home with—but it seemed like if it got too close, then that was it." Upon reflection, some siblings felt that the ill child had kept him or herself distant out of a desire to protect the well sibling from the pain of the reality of the illness. As Erin, 14 years old when her older brother Jim died, articulated: "I think that was something he really practiced, keeping a distance from people, just because he was a sick boy." She explained:

> I think Jim knew that Jim wasn't going to live, and I think he tried to keep a real distance between us. I think that he kind of put up a front. He was only willing to let me get so close because he knew that he was going to die. That was his way of dealing with it and his way of trying to make sure I didn't get hurt. But at the same time, it wouldn't matter if he built a brick wall between us, I would still feel really close to him, and I still do feel close to him.

The well sibling's resentment of the fact that the sick child received more time or attention also interfered with the attachment bond. In the statistical sample, 28% of the siblings were coded as having felt no resentment toward the individual with CF, 40% were coded as expressing slight resentment, and 32% were coded as expressing high resentment. Many siblings stated that the unbalanced competition between them was a barrier in some ways to getting really close to each other. Several individuals were able to understand the reason why the ill sibling received more attention, either because parents took the time for explanations or because the sibling was so sick it was obvious that, as one sibling stated, "the situation demanded it." Most respondents, unfortunately, saw only the inequality and did not understand the reason. As one sibling reported, "Well, this will sound bad, but a lot of times I was kind of jealous. Not of my sister but of how much attention she got. My mother had to give her that attention. But I don't know I understood it for how young I was." Although the resentment, when it appeared in the interview, seemed to have been elicited in direct relationship to the afflicted child's receiving more emotional support, it was rarely expressed directly against the child. Instead, this resentment seemed to fuel anger against the parents. Andy, growing up with two brothers with CF, one of whom was his twin, reported:

I loved my brothers. I mean, you know, of course I did. But I felt they were getting all the attention. I was the little hellion. I would do things to aggravate them and get slapped, but at least I got attention. My mother and father weren't giving me attention. They were, but it was all being projected toward the sick children. And I think they probably thought I should've understood that. But I didn't.

Dennie, 10 years old when her older brother died, pointed out that she does not remember resenting her sibling when her father was too busy to take her anywhere, but instead focused her anger at her father: "He was the one that wouldn't take me." Jealousy was fueled over the sick child's receiving more than his or her share of attention, even if it was medically based and signaled serious illness.

One young man, 15 years old when his sibling died, recalled going through the same battery of tests as the CF-affected child. He stated: "I remember feeling left out 'cause everybody else had something, and I didn't. I guess that's what you feel when you're 9 years old." One sibling "always wanted a broken bone." Dan, now a successful physician, matched his allergies against his brother's illness, feeling that his allergy shots could not compete with the medical treatments his brother received.

Some siblings, perceiving that sickness brought with it increased parental attention, hoped for a little sickness for themselves. Some succeeded, emerging with various chronic complaints such as asthma, constant flu, bedwetting, and so on. Others tried to get attention by annoying or careless behavior and seemed to have had more than their share of childhood accidents and broken bones. Andy reported that, when he was little, he had more cuts than anyone: "I was very accident-prone. I had more stitches than Singer Sewing Machine Company." Others tried desperately to get attention by excelling in sports or schoolwork or some combination of the two. Dan reported that he would compete with his brother, who was the focus of his parents' attention because of his illness:

> I don't want to play amateur psychoanalyst, but I am a doctor, and I can't look back and not see what was going on. I would compete by doing the standard things that other kids would do to make their parents proud, bringing home medals, doing well in athletics, doing well in scholastics. I suppose it could have gone the other way and I could have become a problem child and, indeed, from about 4 to 6, my parents had to move out of one neighborhood because of me. I was just hell on wheels. I guess they expected me to do very poor scholastically. Instead, I went right to the head of the class, and fell into that role of satisfying whatever competitive urge I had.
> I confronted my mother with it a couple of times. I said, "I'm sorry I'm not sick. But I'm not. And that's the way it is." The thing that always bugged me is that most parents would have shot to have a son who brought home all the honors like I did. I was running second in a two-horse race.

Competitive rivalries with the ill sibling generally began to turn around as the well sibling emerged from childhood. Adolescence seemed to be a period during which the relationship was reevaluated and could be enjoyed. Erin recalled how her relationship with her older brother improved as they got older:

> I told you that he and I fought all the time, and we were getting to the point that we wouldn't fight as much, as we were doing more and more together. I was looking forward to being in school with him. I was going to be a freshman, and he'd be a senior in high school. I was really looking forward to that, because then I felt like he and I would have more in common, and I was really looking forward to getting close to him. We were close, but I know we would have been a lot closer. So, I think that when he died, I felt ripped off.

Another sibling discussed that she had always liked her brother, even though the fact that he "got away with murder would drive me up the wall." She remembered how her going away to college had changed their relationship for the better, explaining:

> I was out of his turf. I came back that summer, the last summer that I saw him. I remember his friends telling me how proud he was of his brother. So once I was out of his turf, he could afford to be proud of me. That was a very heartwarming experience. I think that summer we were closer together than ever before.

For those whose siblings died just at this turning point in the move toward increased attachment, it was a particularly devastating and embittering experience.

ATTACHMENT

If the sibling relationship was altered negatively for some, it was intensified for others. For most, although strong resentment may have been expressed, a strong attachment was demonstrated as well. Some relationships became more intense because the sick child spent so much time at home. One sibling stated that her relationship with her brother was strengthened because he was not able to go to school. She reported, "We were his contact with the outside world. He was away from normal friendships, because he was at home. So a lot of his contact would be with me and my friends." Individuals who clearly understood that their sibling was sick, even very sick, struggled with the guilt that this awareness evoked. Bruce, 16 years old when his younger brother died, reported, "I used to always give him my allowance; I guess I felt sorry for him. I used to buy him tons of stuff later on when I had a job. For Christmas I'd overdo it." Some siblings hoped for a little illness for themselves, so that magically the sick child would get better. Struggling with feelings of guilt and sadness, they found it hard to understand why the sibling was so ill when they were not. These existential difficulties were generally kept to themselves, because they feared that there would be no receptive audience. Andy recalled his attempts to make some meaning out of his brother's illness, stating:

> And then a lot of times I got really depressed. I'd say, "Why couldn't it have been me instead of him?" I went through that routine a lot. I felt guilty that he was sick and I wasn't. How did I get the luck of not being sick? It's funny, it took me a long time to even talk about it. I never talked about it.

When the ill child was idealized, either by the parents or the siblings themselves, it was particularly difficult to grasp why the "good" person was sick and the "bad" one was healthy. As with the witch hunts, to live was to be convicted.

There was a great degree of attachment and love expressed in the interview material for the lost sibling. The longing generally revolved around five primary roles that were lost when the sick child died.

Best Friend

Some siblings had been the survivor's closest companion, playmate, sharer of confidences, and best friend. Youngsters had fished together, played baseball together, baked cookies together, and had spent most of their time together. Particularly for younger children, who had not yet moved to peers for their friendships, the loss of the sibling meant the loss not only of their best friend but of their *only* friend. Andy recalled that they lived in a very isolated part of the country, and they did not have many friends outside the family. Therefore, he was very close to his brother Rob, who was a year older. As he recalled:

> I guess I would say he was kind of my hero. Whatever he did, I wanted to do. He was my buddy. When he went to school, I couldn't wait to go to school. And when he died, it wrecked me. I felt that I got too close to him, like me and him were just like—we weren't brothers, we were best friends. When he went away to school for first grade, I was lost.

Memories evoked are of quiet times, close times, with just the children sharing an experience. Dennie, 10 years when her older brother Mike died, recalled one Christmas Eve when she woke up and went into the living room:

Mike was sitting on the couch all curled up, and he was looking at the Christmas tree. It was dark, the lights were on the tree in the living room. We sat down on the couch, and we were all curled up together under a blanket, and we were guessing what Santa had brought everyone. We had the best, nice times like that.

He used to like to cook, and I'd wake up in the middle of the night and hear something in the kitchen. I'd go out and he was cooking, and we'd sit and eat together, because he wasn't supposed to eat those things, and he could only get away with it then. He made the best beef stew and he was just a little kid. We'd eat beef stew together in the middle of the night.

The illness was not always a barrier to the attachment relationship between the siblings. Jenny remembered that her sister would sleep in a mist tent, and many nights she would bring her sleeping bag into the room and spend the night on the floor next to her bed. Some siblings had shared a room with the sick sibling, and the relationship had been their most intense one within the family. For many, the longing and the idealization of the sibling remained intertwined forever, and the loss was irreconcilable. Danelle, 15 years old when her younger sister died, explained how similar their personalities had been:

It was a very unusual relationship. I remember at the eulogy the rabbi said that. Same interests, same everything. Scary in a way. I don't even think we ever argued. I even remember as a kid my friends would come over and we would all play. And usually no one wants their younger brothers and sisters. But they all said, "Come on in, come on in, play."

Vital Link

Many respondents felt that the ill sibling had been the most important link within the family unit. The lost sibling was frequently portrayed as the most lively of the group, the best and the brightest, the energizer for the family. As Erin explained, "I always felt like we had this chain link of a family and there's five links, and I felt like the middle link got broken right out." She described her brother as having been a very enthusiastic person, and that he had been the one to motivate them to do fun activities. She feels that her brother was a "real vital link and I just think things would be a real lot different if he was still alive than they are now." For some siblings, this may reflect the tendency within a family with a seriously ill child to reorganize around the sick individual. It also may reflect the idea that the afflicted child was able to develop fully inborn talent and intelligence because physical prowess was not an option. Knowing that they are very sick and may not live long may also propel these individuals to live life to the fullest, fostering a maturity and ability to love beyond their years. In fact, physicians have noted that children with CF frequently appear brighter than other children (Nickerson, personal communication, September 10, 1990). Whatever the reasons, the lost sibling was a crucial force for the families of many of the siblings with whom I spoke. Rick explained how important his sister with CF had been in organizing family fun and energizing his less outgoing sister, Elin:

> Jill was a very important link. Jill was gorgeous. When she was in the hospital, she was always in burn wards and visiting kids. She was just wonderful, really wonderful. Jill was a bridge, an avenue, a vivacious and very warm and outgoing person. She was an inspiration and a spark for Elin. With that gone, Elin really caved in. When Susie was born, we all galvanized under Jill. She was like a doll for us, and we'd make all kinds of flower crowns and take her down to the fields and treat her like a princess, like a doll, and Jill again was the force behind that.

Surrogate Parent

Bank and Kahn (1982) pointed out that in families in which parental underinvolvement is high, the sibling bond becomes more important. In the families that I studied, with parents so involved with the sick child, this reliance on sibling relationships seemed to have occurred. The finding that those siblings who idealized the lost individual experienced more difficulties as adults (see appendix) is a very interesting one. Although it may lend support to theoretical views on idealization as a defense against envy (Klein, 1957), it may also suggest that, where parental relationships were lacking, siblings functioned as parental figures. Parental preoccupation with their own struggles, both internal and external, often created a vacuum in the parental role. When parents were spending time at the hospital or working to pay for the added expenses of the illness, siblings tried to take care of each other as much as possible. One young woman, the only healthy child with two siblings with CF, recalled that when her brother died, she felt totally alone. When her brother was alive at least she had somebody home at dinnertime when her sister, also affected with CF, was in the hospital.

If the sibling with CF was the oldest child in the family, he or she frequently tried to help out with the missing role, functioning in some instances as a surrogate parent. In those situations, when the individual with CF died, the loss of the sibling came as a double blow, simultaneously removing two roles. Donna, 14 years old when her older brother Matthew died, recalled how he had helped motivate her to do her schoolwork in her father's absence:

Matthew was my everything. Everything that went wrong, I could go to him and he would always make it better. So then I had to turn to Carl 'cause he was older than me. It just wasn't the same. I would come home and Matthew would say, "Well, you better sit down and do your homework, and you're not doing anything until you do." And after that I had nobody to tell me what to do, and so I didn't care. He would have directed me. He would've been my incentive program. He was basically my father when my father was away.

Role Model

When the sibling who died was younger than the well child, the loss was of the source of idealization or the loss of narcissistic supplies. If the child with CF was older than the survivor sibling, he or she was often seen as a hero or heroine, as an identification figure for the younger sibling. This individual was instrumental in leading the younger child out into the world, introducing him or her to areas of interest, and so on. Ralph remembered how much he had looked up to his older brother, and how much he did not want to miss anything they were doing. He reported that his brother taught him things that he has continued to use in his life. If interests were shared, the relationship served a particularly important role. For example, one young man felt that his sister affected him more than anyone else because they were both very artistic.

Several siblings continued to use the lost sibling as a reference point. Carl, Donna's older brother, explained that when he was asked to be a programmer within 9 months of working at his new job, he compared his success to his brother:

I felt that here I am 21, my brother died when he was 21. Although I haven't accomplished as much in my life as he had accomplished in his, I guess I have done all right for myself. When my sister turned 21, I thought about what he had accomplished, and I think that she should have accomplished more. My brother being as sick as he was, and Donna being as well as she is, she should have done better for herself. So I guess even now I use my brother as a role model.

Many individuals lamented the premature loss of the help an older sibling can provide. Tom, who had lost both of his older brothers by the time he was 15, regretted that he did not have anybody to teach him the things that older brothers teach younger brothers. For some, the role of the older brother or sister had been altered by the disease process. Reactions of peers to the stigma of the illness were the source of much pain and confusion for younger siblings, who idealized the older sibling. One young man remembered going to school on the school bus with his older brother when his brother's teeth were "just a wreck." He recalled that some children on the bus teased his brother because of his discolored teeth, and he was very upset that they were doing that: "This was, you know, my big brother." Struggling with a desire to protect the sibling with CF, or embarrassment that the person was not in all ways the big brother or sister, siblings tried to find a happy medium for themselves. One young man, 10 years old when his older brother died, stated:

> He was my big brother, the one I looked up to. I admired him for his intellect and what he could do. He was good with his hands and artistic. As a team, he was the brain, and I was the brawn. He was subject to some teasing and harassment when we were in grade school. I found myself wanting to defend him and kind of drifting with the crowd, which I alternately felt indifferent and guilty about.

Protective instincts usually won out, particularly when the unaffected sibling understood that the relationship might be all too short. One young man explained that he and his other well siblings used to tease his ill sister, but that they always made sure that nobody was ever mean to her. "We were always extra careful of her 'cause we knew she wasn't going to be around forever. So we just tried to be nice while she was here." Some well siblings continued to look to their sick older brother or sister as role models, as they themselves became superior only in physical prowess. Martin recalled how his relationship with his brother changed in some ways over time. Although his brother was very thin and light because of the disease, he was a better athlete than Martin was when they were young. However, at the age of 12 or 13, Martin started to surpass his brother in sports. Nevertheless, his brother retained the role of leader:

> See, he was my big brother but I was bigger than him. So he was my big brother mentally. Physically I was the big brother. But he was the leader of everything, he was the one to decide when to go to the movies or something like that. I would be the protector. I took over that role very early.

Many siblings had a change of status with the loss of the individual. The next oldest sibling often tried to fill the role emptied by the death, with no socialization processes to support this change. Following his brother's death, one respondent articulated that his status within the family structure changed from being the middle to being the oldest child, "with all the benefits and responsibilities that it entails." Ralph felt alone following his older brother's death because he was no longer following in someone else's footsteps: "Now I was leading," he remembered. Some siblings were clear that the loss of the older sibling meant the loss of an effective agent of socialization of the parents.

One sibling recalled that when she became 20 years old, she was the first child that her parents had that had lived to that age:

> It was like, from here on, I was breaking new ground. They didn't know how to react with a person of this age. I was becoming a young adult. They'd dealt with kids from 0 to 19, but from there on, I was breaking ground. They wouldn't know how to react to me, and I wouldn't know how to react to them.

Even if the role realignment was resented by younger siblings, the one who was next in the birth order tried to take over the function of "the vital link" as best as possible. When Rick's older sister died when he was 13 years old, he believed that his role was to take over as the oldest in the family. He tried to maintain the continuity, the network. He attempted to write frequently and give advice to his younger brothers and sisters: "I think I'm still carrying on the idea that I'm the oldest. I think I'm still trying to provide that kind of role model."

Role of "Sibling"

Although the sibling may function informally as best friend, confidant, parental surrogate, role model into the world, and so forth, the relationship is a special one. This uniqueness is exemplified by the title of a book for children grieving the loss of their sibling, *Am I Still a Sister?* (Sims, 1986). Although one may lose individual friends, one has only one father, one mother, and siblings cannot be replaced. One young woman, 16 years old when her older sister died, thought it would be nice to have a sister to be able to talk to. "My girlfriend, and one of my closest girlfriends, both of them, have sisters that they're very close to." The loss of this irreplaceable category haunts survivor siblings and is the occasion for much envy. Danelle, 15 years old when she lost her younger sister, explained:

> People say, "I'm going on a trip, or I'm checking into college, and I don't have a roommate, but I'm going to room with my sister," and they go "yuck." I say to myself, "Oh, you're the luckiest person, because there's no one I would pick over her." People say to me, "You just think that, but that's not even natural. You want to be with your girlfriends more." That's the only time I envy people. And I've always looked for a soulmate.

Some siblings suggested that when they had their own children, it seemed to them that their parents were able to replace the loss of their own child with their grandchildren. But there is nothing the sibling can do. As one young woman reported about her parents, now that she has a child, "I think they think of him as their son, but I still don't have my brother. He just hasn't replaced that."

Chapter 4

The Sibling's View
of the Illness

To unbind what is bound, to bring the underground waters to the surface: mankind is waiting and longing for such as can do that.
—Albert Schweitzer (*Out of my Life and Thought: An Autobiography*, 1964)

Many families with a chronically ill child do not communicate well about the disease. For example, in families with a child with CF, Turk (1964) pointed out the "web of silence" in families in which communication serves to conceal as much as it reveals. The demand of keeping the family secret is a heavy burden for a young sibling and threatens healthy development. In families affected by pediatric AIDS, communication concerning HIV and the possibility of a child's early death is often handled as a family secret within and outside of the family (Fanos & Wiener, 1994). Struggling to come to terms with why they must lie, siblings of HIV-infected children repeatedly discuss themes of secrecy during clinical sessions. As inquisitive peers ask children why their sibling is so sick, it becomes increasingly difficult not to tell the secret. There is often much anger expressed at parents as a consequence of feeling excluded from disclosure. Children may interpret the reason for their parents not telling them the truth to be that they are not important or that they may have done something wrong, causing the parents not to trust them. Furthermore, the siblings may think that the parents will always keep secrets from them (Fanos & Wiener, 1994).

Studies of siblings of children with cancer have shown that children coped better, and felt less isolated, when they were informed about the illness and the treatment program (Kramer, 1984). Families who communicate well before the death of a child tend to communicate well after the death also, and this communication is indicative of how well a surviving sibling will adjust to the loss (Birenbaum , Robinson, Phillips, Stewart, & McCown, 1989).

Clinicians frequently have little information on how parents actually communicate the news of fatal illness to their children, particularly the siblings. An important question is, in families with a fatally ill child: Who tells the children? As Davis (1963) pointed out in his study of families with a child with polio, explanations offered by most physicians are frequently confusing and veiled with ambiguity. This communication pattern, Davis suggests, often marks the initiation of the family into a world in which as much is left unsaid as is said, and in which the "art of hearing between the lines comes disturbingly into its own" (p. 31). It is the physician who frequently suggests to the family that they treat the child and the illness as "normal as possible," which is in fact good for the patient. The impact on the siblings, however, of growing up within a family in which an exceptional situation is treated as though it were normal is of questionable value. It may set a pattern in which dissociation from the illness experience is reinforced in order for the sibling to continue on with "normal" developmental tasks. Whether this learned dissociation lays the groundwork for a traumatic response to the sudden intrusion of the reality of the death has not been investigated.

In this study, only 20% of the families in the statistical sample reported that there had been good communication around the illness. One third of the families were coded as "veiled" communication, in which the sibling may have overheard hints of something seriously amiss, with no discussion or emotional support to help with processing the information. Approximately one half of the siblings reported that the illness had been handled as a "family secret" while they were growing up. For some individuals, simply being in the physician's office at the hospital for the interview brought back years of having been dragged along to the clinic with the sick child and being kept in the dark, confused and worried. One sibling, 14 years old when his brother died, has vivid memories of driving to the hospital with his family, waiting there, and driving home but never really knowing the outcome of the visit or what had taken place. Others recalled that information had been given to them in a way that was not useful. It was delivered at a level of sophistication of terminology beyond their childhood comprehension. One young man, 14 years old when his brother Ray died, recalled his confusion:

> We were all sitting in the car getting ready to go, and the phone rang. Dad goes to answer it. It was mom and she said, "Ray has gone into a coma." Dad hung up, packed his suitcase, called the limousine and left. And we're just sitting there in the car, asking, "When we're going skiing, when we're going skiing?" And they say Ray has gone into a coma. Well, what's a coma?

Others complained that although they were well aware of the eventual fatality of the disease of their sibling, there was no emotional support to aid in processing this knowledge. It would appear that mere cognitive ability to anticipate the eventual loss did not help the survivor sibling.

YOUNG CHILDREN

Younger children were most likely to take the illness for granted and to assume that everything was normal. If there were years in which the illness was under control, it looked as though the sibling just had a bad cold and would receive treatments. One young man, 10 years old when his brother died, stated that he had never really worried about the seriousness of his brother's illness:

> I was accepting that this was a given. This wasn't anything affecting his life—he went to school, we played around, so that was all right. There were visits to the doctor. There were maybe one or two hospitalizations before he got really sick. Again, it seemed like somebody who had a bout of pneumonia or a bad cold, and a period of rest was required. There wasn't any big stigma of chronic illness or terminal illness ever in our minds, at least in my mind.

The machinery that was an integral part of the treatment of CF appeared not to frighten siblings. Rather, some youngsters thought it was kind of fun, with mist tents turning into entertaining places:

> I never really thought of him as being sick, because he played with us. The only time he was sick was when he was in the hospital, and then he would come home and he was fine. And he had that mist tent. I used to go in there and talk to him when he was in bed. It was really stuffy and hot in there. But that seemed normal. I used to sometimes get in with him, 'cause I thought it was kind of neat.

If the home equipment elicited no direct concerns, and the illness might have been a cold, even the name of the disease held no particular terrors. One young man, 10 years old when his brother died, knew the word *cystic fibrosis* and knew that was what his brother had, but it was not mentioned to him that it was a life-threatening disease. He reported: "I didn't know my brother was going to die until after he died. I had no idea it was coming. That's kind of naive, but kids are allowed to be. But I also wasn't prepared." If parents did try to tell the well child about the seriousness of the illness, it was often very difficult for the youngster to understand the concept. Elin, 11 years old when her sister died, explained that she never thought of CF as very serious:

I guess I had this vague idea that it was some mechanical thing that had to get adjusted now and then. Every once in a while it would go wrong, and Jill would have to go back into the hospital and fix it up, and she'd come out and be as good as new. I can remember a couple of weeks before she died my parents told us, "This is very serious, there is a very good chance that Jill is going to die." And I was saying, "Well, sure, there's a chance that you're going to die when you have a cold, right?"

The concept of severe illness was difficult for the children to grasp because they had grown up with it. Because siblings affected with CF often appeared so normal and able to live an active life for the most part, the well siblings found the danger and severity of their siblings' condition hard to accept. Elin found the seriousness of the illness difficult to believe because her sister was very active and healthy—outside of her hospital stays, she was not sickly. She slept in an oxygen tent, but that seemed normal to Elin. She explained: "That's what you'd grown up with, so it didn't seem strange." The children seemed to struggle to comprehend the contradiction between the normality they perceived and the information they received from their parents. Even when the sibling was aware that the child with CF seemed very weak, had a poor complexion, a big stomach, yellow teeth, and could not digest food without difficulty, still the contradictions remained in the minds of the well siblings, as one reported: "It was hard to understand, really. Until he died. He was sick, but children don't die." A few perceptive youngsters were able to grasp the severity of the illness, particularly if the sibling was obviously sick. One young woman, 10 years old when her sister died, explained: "I can remember her one day walking up the stairs to school when she was blue. And we only lived across the street from the school." Her sister's difficulty in taking in enough oxygen caused her skin to take on a bluish shade, and this symptom alarmed the young girl. Another young woman said she was glad she had not known. At 12 years old, it seemed appropriate for her not to know; however, she felt that she would have been angry at her parents for not telling her if she had been older. Occasionally, it was a blunt remark from a relative outside the immediate family that informed the sibling that their brother or sister was going to die. Others recalled reading that children with CF did not live past teenage years. For those who wanted more information, it was not an easy road. One young woman, who lost three siblings to CF when she was 3, 5, and 10 years old, explained: "For a lot of time I would ask mom and then I thought, well, she's not telling me everything, so why should I ask her? It felt like she was hiding things from me. Then I started keeping things to myself."

Only one sibling, Andy, 9 years old when his older brother died, complained that his mother was too open about the eventual death of his brother. He lamented, "As a matter of fact, that came up too frequently, and it just upset me." Several young children remembered being told openly, but the communication appeared to have been bungled. Sally, for example, recalled that when she was about 10 or 11 years old, her mother, "maybe in a moment of weakness," told her that her brother may not live past 18 years of age. She recalled this "nightmare" memory following this realization:

> We were out on the swings playing with the kids from the neighborhood. The kids started bullying my brother, and knowing this kid had something in mind, I dragged him aside, sat on his head, and said, "Don't say that, my brother might not live past the age of 18." The kid jumped up and started yelling, "Ted's going to die when he's 18." Ted ran home crying. I didn't go home for about an hour. I didn't even think they'd ever want to see me again. Of course now I can say, hey, it wasn't totally your fault. You don't go from nothing to death in one afternoon.

ADOLESCENTS

Those siblings who had been adolescents at the time of the death seemed similarly confused. Some individuals reacted much as their younger counterparts did, accepting the unusual as normal. One young man never really thought about the fact that his brother was sick, other than the fact that he had to sleep in the "funky" tent at night. "I didn't even know what it was. I still don't know what it is." Although the adolescent group in the sample was more likely than younger children to understand that the sibling was ill, they, too, frequently did not grasp that their siblings with CF would eventually die. Rick, 13 years old when his older sister died, recalled:

> This sounds crass, but my awareness of it was not as much as it should be. I do have vivid memories of the hospital, of her going in and out, but from day one it seemed like just a natural part of the routine. Jill's sick again, we gotta take her to the hospital. She'll come back.

In fact, some youngsters were able to turn the pill-taking regimen into a game, happily fetching green or pink pills for the sibling. Jenny remembered:

> I had one of these ornaments on a Christmas tree—the little bells—and I used to keep them in my room. I gave her a bell, and I was like her little servant. Whenever she needed anything from bed she'd go, *ding, ding, ding,* and I'd run up there and go down and make her something, whatever she wanted.

It would appear that it was rare for parents to talk frankly with their well children about the illness. If they admonished siblings to be careful when playing with the sick child they rarely offered any accompanying explanation. Some siblings gleaned information from overhearing conversations between relatives. One young man, 14 years old when his younger brother died, commented that his parents never really told him what the problem was and what they were trying to do about it. He picked up little hints through conversation with his grandparents. Furthermore, siblings rarely discussed the illness with the child with CF. If it was ever mentioned, the affected child's discomfort became readily apparent. Danelle, 15 years old when her younger sister died, reported the one brief exchange between the two of them on the seriousness of the illness:

> I remember she said to me, "I know what I have." I didn't say anything, because I didn't even know. That's what she said. The way she said it was, "and I'm resigned to it." And it scared me. Just like that: "I know what I have." Not sad. Just straight.

Some adolescents were alerted that something was wrong by the tone of their parents' voices while they spoke with a relative or close friend over the phone. Tom, 14 years old when his older brother Bert died, stated:

> I knew something serious was happening, but I didn't quite know what was going to come of it. I guess I didn't want to face it. I heard a conversation on the phone. I didn't hear what was going on, I just heard the tone. It was when Bert was in the hospital, one of the last times when I realized he was real seriously ill. It wasn't a conscious thing but I knew it. It wasn't something that was discussed. I think that my parents wanted to be as hopeful as they could.

In particular cases, adolescents were aware that there were private conversations going on from which they were excluded. Other parents held private conversations with the well siblings but emphasized the positive aspects. Upon reflection, siblings assumed the parents did not want tell them that the ill brother or sister was going to die. The well siblings, however, wished that they had been informed. As Tom remembered, "It was like holding your breath and not wanting to know the truth, but knowing it at the same time." Some siblings suspected that something was very wrong, because the child was sick for a long time before he or she died. Looking back, there was much anger against parents for not divulging that the sibling might die. Many respondents felt that more conversation would have eased the burden of veiled fears and concerns. Tom wished there had been more discussion. He remembered, "On a short-term it may have been a problem, but long-term, it definitely would have helped. I do feel that certain things would have been more comfortable. I would not have been as fearful of certain things. I may have been concerned about them, but not as confused. I wouldn't have hidden from them."

Adolescents were more able to empathize with their parents' distress. Looking beyond the mask that their parents wore, some respondents perceived a gap in their close conversations. Danelle remembered sitting down with her mom and having "long soulful talks about stuff, but not the illness—nothing, nothing. That was real hidden." She continued:

I was always very optimistic and bubbly and energetic. I didn't really understand the disease my sister had, that it was fatal. So I kind of lived a happy life. My parents tried to do it that way. They didn't tell me that. But I think I'm pretty sensitive, and I was tuned into what was going on, because I can see sad faces. To tell you the truth, you said, "what was it like?" The one word I can think of spontaneously—I would say, hell. A living hell. For everyone.

The adolescents were more likely than the younger siblings to contradict themselves during the interview, and were more likely to blame themselves for their difficulty in accepting the truth:

I just knew something was bad. Serious. But I thought she'd get over it one day. I just didn't want to face it. I knew what the illness was, but I couldn't look it up. I didn't want to know. I thought if my mother kept working real hard, it would get better. But I really do think in the back of my mind I knew. I'll tell you why. I saw her suffer so much and I said to myself, "Nobody can suffer this much, all the throwing up and everything. How much longer is this gonna go on?" And I just read it in everyone's eyes. It was right there. No one even had to speak.

Confused and frightened, Danelle worried that maybe she, too, had CF. Thinking it might be contagious, she once asked her mother for reassurance. Her mother abruptly turned around and said, "'Of course not.' That was the end of that discussion." Danelle clearly understood that the topic was not to be brought up again. When parents disagreed on how much should be told or in what way, the siblings received jarring information without an opportunity for ongoing discussion. The coping styles of the parents frequently conflicted, and the sibling suffered:

I think my parents were at odds. My mother said I should definitely not know until it happened. My father said that I should have been told. So they disagreed. My father respected my mother's wishes, but he tried twice to give me a hint. I came back from camp and he said, "You know, your sister was so sick, she had pneumonia." So I said, "Oh, that's awful." He said, "She was in the hospital for a week." I just said, "Oh." Then he said, "One day she is just going to drop dead with all that coughing." Those were his words. And it was like a jolt. But he was trying to say, "Don't think there's hope because there isn't."

Sometimes parents avoided a frank discussion in an attempt to protect their well children. Other times it was the siblings who were trying to protect the parents. Fears that parents would think they were being silly, hypochondriacal, or selfish kept many worried siblings from raising any questions. Instead, they kept everything inside, bottling up fears. In the absence of open communication about the genetic aspects of the illness, various myths and fantasies flourished (Fanos & Johnson, 1992). One young man was told by his mother that if he had children they would all have CF. At the time of the interview, he still believed this to be true. Sally, 18 years old when her younger brother died, remembered struggling alone with questions she could not direct to parents too overwhelmed to listen: "How many bizarre things did I believe as a child? I don't know how much time I spent thinking when I was 13, 14, 15, how do I know I don't have it? Why him and not me? And there was no one there to …even if I had been able to put the questions into words to sort things out."

Many well siblings feared that they had CF. As young children, many had been subjected to tests for CF in which they had been wrapped in plastic bags and left alone on a cot in a clinic room to sweat for a long time. This experience generated terror that they might have CF: "I remember when I was a tiny little kid, and nobody would tell me why. I think if things had been more out in the open it would have been a lot easier for me to deal with." One young man remembered going into to the hospital for his test, and the scary expression on his parents' faces while they waited for the result:

> The only thing I remember about coming to Children's is that we were put in this room. We were wrapped up in plastic bags and made to sweat, and it was hot. So hot. And it seemed like we stayed in there all day. Didn't know what the hell was going on or what. I knew it was important to my mother and father because they always had this look of dread on their faces.

One young man recalled being told by doctors that the score on the test was 90, whereas his sibling's score was 70. He remembered that this meant that he was more likely to have children with CF than the sibling who received a lower score. For this young man, as well as for several other individuals, assumptions made on the basis of results of childhood testing shaped future plans for marriage and having children.

ADULTS

Individuals who had been at least 18 years old when their sibling died generally had more years to read cues concerning the seriousness of the illness. Constant coughing, great difficulty in breathing, and other physiological markers that were too difficult to ignore were more likely to penetrate the siblings' defenses. One young woman, 22 years old when her brother died, remembered a summer evening when her mother let her borrow the car. She was planning to take her sick brother and his best friend to the nearby root beer stand. She pulled up alongside the porch in order to pick them up, and had the following frightening experience:

> He said, "I can't see you." It was like my heart stopped. I said, "Oh my God, he's blind." I said, "What do you mean you can't see me?" It was just a very short distance. He said, "I can't see where you are." I said, "I'm right here in the car. See the car?" "I can't see the car." Then I can't remember. I must have walked him to the car and I think that was the first time that I realized Mike was getting worse. It kind of hit me right smack dab in the middle of my forehead, he's not getting better. Maybe I blocked it out of my mind, because when he died I still went. ... My sister told me he was dead, and I said, "He's not dead. Why would you say that? How can you say that?" I think my exact words were, "You're lying to me."

If adults were more able to perceive accurately the seriousness of the illness, some siblings still struggled with their own internal ability to believe that death was really coming. One young woman, 18 years when her older sister died, explained:

> We were brought up to know that there was a problem. My parents never tried to hide it from us. But I never really thought about it. We always played, and it never seemed to bother her. If she had a bad night sleeping, that would kind of affect me, because I was sleeping in the same room. But it really started to bother me when I got in high school, because that's when she started getting bad and lost a lot of weight and everything was starting to go downhill at that point. That's when it really started to affect me, but I think I blocked it out. I didn't want to face up to it.

Some adults blamed their difficulty in comprehending the possibility of their sibling dying on their parents' inability to tell them the truth directly. One young man wondered why his sister coughed when none of her friends did. He thought that it would have been hard for his parents to tell him that his sister had a fatal disease. Roland, 20 years old when his younger sister Karen died, had many questions about CF but was unable to discuss his concerns. Thinking that his sister had something like asthma, he assumed that she would be okay. Later on, as he became older, and she was getting worse, he asked his mother and father:

> "What the hell is cystic fibrosis?" "Well, she's got a lung infection or a lung disease, she has no pancreas, you have to slap her on the back to loosen up the phlegm." Well, that's all very interesting. But it never really concerned me. I didn't think it was a danger to her immediate health and I always

thought that she was going to get better. And then maybe about a year before she died, we realized that it was really serious. When she had to stay in the hospital for a while, we came to see her once or twice. They [his parents] had come up by themselves. We had stayed home. It wasn't until when I woke up the next morning. Mom came in, started crying and said, "Karen passed away." And that's when it hit me that this wasn't an asthma attack. It was something far worse.

Many siblings had a sense of impending doom even if there had been no discussion within the family. One young man, 19 years old when his older brother died, felt that everybody knew that something bad eventually was going to happen. "But it was always underlying, it was unsaid, it was heard here and there." Some siblings remembered one instance when they became alarmed by something that was said by a parent, often at an inopportune time, with no further explanation offered. One young man knew that his brother was sick since he slept in the tent, but the fact that he was seriously ill never registered. He remembered one day having done something "awful" to his brother and his mother screaming at him: "You have to be nice to him, he's very, very sick," and I said, "What's the matter with him?" This young man cannot remember his mother's response, but it wasn't until years later that it dawned on him that his brother was going to die.

There were many reasons not to talk about the illness. One sibling tried to understand why he was reluctant to bring it up: "I don't know if that's because I knew that if I did bring up a subject, help would be unavailable, or it would make the matter worse. I don't know the reason why I kept it to myself." Many siblings protected their parents or had enough unpleasant experiences trying to broach the topic within the family that they gave up. One young woman recalled that she had no one to talk to. She didn't want to worry her parents, and she couldn't talk to her grandfather because whenever anybody mentioned CF, he would begin to cry. Other siblings searched for confidants outside their family and had a larger radius to draw from than their younger counterparts. One young woman recalled that when she was 25 years old:

> I didn't know who to talk to. I knew that she [her sister] was talking to a minister who was playing backgammon at the hospital with her, so I didn't want to talk to him. The Catholic priests around here are not any good. My high school principal—I didn't feel as though I could really talk to him. So I ended up calling the minister's wife and talking to her and saying "You know, she is not going to last, and I don't think my parents realize that."

Most siblings did, however, stay within the confines of the family, and it was not unusual for them to be concerned about their own health for years. Sally worried throughout her childhood that CF had finally developed in her. She recalled, "I was concerned that I had CF. Not caught it, because you don't catch it, but that it had been there all along, and it had decided to bloom inside me. I thought about it off and on for five, seven, eight years. Wondering if I'm going to get it." From the age of 15 to her late 20s, she was terrified that she had the same disease. "I heard that cystic fibrosis was a disease of very young children and young adults, and I thought, oh no, I'm a young adult."

Having grown up in such a closed and tense environment, many siblings wanted to get out of the home as soon as they could. As one young man reported:

> When I was young my brother and I were just so disturbed about the lack of dialogue in the house, we all decided that we were definitely going to go to college because it was the best way to get out of the house forever. And we all did go far away to school. I think I went farther away from home than anybody else in my graduating class.

Most individuals wished that there had been more open communication, lamenting that they should have been told that the illness was terminal and that some day their sibling would leave them. There were so many mysteries happening all the time:

> All we knew was pneumonia four times a year, but why? There was always that question, why? And it was never answered. It was always more of an evasion tactic. They figured it would go away. Well, it never did, because it kept happening. And I think that they could have treated it like the subject of sex—give them what they can understand, and they're going to retain what they're ready for.

Some respondents wished they had known so that they could have done more for the sibling while he or she was alive:

> I don't have that many strong statements to make, but they never told me that he might die. I've felt that way for years, that I wished I had known that he might die. I would've written him more letters, I would've gone down to visit him. I would've done more things, even though I had little children and I was so busy. But that was my only brother.

One young woman, 23 years old when her younger brother died, remembered that no one beyond the nuclear family was supposed to know about the illness. She wished that she could have been honest with visitors to the home about what was happening:

It was so depressing. There was all the equipment around the house. He had the board, and he had the pump that would pump the mist in the tent at night. People would come over and they'd want to know what it was and I'd find myself making up stories about what these things were, like the exercise board. I can remember saying we race our little cars on it. I just wish I could have felt that I could have told them what it was for.

Often the best friends of the individual with CF found out about the illness only after the death. One sibling remembered that when she was in college she wanted to watch a medical show on her friend's television. She could not bring herself to tell her friend why she was interested in the show, because frank discussion had been so taboo within her own family. Another young woman recalled that it was not acceptable to talk about her brother's illness. She reported, "Even when he was making these trips to the hospital every few months, my mother refused to tell people. It was crazy, really crazy." This young woman could not even tell her roommate about her brother's illness, and recalled the shock her roommate felt at the funeral. To this day, although she would like to help out by raising money for a cure for CF, she will not become involved in fundraisers because she still does not want anybody to know that her brother had CF.

Siblings also rarely spoke to each other about the illness, protecting the sick child from painful disclosure. Sally, 18 years old when her younger brother died, recalled:

I don't remember understanding anything. I don't remember knowing that he was ill. I remember we used to say, "Watch, he can take 14 pills at once after every meal." We knew there was something, something you didn't talk about. You didn't talk about it to him, because you knew inside that there was something wrong. And you didn't want to upset him.

Chapter 5

The Ordeal

Watchman, what of the Night?

—Isaiah 21:11

Although the impending death of a sick individual may be apparent to outsiders, the view from within the family may be quite different. Only 25% of the individuals in the statistical sample reported that they had known that an early death of their brother or sister was possible. Forty percent had some suspicion that something was worrisome but there had been no discussion in the family about the possibility of death. More than one third of the statistical sample reported that the death came as a complete shock to them. In fact, the actual death bore all the earmarks of a traumatic event in the lives of these individuals, giving rise to many of the sequelae associated with posttraumatic stress disorder (American Psychiatric Association, 1994; Terr, 1991). Although siblings shared some reactions, there were concerns and responses that appeared to be related to developmental capacities.

YOUNG CHILDREN

Young children spoke of the frightening loss of family stability as the sibling become very sick and was hospitalized. With parents spending more and more time at the hospital with the sick child, their brothers and sisters were often left on their own. Friends, neighbors, and relatives, wanting to help out during the crisis, divided up siblings. One young woman went to stay with a friend from school and that became her "battle station." One young man, 10 years old when his 12-year-old brother died, reported that there was "no public announcement" about his brother's prognosis or state of health at any time, and he was never consciously aware that his brother was going to die. He reported:

> But in reality the family lifestyle was being disrupted, particularly during that crisis period. It was being broken up. Everyone was in a different direction. I was staying here, and she was staying there, and she was staying somewhere else. The siblings were separated, my parents were running up and down to Boston, and the whole thing was in truth destabilized.

Most siblings were kept in the dark about what was going on. Younger siblings were left at home with a brother or sister only slightly older. Questions were brought to the older sibling who generally had just as little knowledge of the situation. Dennie, 10 years old when her brother died, remembered waking up one morning and realizing her parents were not home. Frightened because it was very early in the morning and they were not there, she ran into her other brother's room. Both youngsters tried frantically to orient themselves. She recalled:

> We knew something was wrong and we were scared. I don't really exactly remember why, but I remember we were crying. I think I was scared because I didn't know what was happening, why mom and dad weren't there. But then after that I don't really remember anything until the funeral.

For those siblings who had accepted the illness as normal and thought that everything was under control, the death came as a complete shock. One young man, 10 years old at the time, recalled the way he found out his brother had died. He reported that his father's way of dealing with the situation had been to shelter the children from the knowledge; his mother refused and said that they had to be told.

> It was my first summer at sleepaway camp. I got a call from the camp office that I had a phone call. I was all excited, 'cause you don't get a call at camp very often. So I rushed up there. I sat down in the camp director's office and I'm starting to run off at the mouth about what I'm doing. [His mother said] "Listen, Dale has been very sick, and last night, he died." Something to that effect. She said something about his having died the evening before, and a little description of the scene. It was all very sudden and very shocking to me. The camp director talked to me afterwards about how he had lost a brother a couple years ago. I was still shocked at that point, I wasn't really interested in what he had to relate to me about the situation.

For some siblings, the events leading up to the death were reported as hypercathected images, the disturbing reality of what had happened jarring with the beauty of the natural setting or of that particular day. Ralph, 10 years old when his older brother died, remembered the last time that he had seen his brother in early December, right before Christmas:

This particular day is very vivid in my mind. It's very, very clear. I didn't go to school, I don't know why. It was a winter day, the sun was out, and it was bright, and the snow was a white blanket. It was a real beautiful day outside. Inside, to me, it was just, oh, they're going to take him to the hospital for a stay. I was standing in the kitchen, and they left. They drove out of the yard, and I watched them go down the road. Then I went outside and took a walk out in the field in the snow.

The next picture that he recalls was the night that his brother died. His parents never took him on their visits to the hospital, because hospital regulations prohibited children from visiting. Ralph always wanted to go, and felt bad that he could not go with them.

But the next scene is the night that he died. They went down that day with some friends of theirs. My mother's sister was having a Christmas party and we went over there and spent the day over there. We came home that night and the folks had gotten back and they said that he'd died. It hit me but it wasn't until later in the night after I'd gone to bed that I woke up screaming, just woke up screaming, that was real bad. Thinking about it. You know it hardens you down to life and death at a young age.

Only a few siblings were able to be present at the death. One sibling remembered his brother was making out his will to everyone and that he was given his dying sibling's coin collection. For the majority, however, the death took place away from them at the hospital, and receiving the news of the death was recalled with dismay. Andy, 9 years old at the time, recalled the minister coming to their home:

He's a nice guy, real nice guy, and he said to my [father] … I remember these words—he says, "Can I talk to you for a minute?" And I just got these chills up my body. I knew something was wrong. Because he never came to the house, never. And they went outside in the driveway, and the light was on in the car, and I could see my father crying. I knew there was something wrong, I just knew it. I went up and hid in the attic. I didn't want to hear it. They couldn't find me. I just wasn't ready for it.

Some siblings were frightened by the prolonged and mysterious absence of their parents, while others were scared by witnessing their parents' deteriorating emotional state. One young woman, 10 years old when her older sister died, recalled:

I was hurt, but I didn't really understand what was going on. I saw more the reaction of the rest of my family than myself. If I was scared, I can say I was scared through the eyes of the rest of the family, seeing how they reacted around me, seeing them broke down. I just sat back and said, "Well, what's going on around here?"

Siblings questioned the natural order of things if parents were this upset. One young woman, 5 years old when her sibling died, thought that parents were the ones who were supposed to comfort children. When she saw her parents unsettled she thought, "They can't do that, they're not supposed to get upset." Others cannot remember anything about that period, especially their feelings at the time of their sibling's death. The wake and funeral also were very difficult experiences for them. Memories that are accessible abound with images of parental breakdown. One young man, 9 years old when his younger sister died, could not remember his feelings at the time: "I really don't recall. I would assume I was sad. I remember staring at the coffin. I remember seeing my father cry. And I can remember running my hands through her hair. That's about it. I don't remember any emotions or anything like that." Another sibling, 11 years old when his younger sister died, struggled to recall his mother's response following the funeral of her daughter: "I remember at the end, at the cemetery, that's when she let it all out. I just remember a split second of that." The death was very difficult for them to understand cognitively. One young woman, then 10 years old, knew that her sister had died, but could not understand why or if she would return: "I can picture right now standing in the funeral parlor and looking at her. But do you really know if she's dead? And I used to stand there and say, well, she'll come back." The realization of what had happened could only penetrate for a while, and then the child would divert him or herself by playing. Elin, 11 years when her sister died, remembered that on that day, her parents brought all the children over to the local YMCA. She recalled looking around at all the people who were very quiet, and knowing that something bad had happened. Every hour or so she said to herself, "God, she's dead, and then I'd have to go running off to the playground or something." Some youngsters re-experienced the death many times over the ensuing months, the reality coming in waves, eluding final resolution. One sibling reported:

> I think that every day that kind of surprised me. Every time I would think of what it meant, it was like a new shock. I had to pinch myself to remember that not only today and tomorrow, but every single day, she wasn't going to come back. The initial kind of hysterical grief about it didn't seem to last that long. It turned into more of a long-term nausea about the whole thing.

Several youngsters had nightmares that continued for years that their sibling had been buried alive somewhere. One young woman used to pray that she would dream about happy things. She had seen her sister lying in the coffin and this visual memory persisted throughout her childhood. Two little girls from one family, told by their parents that their sister had gone up to heaven, kept silent watch in the backyard for months, worrying that she would fall off the clouds with no one to catch her. One young woman, furious that her parents had not even told her that her sibling was in the hospital the week before, found out from neighbors that she had died. She had continuing nightmares that her sister was alive somewhere, and alone. She recalled:

> I had dreams like that for years. I didn't believe it. I mean I knew it, but that was a fear. I was thinking "Gee, something happened. They took her in for this operation and they messed up somehow and they've got her in some kind of coma somewhere." I can remember looking at her, and my first reaction was, "You're faking."

If parents did try to explain what had happened to their children, siblings still struggled with the concept. One young woman, 10 years old when her sister died, remembered that her parents told them that their sister would not be with them anymore, that she would be in heaven. "They tried to go through everything," she said, "It was like you knew it, but you didn't know it." Only a few of the siblings felt that they had received any parental help with mourning. If parents did try to reassure the siblings, attempts were ineffectual because they were given on an adult level, addressing concerns that would emerge at higher developmental levels than those achieved by the children. One sibling, 11 years old when her sister died, explained: "My parents tried to let us understand it and reassure us that everything was okay. She was happy, she wasn't in pain anymore, but those were grown up things. Mine was just how miserable I was about it." Parents counseled their well children to be "brave little soldiers," and neighbors advised them to be strong for their parents. They were left alone with their grief, younger children in some families not even believed to be in pain. Dennie, 10 years old when her older brother died, felt that nobody cared what she thought:

> I remember Nancy saying something at one time, "Well, you don't under-stand it," or "you weren't close to him anyway," or something like that. I felt really left out that nobody cared what I thought about the whole thing. I don't remember exactly what she said, but it was "You don't have any feelings because you're too little. We don't have time for this, we're all too sad." I always felt like I didn't have any right to be crying in front of them.

She remembered sitting by herself in front of the TV and feeling that everybody was wrapped up in themselves: "Everybody felt bad, but no-body knew that I felt bad." She recalled her parents "clinging together at that time. They were very much into each other, and not much into us, because they had lost something together."

Older siblings, engaged as they were with their own coping strategies, seemed not to have been any help at all, at times actively interfering with childhood strategies, creatively devised for the occasion: "I had a doll and I used to think of her as my sister and think I'll take good care of her and stuff. Sally would be mean to the doll, and it hurt me more than anything, 'cause she thought I was being stupid." This lack of sibling support differs from what we know through prospective studies of the reliance on siblings for children going through parental divorce (Wallerstein & Blakeslee, 1989; Wallerstein & Kelly, 1980). In families who have lost a child, the lack of support may reflect the fact that individual coping styles with death are so idiosyncratic that they more often conflict than intersect. It may also arise out of the entrenched denial mechanisms that had been operating within most families for many years. If nothing is wrong, and nothing happened, how can one seek support? How can one speak of the unspeakable?

Some siblings were helpless captives of their parents' preferred styles of coping. Ralph, only 10 years old when his older brother died, poignantly described one day about 2 weeks following his brother's death when his brother's friend called and invited him to go snow shoeing:

> I remember my father saying, "You gotta get out and go." He was pushing me. He says, "You can't sit around here, you gotta get out and do something." I remember getting real mad. I was trying to get dressed, and I wasn't doing it 'cause I wanted to, I was doing it 'cause they were making me do it, and I was resenting that. I was getting dressed, and I was putting boots on, and he was yelling at me, "No, you can't go out half dressed, you gotta put every-thing on right, and you gotta go."

Peers seemed to have been unable to know how to help, not yet having learned acceptable ways to give support. One sibling explained that it was very difficult at 12 years old to deal with the death, "'cause you don't have any support groups or anything. You just want to know that somebody else can share that feeling with you, or at least attempt to understand what you're going through, and there wasn't that for me." Embarrassed by the attention of their peers, some preferred that no one know. If the family had been different before, the death set them further outside the realm of ordinary experience, and their classmates responded with unfortunate curiosity. Andy, 9 years old when his brother died, remembered going to the schoolyard and being pointed out as the one whose brother died. "I just felt like an object. That was the worst thing." Many siblings became very angry. Some individuals were angry at a God that could allow this to happen to their siblings. Some individuals resented peers for having healthy brothers and sisters. Some were angry at themselves for "getting back into the swing of things" too soon. One young woman, 12 years old when her sibling died, reported: "I guess you have those puritanical black draped ribbon in your mind. I thought I should go back to school and not laugh and have fun. But then I ended up having fun, and I had a little guilt about that."

One sibling was put into an awkward situation by an insensitive teacher who asked across the classroom about his brother's health. This forced him to have to report to the entire class that his brother had died. Several youngsters received help from a thoughtful neighbor who was able to take the time to talk. Dennie, 10 years old when her brother died, could not believe that he was never coming back, because he had gone away to the hospital so many times and returned. Her next door neighbor was the one who helped her understand what had happened. She recalled, "It sank in when she talked to me about it. I'm sure mom and dad told me, but they just didn't take the time to sit down. They had enough to think about. I don't think they realized that it might have bothered me." Ralph, 10 years old when his older brother died, was taken outside by his brother's best friend, Dan, and helped tremendously by an incident engraved in his memory:

> This was in the winter time, probably about a couple weeks later. I was all by myself 'til I found them, 'cause they'd gone ahead. I had to catch up. I remember coming back down through the woods and Dan was saying something about "you gotta let things out, some physical thing in there." He felt real terrible about it. I remember the two of us were standing in this little clearing and he just started yelling, just like letting feelings out. I don't recall that I did the same thing, but it was the start of a new beginning of continuing on.

Most siblings were left on their own, alternating between feelings of sadness, anger, and fear, as we shall see in the next chapters.

ADOLESCENTS

The death came as a shock to many of the adolescents as well. For some teenagers, the way that the news was received was as difficult as the fact of the death itself. Jenny, then 14 years old, remembered her mother coming into her room several days before the death of her older sister:

> My mom goes, "You know, we're going to have to go pick out a casket." I just went, "Oh my God." She just shocked me. I had no idea how sick she was. Afterwards we talked about it and she goes, "Well, I was just trying to prepare

you as well as I could." That wasn't preparing me. That shocked me. That was the first time that I realized that she was sick.

Danelle, only 15 years old when she lost her younger sister, recalled with dismay the way her parents handled the final hours in the hospital:

> I saw her just the night before. I just remember her putting her head up, and my mother saying, "When you come home, what do you want for dinner?" She said, "I don't want meatloaf." My mother turned away in tears, and I still didn't understand. Then we went out to dinner. My father stopped eating in the middle of dinner and said, "I don't think I can take this." I still didn't understand. Then during the night I think she died. Then the next day they woke me up. And my father pretended like nothing happened still.

A few individuals were present at the bedside while the sibling was dying. Some have poignant memories of the last few hours or days, when feelings of closeness and love were directly expressed. One young woman remembered holding her dying sister's hand and crying, and her ill sister trying to comfort her. Siblings expressed a great deal of guilt over the way they had handled the death. If they continued on with daily activities, out of shock and incomprehension, they looked back with amazement at their behavior. Tom, 15 years old when his older brother died, remembered the morning his father came downstairs and told him that his brother had died. Since he had an early morning paper route, he delivered his newspapers, about which he now feels bad. Rick, then 13 years old, remembered the day his older sister died:

> My parents drove back and I went out to see them in the parking lot and I said, "Well, how's Jill?" and Dad was crying and he said, "Jill died today." I said, "We used to have 5 kids in the family, well, now we have 4." That was it. Then I left and my sister was just totally bonzo, gone, and I went out and played baseball that day.

Many siblings became very angry that something so unnatural could happen to them and their sibling. Donna, then 14 years old, recalled:

> My mother just grabbed the phone out of my hand. I guess it was Dr. Shwachman who told her that he had died. I was standing in our dining room. We had a partition, it was like plaster, and I just went up and I kicked that wall so hard. I said it wasn't fair. I said he never did anything wrong to anybody. It was hard getting through those next couple of days. Just to get through those next couple of days was a job in itself.

Some adolescents still struggled with the difficulty of believing that the sibling was gone forever. Kathy, then 13 years old, could not believe that her sister had died, convinced that the doctors had hidden her in the hospital. "For years I always looked around corners, waiting for her to come around a corner." Even seeing her at the wake did not help convince her: "I thought it was a dummy. 'Cause they don't look real ... it just didn't look like her at all. Not at all."

The wake and the funeral were an ordeal for most. Parental responses were at times frightening. Danelle, 15 years old at the time, recalled that her mother was composed until they got to the synagogue. Remembering that day, she reported, "I just remember the rabbi hugging me and I started to cry, and that's the last time I ever cried. But then my mother at the funeral fainted. And she screamed. I remember that scream. Oh, that's what stays with me. I hear that scream."

Upon going back to school, siblings worried about the reactions of their peers to the news. Some individuals hoped that their classmates would not find out what had happened, because it was a time when fitting in with the crowd was essential. Tom, then 14 years old, recalled:

> I remember the week and the wake and the funeral being horrible. I didn't like the attention that was the wrong kind of attention. I felt that I didn't want anybody to know. I didn't want my friends to know and I didn't want kids in school to know. I definitely remember it as something that I was really embarrassed about, which caused me a great deal of guilt later on.

On the other hand, when Doris, 15 years old at the time, first went back to school, she felt that everybody should be aware of the death and that nobody should be laughing: "I didn't see why everybody should be so happy, I didn't like that at all." The ordeal was such that Donna, 14 years old when her brother died, stated that she could never go through that again, including her own dying: "I don't ever want to die. I don't ever, ever want to die." Siblings who were adolescents at the time of their siblings' deaths were more likely to express anger and question why it had happened. The following sentiment was fairly typical for the adolescent group: "I'm still angry. I still don't understand. I want to know why. I'm going to ask that 'til I die. I don't want to say it's unfair, because life's not fair, that's a stupid thing to say. But it's not fair. Someone who is so good and kind, something's wrong somewhere."

It was the adolescent group that questioned their religious upbringing, and belief in a benevolent God generally fell by the wayside under the stress. Tom was certain that this anger is why he was no longer a practicing Catholic. He remembered the people at the wake making him angry by trying to reassure his parents that his brothers must have known they were special children. A related question which emerged frequently for this group was not why did it happen, but more specifically, "Why did it happen *to me*?" The sense of being different, set apart, elicited anger at having had an experience that no one that they knew had gone through. This sense of stigma may reinforce a tendency to deny the trauma. It also can contribute to the sense of isolation for the siblings: "It was just strange because nobody else my age had ever dealt with anything like that. I just didn't feel like any of them could possibly know what it was like. I think I probably closed a lot of people out, or I don't think I tried to get to know people like I should have."

Finally, siblings were not able to be helpful to each other following the death. Erin remembered having only one meaningful conversation with her well brother in their family room around the time of their sibling's death: "Ever since then there really hasn't been anything."

ADULTS

Individuals who were 18 years or older at the time of the death were very upset as well. However, unlike younger siblings, they were more likely to attribute their difficulty in envisioning the death before it actually happened to their own denial. One young man, 18 years old when his sister died, knew that her illness was serious toward the end because his parents became very concerned:

> I can remember her leaving the house and saying how she knew this time she would never come home again. I can picture that. Her going downstairs to the door. And I think my reaction to that was denial. Then she went into the hospital and I didn't go. Then I went sometime later before she died. It was to go the last time to see your sister. They brought me into this room and she was hooked up to these machines and it was just amazing, I mean I just couldn't believe it. I still have this picture in my mind of that. Terrible last time to see your sister and really not to have any idea of this is what you're going to see.

Some individuals had visited the sibling every day during the final decline. One sibling kept a vigil for nine weeks, visiting her sister daily and falling asleep beside her bed. One young man would carry his dying sister when she could no longer walk. Some siblings were able to express much love during the final hours:

> When my sister and I last said good bye, I felt as if for just a little while our souls became one. For a moment there, we actually touched our souls together. We both knew it was our last good bye and we cried into each other's

eyes. We were so close, we just couldn't get any closer. We held each other, we held each other so close. We just united our souls.

Although the deaths were extremely painful, siblings were able to remember the episodes in great detail. One young woman, 18 years old at the death of her younger brother Bob, remembered her father standing in the kitchen and telling them that their mother could not accept that Bob would not be coming home. That's when she began to become scared, and did not know exactly what she was afraid of.

> I don't think I'll ever forget when we were there and he was breathing real irregular, like it would take him 5 minutes to take another breath. And we're just all sitting there watching him. The doctors are discussing whether they should do a tracheotomy or not because he's having such trouble breathing. Then they're saying, "Well, there's probably no point, because he'd never survive the strain of doing that." I'm thinking of all these TV medical shows that I've seen, and saying, "Gee, they'd rush in and save these people. Why aren't these doctors? They're just standing there." I expected a flurry of all this activity. Then they said, "Why don't you go and have some breakfast? He'll be okay for awhile." My dad didn't want to go down, but we went down anyway. We were down there and my father was real nervous. He says, "I think I'm gonna go back up." My mom was talking to [my] uncle, and I said, 'Well, I'll go with you." And we go back up and walk down that corridor and the nurse is there. We walk by her, and then she says, "Oh, by the way ... *By the way* ..." I can still to this day hear her say that. And she says, "I'm sorry, he's gone." I'm standing next to my father, and I could see my father shrink 20 feet. He just turns to me and says, "Go get your mother." I remember going down the hallway. The elevator door opened and my grandmother and my aunt were on their way up to visit, so I just fell into the elevator and said that they said he was gone. My father went in the room, and I'm thinking, I have to go down and get my mother. Then I go into the cafeteria and have to face my mother who'd been there every minute with him for 2 months, and the one time she's not there. ... Then trying to get an elevator and the elevator wouldn't come. That whole scene just goes over and over a lot of times.

Some ill siblings looked to their well brothers or sisters to help them make life-and-death decisions. One young woman, only 18 years old when her older sister died, recalled a conversation they had: "She told me that she had the option of getting a tracheotomy, and that would probably extend her life. And she had to make the decision. She was asking my opinion and I said, "I can't. It's a decision that you have to make."

Several siblings, barely adults themselves, were the ones to spend the final hours alone with the dying person, a memory that will haunt them forever. One young woman, 21 years old at the death of her 27-year-old brother, recalled:

I spent the last night with him. It was the longest night of my life. Very, very strange. He screamed at me that there is no God. Then 5 minutes later he says, "Yeah, there is, don't listen to what I say." I had already decided that there wasn't. He rambled on that night. I can't remember what he talked about. Just screaming at me, "Where's God, where's God now?" And I kept saying, "I don't know, but I wish he'd get here fast." And he didn't get here 'til the next day.

Occasionally, a well sibling had to confront his or her inability to do anything either to halt the disease or to comfort the sibling. John, 28 years old at the time, remembered that he went to the hospital to visit his 19-year-old brother: "He said, 'Please help me, can't you help me? I don't want to die.' I just started crying. I said, 'There's nothing I can do.'"

Often overwhelmed with their own feelings, parents were generally unavailable to help their adult offspring. It was not unusual for the sibling to be the family member to provide emotional support. One young woman, 18 years old when her brother died, remembered that in the first few days after the funeral her mother kept asking for her son. They had to tell her repeatedly that he had died. Some parents turned to their offspring to make arrangements after the death, thereby reversing the parent–child roles: "They suddenly became the children and I was supposed to be the parent, and I was supposed to make the decisions." One young man, 19 at the time, recalled:

I just remember the next morning at about 7:00 my mother was screaming downstairs. I knew that something big was up. So I went downstairs. I was holding her and she told me what happened. Then I had to call my brothers and tell them about it. I knew my mother needed me like she never did. So I just held her and let her cry.

Unlike younger siblings who had been upset seeing their parents cry because it seemed so unnatural, older siblings were angry that their parents did *not* cry. One young woman, 22 years old when her younger brother died, stated: "I was mad at my mother because my mother didn't cry. Visibly cry, where I saw her. Then one night about a week after Mark had died, my mother packed all of Mark's things away, put them in boxes, and put Mark away." Some siblings were annoyed that it was the first time they had seen their father or mother cry. They had watched their parents' denial and were upset that their parents waited until the death to express their emotions. As Mark's older sister, then 28 years old, reported:

I was upset at my father because it was the only time I'd ever seen him cry, and it upset me terribly. But it made me mad because he never admitted that Mark was sick until that morning. He went about his life. And I was upset at him that morning. I thought, you've got a hell of a nerve to cry. I was really angry at him because of it. 'Cause he'd gotten up and gone to work this morning, and he knew he had been on the critical list all night and it was just another day. Then when I had to call him it was like, "What are you talking about, there's nothing wrong with him."

Older siblings also received very little help with mourning. Parents protected their children, and children protected their parents, each trying to shield the other from having them witness their grief. Some survivor siblings, seeing how their family handled the loss, promised themselves that they would treat their own children differently. One survivor sibling recalled:

We all reacted in our own little world. We should all cry together. I mean, God forbid you should see your father cry. I want so much for my children to see their father cry. I want them to know it's okay for a man to cry. And they have to be so strong. Why do you have to be so strong? You just lost your son.

Siblings rarely could help each other. Frequent complaints were mentioned that the other had been "off in her own little world." Some parents, unable to tolerate the first holiday following the death, went away somewhere, leaving the adult sibling to fend for him or herself. One young woman remembered her parents' absence at the first Christmas: "I felt like I had nobody then. My brother died, and they went away. My family was gone." A lucky few, who were married at the time of the death, reported receiving emotional help from their husbands or wives. But even at best, it took a long time for the sibling to process all the emotions that flooded his or her thoughts. One young woman stated that for a long time she was "sad and mad and everything else."

Chapter 6

The Aftermath

A world that can be explained even with bad reasons is a familiar world.
—Albert Camus (*The Myth of Sisyphus & Other Essays*, 1955)

For several families in my study, the death of the sibling meant that the secret was revealed and defenses could be dropped. As one young woman explained, her parents became much more open with their feelings following the death. She felt it was only then that the barrier finally came down, and her parents were able to talk about how their experiences with the sick child had affected their treatment of their other children. "It was like the dam broke. The whole family just sort of opened up and went, 'Oh, you felt like that too?'" Generally, however, communication patterns that had been in place for years during the illness period persisted. Whatever dynamic had been in place throughout the sick child's life tended to remain static or, if there was a change, became heightened. If family life was difficult before the death, it was further torn apart by the final crisis. Rick lamented that the death of his sister permanently altered the whole structure of family life, and it was not positive.

Interesting gender differences emerged in long-term responses of fathers and mothers. In the statistical sample, 20% of the siblings felt that their fathers had withdrawn further following the death, while only 1 father was perceived as having refocused his attention on the survivor sibling. Only 1 mother was rated as having withdrawn further, whereas 4 respondents reported that their mothers had refocused the attention on them after their sibling died. The majority, however, reported no major change in the relationships they had with their parents prior to the death.

Fathers frequently threw themselves into their work, remaining remote. Andy, 9 years old when his sibling died, remembered his father became more withdrawn and spent most of his time in his basement workshop. "He really went crazy building things, he was constantly building things." Siblings complained that fathers kept everything inside. Several individuals recalled their mothers telling them that for a long time their fathers did not even come home. If they were home, they were either remote or angry. Jenny, 14 years old when her sibling died, remembered her father's response: "I hated him, 'cause he was awful then, just never around, always at work. He was so cold, he had one expression on his face. He just walked around, he never smiled. All he cared about was his work. Just depressing to be around." Danelle, 15 years old when her sister died, felt her father became much more short-tempered. He worked very late hours and appeared to be emotionally drained all the time. What actually was going on in the minds of the parents following the death was generally not accessible to the siblings. However, the impact was felt, and frequently was the loss of parental resources once again. Rick, 13 years old when his sister Jill died, reported how his parents changed for the worse: "One of the bad things that happened when Jill died, it forever altered my father in a way in which it alienated him from his children. For whatever reason, I don't know the whole story, I never will, it permanently put the death knell on my mother and father as potential for the rest of their lives in that way."

Most siblings felt the death was experienced by their mothers as overwhelming, because so much of their lives had been wrapped up in the care of the sick children. Erin, 14 years old when her brother Jim died, suggested that it must have been devastating for her mother, because she had a full-time job taking care of Jim, and then "all of a sudden she didn't have any job and she didn't have any Jim. So I think that really left her in the lurch. Totally empty-handed."

The relationship between the parents also floundered. Mothers were frequently left to their own devices, as fathers often retreated to work, even during the handling of the details of the death. Erin felt that her father became a total workaholic. The day after her sister died, the family had to go select flowers for the casket, but her father went to work. Her mother felt that was the one time that she really needed him, and he was not there, and divorce became a very real possibility. Her mother never forgave him for his response. Some relationships seemed to experience difficulties because each individual parent had a preferred coping style that frequently conflicted with the other's. Fathers tended to be able to compartmentalize their grief and immerse themselves in their work, whereas mothers wished to process emotionally what had happened and sought increased closeness with their husbands. At a time when intrapsychic needs were severe, coping conflicts were not bearable. One young woman, 19 years old when her sibling died, recalled that her mother cried all the time and always wanted to talk. But that was not the way that her father wanted to deal with it. He would open up somewhat with her mother but essentially preferred to handle his pain in his own way. "We were all trying to deal with it in different ways and relying on each other." Some fathers turned to alcohol and tried to stay away from home, a reminder of their own grief and loss. Struggling to put their lives back together, siblings rarely received help from their parents, who were engaged in their own fight for emotional survival. Danelle reported: "I remember a period when there was a lot of shouting going on. A lot of shouting. It used to kill me. It was like 1 year of shouting." Several siblings, accurately sensing that parental response to the death was going to cause further havoc, dreaded the loss of the sibling because they knew it would cause the family to fall apart even further. As one sibling recalled:

> Well, I knew once she died, boy, it was going to be hell to pay. And it was. Anger's been a part of our lives since we've been born. So that's normal to be angry about everything. I guess they were locked in their own grief and never thought about anybody else. They still are. They'll never get over it. You don't get over your own kid dying, you know. There's a limit to some things.

Several fathers turned to mistresses as an alternate escape, in an attempt to avoid reminders of the pain within their own family. Many siblings remembered months when their parents fought over the husband's girl-friends, glasses were thrown about, and there was a lot of yelling and screaming. Some were afraid for their mothers. Others were afraid for their fathers. Some were afraid for both. Peter, 12 years old when his sister died, recalled his father's response to her death:

> My father took it real bad. Definitely. That's when he went on his sprees, drinking, and stuff like that. And he really couldn't handle it. Even when he thinks about it now, he can't handle it. You can see in his face, like he hates everybody. He used to take off a lot, when my mother and he would get in a fight or something and be gone for the night. Cops just had to chase him. They chased him a lot of times, coming from my sister's grave.

Siblings speculated that their father's anger arose out of blaming them-selves for their child's illness and death. It seemed to many respondents that their fathers struggled with the question of why this had happened to them and to their children. One young woman stated that her father admitted that he was just a person who was always angry. She believes that much of his anger stemmed from losing his daughter. She described it this way: "It's a feeling of hating everybody. Not so much hating everybody, but hating the world. Why did it have to happen to me? Why did it have to be my daughter?"

Some perceptive siblings were able to see the pain behind the anger. Peter, 12 years old when his sibling died, believes that his father blamed himself for the death. "You can see it in his eyes, that he really hurts, and he wonders why it was happening, 'Was it me, or something I did?'" Guilt and blame shifted back and forth among family members. Sometimes parents blamed themselves; sometimes they blamed each other. Siblings perceived that parents felt guilty about the genetic responsibility for the disease. Parental guilt and blame is, in fact, a common response to having a child with CF (Fanos & Johnson 1995b). One sibling felt that her mother could not tolerate blaming herself, so she had to blame her husband. A young woman, 28 years old at the death of her younger brother, remembered her mother focusing on specific things she should have done, "My mother blamed herself. She said, 'Well, I should have done this and I should have done that.' And I said, 'Listen, mom, you did everything that you possibly could. You took him to the best doctors. He had the best care. Anything he needed, he got.'"

Struggling with guilt, parents often turned against each other, while sensing the futility of the search—as one respondent speculated, they knew deep down that it was nobody's fault. For many siblings, it was a short distance to a bitter outlook on life. Danelle told me, "They're still asking the same question. And I think my father just says, 'Hey, that's it. That's the way life is. Life isn't fair. Who says life is fair?' And my mother feels so beaten down that it's just sad." Overwhelmed with the inability to find answers to the large question that haunted most parents, some turned in desperation to their survivor children. As one young woman, 15 years old at the time, recalled: "After she died, all I heard was, "Well, you wanted her dead anyway."

Why would parents turn their anger toward their own children? Several lines of thought may contribute to our understanding of this process.

1. The final weeks of the dying child's life generally leave the parents emotionally depleted and physically exhausted. Yet the parenting role is not over. Their other children need them, and parents must pull themselves together to function and to give when what they may most want is to be left alone to grieve. Some parents may have the need to withdraw and recoup their energy, and the demands of their surviving children interfere with this recovery. Survivor siblings have an increased need for emotional time and support at the same time that their parents have an increased need to be left alone.

2. When the child's suffering reaches certain limits, the thought crosses most parents' minds that the end would not be as cruel. Death wishes for the child are common, and guilt over these unacceptable feelings is difficult to handle. Therefore, the parent may focus on statements made by their well children in the past that they hoped the sibling would die.

3. Parents often feel that they are being punished for some wrongdoing in their lives when they have a child with a genetic or potentially fatal illness. Books such as Kushner's (1981)*When Bad Things Happen to Good People* attempt to counter this sentiment. When guilt is high, it generally spills over to blaming others as well as the self. If fathers readily blame their wives, it would be a short step for wives to blame their children.

4. Parents found well siblings to be poor substitutes for the idealized and longed-for lost child.

5. Siblings are reminders of the trauma of losing a child. If survivors generally try to avoid situations that activate traumatic memories (Van der Kolk, 1987), parents must have difficulties in engaging with their other children.

6. To love the survivor sibling is somehow a betrayal of the lost child's memory. In order to reinvest emotional resources in the living, the dead must first be mourned. If a child cannot be mourned by the parent, this process will be blocked.

Siblings resented the way their parents had handled their own grief. Their descriptions appeared to be classic defenses against mourning. Several parents memorialized their lost child, commissioning portraits to be hung on the wall, infuriating siblings:

> My mother has a painting of my brother that she had done from a photograph, one of those over-the-mantel kind of portraits, which I hate. I've always hated the thing. When I go to my parents' house I see it, and I think how much that picture dominates the house. I think it would be better to put it someplace less conspicuous, maybe take it down altogether.

Some parents admonished the survivors to keep away from the possessions of the lost child, explicitly freezing the mourning process for their other children. As one perplexed young woman reported about her parents, "I mean even today they'll say, 'Don't touch that, that's Melanie's.'"

IDEALIZATION

Some parents idealized the deceased child, making it impossible for survivor siblings to live up to images of perfection. Adolescent when her brother died, one young woman recalled that her mother always asked her why she could not be more like her brother. Joan, 7 years old when her brother died, remembered her entire childhood years as being overshadowed by his memory: "He was the paragon; you competed with a ghost." Joan's younger sister, 5 years old at the time, recalled her mother's emotional distance from her throughout her childhood. Desperately trying to get some attention, she would put little drawings throughout the house, so that maybe they would have to think of her. She reported, "If my drawings are all over the place, I'm here, here I am, I'm the one with the thing on the refrigerator, I'm here on your bed and on your notebook." For some, the process of idealization on the part of the parents had begun long before the death. One young woman, 15 years old when her older sister died, explained:

> If I didn't do exactly what she did, I wasn't any good. I was always compared to her. It had to be her way, "She's smarter than you are in school," all this stuff. I had a friend of mine go down there one time after my sister died and talk to my father. He yelled at her and told her never to come back to the house, 'cause she told him to stop comparing me to her. 'Cause I wasn't her.

The idealization of the sick child seemed to arise from varied sources. Because the child with CF had limited physical energy, intellectual and artistic interests and skills were frequently developed to a high degree. Also, the child received a lot of love, providing a nurturing environment for any latent talent to develop. In addition, parents may have idealized the sick child as a way of handling unacceptable feelings of resentment and guilt toward the child. That those parents who did so may have had their own internal reasons is suggested by one articulate sibling who was 15 years old at the time:

> My mother has built my brother and sister up to be saints. And my recollection of my sister was not a saint. She fought with me constantly. They never got along. They were at each other's throats constantly to the point of really, really fighting, and frightening me as a little kid. I have to say I resented after they died the comparisons that were made, forgetting that they were normal, and finally saying to her, "Geez, you're going to ruin any love that I had for them."

REFOCUSING

Some parents refocused their attentions on the survivor sibling following the death, transposing tremendous fears of something bad happening to yet another child, arousing resentment again. With parental anxieties heightened that bad things can really happen to their children, they turned with fear to survivor siblings, particularly adolescents. While she was growing up, Jenny found that her mother never had time for her. Right after her sister died when Jenny was 14, she felt that her mother became "petrified" that something would happen to her. She became extremely overprotective and wanted to know exactly where she was going when she left the house, and with whom she would be spending her time: "If I was 2 minutes late she'd go, 'Call the police, what am I going to do?' and that just made me feel 'Stay away, what are you doing?'" In some cases the overprotection lasted through to the present. One young woman, 15 years old when her sister died, stated:

> If I'm overweight or she doesn't think I look good, she can't deal with it. Her throat constricts, and she almost stops affection for me. It's hard, very hard. She'll say, "When I see that you're overweight I say, 'Oh, no, I'm gonna lose someone else. You're going to get horrible diseases.'" So she has become much more overprotective, to the point where it's suffocating. Here I live on my own, and she'll say, "I don't care where you are or what you're doing, but I need to hear your voice." That's no good.

Blos (1962) considers adolescence a second individuation process, with the developmental task being the successful disengagement from parents, realization of limitations of parental imagoes, and so forth. It is normally the time when the adolescent tyrannizes the home and freely displays outbursts of anger in support of evolving a separate identity. Because of the death of a sibling during this stormy period, the adolescent experienced a conflict between his or her own developmental needs and concern for the parents. One sibling recalled that after his sister died he felt very responsible for being with his mother. "I can remember my father making a statement at one point that he was going to be there with my mother during the day, and I would be home at night with my mother, and I took that very literally and felt that I couldn't leave her." Those parents who suddenly refocused around their survivor children after they lost their child placed an added stress on their offspring and added resentment to longstanding anger. Not recognizing that there appears to be a critical period for imprinting, parents must have been sadly disappointed at the sibling's reactions. One young woman, 14 years old when her older brother died and 16 when her older sister died, recalled how her mother had often stayed with her sister in the hospital. Her father worked nights, so she was left alone.

> I basically grew up coming into an empty home from school. The problems started after my sister's death, when my mother then wanted me to come in and make up for the difference of the loss of the two kids. Emotionally it wasn't there for me, the relationship had never developed. It was like, I

needed you 10 years ago, not now. By that time I had built up some very strong emotional ties with other people in my life and she wanted them to stop. My sister died, my mother stopped working for a very brief time and expected me to be the little 7-year-old that would come home and tell Mommy what she did in school, and to be there, and I wasn't willing to do that.

Separating from parents was accomplished with increased difficulty, sometimes due to the sibling's own premature sense of responsibility for parents, and sometimes due to parental inability to allow their adolescent children to grow up. Danelle reported: "I've never had my own life, to tell you the truth. My parents just can't let me go." Those respondents who were 18 years or older at the time of the death shared some of the same difficulty in handling the refocusing of attention onto them, although there was less anger and more sadness mentioned. Dan, 19 years old when his brother died, remembered that he would return home from college during the summers:

I was away at school. I mean the fat was in the fire so to speak. Whatever was done was done. The major rift was with my mother, because she was always favoring my younger brother, for reasons which even though at a young age I understood, I didn't like 'em. I understood that there was no malice in this, but it prevented my mother and I from being as close as my brother and my mother were. And when I would be back in the summer, we would look at each other, and we would want to have that relationship. But it was too late to do that.

Older siblings were more likely to experience a kind of role reversal, where they suddenly bore primary responsibility for parents who could not cope with the death. One young man, 19 at the time, recalled that when his father was absent all the time, his mother leaned on him to replace the role emptied by her husband: "There was a big question about who was the father, who was the mother, and who was the son. And that is exactly what is going on with my mother now." Several young women regretted having been trapped at home for what they thought would be a limited period of time to help out with their mothers. Struggling with wanting to move back out and have their own lives, they were very concerned about what would happen to their parents. But most siblings were able to understand why their parents were the way they were, and less anger was expressed in the interview concerning separation issues. One young woman, 19 years old when her older brother died, explained:

They're still very protective, but that's understandable. I'm the only daughter left. And I think I'm equally as protective of them. We really need each other now, and we have to be in contact at lot. They are probably too protective of me, or just too concerned about my happiness and welfare, but it's easy to see why.

SUBSTITUTION

Some parents tried to replace the lost child by substituting one of their other well children. Similarity to her lost older sister spared one young woman, 9 years old when her sister died, from her father's anger, which appeared to be displaced onto all his other surviving children. She recalled, "I was close to my father in a lot of ways because he always claimed I was like my sister. So that made a big difference. He always used to tell me I was like her. In fact, my grandmother calls me [by] her [name]." In general, however, any change in behavior that was reminiscent of the relationship between the parent and the lost sibling was the occasion for much anger. Jenny, 14 when her older sister died, recalled the way her mother used to treat her sister and the change following her death:

> Every night and all the time she was always hugging and kissing her, and they were just so close. She never did that to me when I was little. Then when she died, she came up to me and started hugging me and I just thought, what are you doing? I still to this day—and that was almost 3 years ago—do not like my Mom hugging me. I don't like it at all. She's come up to hug me and I'll just back away real bad.

Those who were adult at the time of the death were less likely to serve as substitutes for the lost sibling, as they were more secure in their own identity than were the children. With personalities and talents so formed by this time, parental attempts could be resisted with greater frequency. But many still had to struggle with pressure from parents to try to replace the lost individual:

> I always thought it should have been me instead of him. I just think he had more to offer people. I can remember when he died my father looked at me one day at supper and said, "Well, you're going to have to carry on now, keep things lively at the dinner table, and keep the jokes going." And I said, "I can't." It was a long time before I could accept myself as myself. Not being compared to him.

With no model for a healthy grieving reaction, the majority of siblings seemed unable to begin the process. If depression in the parents had not been visible to the siblings before the death, it was not visible afterward.

If parental depression was not discernible, it becomes important to ask: (a) Was it present but siblings were too absorbed in their own concerns to see it? (b) Was it present but not acceptable to be shown (i.e., do the demands of bringing up children in a home in which one will die make sadness a secret to be hidden to keep the appearance of things normal)? or (c) Was it present only in defended form; that is, is there something about the genetic transmission of CF, with both parents as carriers of the gene, that elicits parental guilt on such a level that to feel compassion for themselves is impossible? In other words, does guilt block an ability to mourn? What is important for the siblings is that for whatever reason, parents seemed to have hidden depression, and siblings appeared to have inherited a model of avoiding feelings of sadness.

Chapter 7

The Next Year

Slowly the poison the whole blood stream fills.
It is not the effort nor the failure tires.
The waste remains, the waste remains and kills.
　　　　　　　　　—William Empson (*Missing Dates*, 1949)

As difficult as the illness and death of a sibling may be, one might expect the period that followed to be one of relief or even recovery. However, the siblings I interviewed reported that they found the weeks and months following the death of their brother or sister fraught with difficulties. Van der Kolk (1987) pointed out that an individual remains fixated on a traumatic event until it is integrated into his or her experience. Traumatic memories, unable to be avoided, return in various forms, including reenactments and nightmares. He explained that the nature of the trauma, overwhelming as it is to the ego, makes psychological integration difficult; dissociative processes are mobilized as defenses against severe stress. Finally, he pointed out that these individuals have difficulty warding off feelings of anxiety and aggression.

In this study, although many concerns were shared by siblings of all ages at the time of the death, different issues were emphasized depending on developmental stage at the time the loss occurred.

YOUNG CHILDREN

A heightened fear of dying was a major concern articulated by young siblings. Just as their early memories had included themes in which there had been a threat to the self, repetitive dreams played out the same concern. For many individuals, their dream life was the only outlet for memories; it was not uncommon for siblings to remark, as one respondent put it, "I swear one whole year of my life I forgot." Dennie, 10 years old when her older brother died, recalled a terrifying dream of being stalked by a man in white who pursued her over the slippery hardwood floors in her house:

> It was just coming, walking like this, very rhythmic. In my dream it was a man with all white clothes on and white shoes, and he was after me. I would run up the stairs and I was sliding all over the place. I'd slide down the hall and then I'd get into Mum's room. And she had this desk and I'd hide inside the desk. I would just be holding my breath, because I knew he was coming up the stairs. I could hear his footsteps. He kept coming and coming, and I was so scared. Then he'd see me. I never saw his face. All I saw were all his white clothes and his white shoes, and then it wasn't bad. He didn't hurt me or anything. Then I'd wake up. But it was so scary up to that point and then nothing really happened. And I've had dreams like that ever since. I was so scared until he actually saw me, and then I wasn't afraid of him anymore.

The commingling of the man in white, perhaps an image of a doctor, and death, is of interest. The realization that this figure was not in fact stalking her was of great relief to this young woman.

The effect on three young children, who lost their 11-year-old brother to CF when they were 10, 7, and 5 years old, illustrated the impact on the whole family. The oldest son recalled that immediately following his brother's death, he became very afraid of dying. He thought: "Hey, wait a minute, I'm going to die. We're all going to die. Somebody says, it's just like going to sleep. All right, I can conceptualize going to sleep. But I wake up every morning, and it only seems like a moment of time has gone by." Sometimes he would go to bed and before he would go to sleep he would try to find a solution to that problem. He remembered being terribly confused that maybe his brother was not really dead but somewhere else: "There were dreams where I'd think about death, or being buried alive. I had a lot of fantasies or ideas that maybe this whole thing is a dream and I'm gonna wake up, or maybe he's not really dead, he's somewhere." His sister Joan, who was 7 years old at the time, also recalled her dreams:

> Ghost-type dreams, where I would see my brother, or think I saw him, think I heard him. At that age my imagination was still pretty good. I remember I was watching a lot of TV programs like Bewitched. I thought that he would pop back in somewhere or I'd see him some place or I could talk to him. I would imagine that he was still around 'cause he wasn't dead that long so that I could still sort of talk to him, or that he might come back.

Some of Joan's other dreams illustrated her struggles with the abstract concept of the death. She reported that she used to have dreams of geometric shapes altering their form:

They were squares or geometric figures, and they were big. They'd go back and forth and back and forth and back and forth. I remember having those dreams. They scared me at first, and then I thought they were neat. I think there were colors, although I don't remember. And they stuck in my mind 'cause they were so weird.

When I asked her what she meant by going "back and forth," she continued: "Getting bigger and going away. It wasn't ever a figure, it was a form, usually a square or a triangle or something."

Her youngest sister was only 5 years old at the time of the death. She too had fears of dying and remembered the terror with which she contemplated what her own death would mean. The worst part for her was that she would have to leave her parents. Repetitive dreams continued until she was about 12 years old:

There was one like being in a dark place, and then getting out of the dark place and being in a nice green area, palm trees and things like that, and playing, but then realizing I couldn't get back home, and that frightened me. Then I had a few dreams of my mother dying, and that upset me. Most of them were just thinking about it. Thinking about it would scare me the most.

She was very afraid that she would die when she turned 11, the age her brother had been when he died. "It would occur to me that I was the same age when my brother had died. I thought, uh oh, am I going to make it to the end? I still think I might die an early death." When I asked her if there was anyone (particularly her parents) with whom she discussed her fears about dying, she replied: "Once or twice I did, but I really didn't talk about it that much because I was a little embarrassed by it. I didn't think it was rational. I thought, this is ridiculous. I just didn't want to bring it up with them [her parents]." She feels that although there was a lot of love expressed in her family, anxieties were difficult to dissipate: "I did express fears to my mother, and she would be comforting, but they would always recur, and I just didn't see any point in discussing it with her further."

Another young woman, 10 years old at the time of the death, remembered sitting alone for hours in front of the television screen. She described her dreams:

It's hard to explain but everything is so nice and serene and very smooth and calm, and then all of a sudden, everything gets like static. I just get so upset, and I can't control anything anymore. I can't get back to being calm. I don't know where it's all coming from, and so therefore I can't stop it. I had that dream all through my teens and I used to think I was going crazy. Sometimes I would feel like I was losing control freshman and sophomore year. Losing control of myself. Like sometimes I was way, way inside somewhere, and looking out of my head. I thought that was so weird. I tried to explain it to mom and she didn't understand. My body was normal and everything, but what's really me was this little tiny thing inside my head looking out of this big body. I seem very small inside this big body, and everything was so big outside.

Because of the intense preoccupation with what was going on in their inner world, many siblings had a great deal of difficulty concentrating in school. Unfortunately, many individuals were not able to sense the connection between their difficulties concentrating and their preoccupation. Instead, because they were not doing well in school, they concluded that perhaps they were stupid, which damaged their self-esteem. One young woman, who lost three siblings when she was 3, 5, and 10 years old, described herself as always being very quiet in school; she just watched everything that was going on. She had a difficult time in school, and was never better than a C-average student. She had to repeat the first grade because she was having such a hard time. Pondering the question of whether her school difficulties were related to the deaths of her siblings, she wondered: "Who's to say whether it was that directly or maybe something else that was bothering me? Or maybe I'm slightly retarded. Who knows?" But her nightly dreams following her sister's death gave us a clue about the source of her distraction:

I used to have dreams like there was a war. They were bombing our house and dad was running through picking everybody up, trying to get us all in a safe place. And I kept telling him, "No, go on and get the others, get the others." I had dreams I was running through a graveyard sinking into the ground. At first it started out just running down a beach and then all of a sudden it got real dark out and then there were all these gravestones and then the water turned red like blood and we were running and I fell behind and she started sinking into the sand and I went back to grab for her and I started sinking into the sand and we both turned to grab each other and we kept going down and down and down.

Bewildered when her last sibling was taken away to the hospital only to die a few hours later, she thought, "Why did they bring him to the hospital? Maybe he wouldn't have died if he wasn't in the hospital." Then she started fearing going to the hospital. Another young woman remembered having frequent daydreams in school when she was young, again not sure of the connection with her older sister having died:

I used to daydream a lot. I got in trouble in sixth grade, which is the year she died, I think. I got in trouble a real lot that year for daydreaming. They'd be reading through a book, and I would never know where they were, because I'm off daydreaming somewhere. I don't know if it was because of that, or if it was just because I was at the daydreaming stage. I was the only one in the class that was ever lost though.

She also developed symptoms of epilepsy 1 month after her sister died, which she interpreted as a consequence of the trauma of her sister dying. A young man, 11 years old when his younger sister died, was diagnosed with epilepsy about 3 years later. It is tempting to speculate on the possible connection between the timing of the onset of such neurological disorders and the facilitating aspects of trauma (Van der Kolk, 1987). There were other somatic disorders reported by siblings during this difficult first year—one respondent, for example, 10 years old at the time of the death, had severe intestinal cramping. Other youngsters had numerous accidents. One sibling fractured his arm while sledding right after the death, another had a concussion riding his bicycle, a third broke his leg during the next year, a fourth ran into a tree, and a fifth broke his hand by tripping over his hockey stick.

Van der Kolk also pointed out that risk-taking behavior can be seen as voluntary exposure to dangerous situations in an attempt to rework the trauma. Whether the accidents were the result of distraction or risk-taking behavior is difficult to separate. However, some siblings were quite explicit about their motivation. The following young man illustrated the connection between a conviction of dying young and his devil-may-care attitude.

Peter

Peter was 21 years old at the time of the interview and was 12 years old when his older sister died. One of his earliest memories was of feeling frightened when he saw a woman in a wheelchair at a beach house where they were vacationing. He was scared seeing his sister in the hospital, with "all the stuff hooked into her," and seeing the other sick children frightened him as well. His sister died when she was 16 years old. After the death, his father went on drinking sprees and "chased women," and the police often followed his father home, coming from visiting his sister's grave. Peter would sit there day after day and think, "why couldn't it have been me?" He recalled that he kept these thoughts mainly to himself. He had nightmares in which he saw his sister and thought she was with him in his room. Terrified, he would ask to sleep between his parents, but they would not let him, so he would try to jump into the bed and lie between them. If they did not allow him into their bed, he would sleep on their floor, but he would not go back to his own room. He also had nightmares that "something's coming in at me, too early, too early coming in at my face." He tried to talk about his anxieties with his mother but she would scream at him, "Why are you always having to bring up stuff about it?" Over the next several years, he broke his elbow and had other minor accidents. He started drinking in seventh grade. Shortly before his sister's death, his parents had bought her a car, but she died just before they were able to give it to her. It greatly disturbed Peter that she had to miss out on enjoying her car. After turning 16, the age his sister was at her death, he got into a "million" accidents in the car he inherited from her. When I interviewed him, his best friend with whom he drove around while they were drinking, had just been killed.

> Me and this one boy, the one who got killed, were keeping up pretty good together. Like you'd get really down about it. I wasn't afraid of it. It didn't bother me. But I thought—and I still do—that I was going to die young. That's what me and my buddy used to talk about. We always thought we'd die young. I don't know, it seems like I'm always trying to push myself, push myself in a car. See how far I can go.

Even at the time of the interview, Peter continued to drive recklessly. However, concerned for the safety of others, he now only drives like this when he is alone.

ADOLESCENTS

Siblings who had been adolescents at the time of the loss shared many of the concerns of their younger counterparts. Although they recalled fewer nightmares of death and dying, they shared a conviction that they would die young, usually by some sudden and unexpected way, an accident perhaps. Unfortunately, the possibility was only too real, for, unlike younger children who had accidents while playing, adolescents were able to drive a car, and their risk-taking behavior was therefore potentially much more dangerous. Drinking problems were frequent, and some began to abuse drugs and got arrested. Although younger siblings recalled difficulties concentrating in school, adolescents struggled with problems of motivation. Long-range goal formation was the last thing on most of their minds. Some expended energies trying to be the peace maker for their squabbling parents. Somatic complaints emerged, many of which persisted for years. Adolescence is the time when developmental tasks include a move to peers and intimacy, thus the impact of loss during this period was considerable. The following cases are a few examples.

Erin

Erin was 14 years old when her older brother Jim died. Her family had been very close while she was growing up, although she would describe her father as a workaholic. Jim was a very sensitive person, and enjoyed spending time with her and her girlfriends, particularly because it was physically difficult for him to keep up with their healthy brother. Toward the end, Erin began to face the fact that he might die. She was devastated when he died. Her father threw himself into his work more, and her mother spent hours sitting around the house crying. Erin was angry. Partying through school, she was drawn to the wrong crowd: "Well, at the time that he died, I hung around with some derelicts in the neighborhood. We were all into causing trouble, and we caused a *lot* of trouble. And you know, those people were my so-called friends, but they're really not the type of people that I would invest my time in now."

What bothered her most was that she was going to go to high school and her brother was not going to be there. "All his friends were there and he wasn't. I think I was even given his locker. Jim had real good friends, and they watched out for me, but it wasn't the same." Looking back now at the pain her behavior must have caused her parents, she feels guilty about adding to their unhappiness during those years: "It was a time in my life when I was 14 and I was belligerent and I was a brat. I was doing things like smoking pot that I shouldn't have been doing, and I think that caused extra problems for my parents, because I was hanging around with kids that I probably shouldn't have been hanging around with."

When her time came to leave for college, she felt badly that she was able to do something Jim had never done. She wished she had a closer relationship with her surviving brother now, and believes that he still feels tremendous guilt over his relationship with his lost sibling.

Jenny

Jenny is a 17-year-old who lost her older sister Paula to CF several years before the interview. Growing up, she was "the bad one," while her sister was "perfect." Her earliest memory is of trying to get her mother to play with her, to no avail; basically she "grew up alone," despite playing sick constantly in order to get some attention. Paula's actual death came as a complete shock to her. In fact, she learned of its probability when her mother came into her room the day before and told her that they would have to buy a casket very soon. Following her sister's death, her mother's attitude changed completely toward her. She frequently tried to hug Jenny in the same way she used to hug Paula. This annoyed Jenny a great deal because prior to Paula's death, her mother did not hug her. Turning to her boyfriend, Jay, sustained her emotionally through this difficult period:

Me and Jay went out for about 8 months, and he just helped me through everything, he was just wonderful. I'd run away. He lived just a couple miles away and I'd go right over to his house. I'd go through the forest because I'd want to avoid the road; I was scared my mom would be out. So I'd go the back way through the dark woods and I didn't care. I'd go over to his house and his mom would make up the bed on the couch, she was really sweet. Or he would let me stay in his room and he'd sleep on the couch. He was so nice, so good to me. He was the first person that ever took care of me, and I got really attached to that.

She dropped out of school twice. At the end of her sophomore year, her parents sent her away to boarding school. Fourteen months before our interview, Jay had broken up with her.

All through our relationship I would like take advantage of it. I loved him, and I still do. I'll never stop loving him. A lot of times when we were going together I'd break up with him, and he'd just come running back to me. I kind of took advantage of that. Then the one time he broke up with me, it was for good. And I tried for about 8 or 9 months to get him back. Then about a month and a half ago he moved to New Mexico. But I don't care. Sometime, if I'm 20 or 30, I don't care how old I am, I'm going to get him back. I don't care what anybody says. One time when I had a knife and razor blade, and I was cutting my wrist, what made me stop was thinking, "Oh my God, if I do this I'll never be able to get him back," and that's what made me stop that time.

She was in a psychiatric hospital for 1 month, an episode she considered a total waste of time.

That was what made me start cutting on myself, because people in there whenever you're not feeling good do that, and I'm all, "ooh, this does make me feel better," 'cause it gets out your aggression too. Then I got out for a week, and I was kicked out of the house, and I was very suicidal and went back in for a week. I know that if I did not go back in the hospital for that week I wouldn't be here now. I can promise that, because I was the most depressed person.

When I asked her why she had been "kicked out" of the house, she said it was her fault, because she was just "messing up" and did not care about anything. She has yet to resolve many issues around the relationship with her sister and her handling of the illness:

The worst thing about me is that I have the worst guilty conscience. Like still I feel like Paula's death was my fault. My conscience will carry anything. I used to feel guilty like how I tried to make my mom do things with me when she had so much other things to do. You know what I mean? I just wish ... I feel guilty so many times. About everything. I don't know why.
Like there were times when she'd [Paula] ask me to get her something and I wouldn't 'cause I was mad at her because she got all the attention. So I wouldn't get her something. Or she was coughing, and she didn't feel good, and she wanted me to go get her something, and I wouldn't get it. And I still

hate myself for that. My mom is trying to make me feel better. She says that was okay because Paula more than anything really wanted to be a normal child. But there's a degree of being normal, there's just so far ... I don't know.

About 6 months after her sister died, Jenny's throat swelled up so that she could not talk and she could hardly breathe. "I mean if it had swollen up much more," she continued, "I would have choked to death." Feeling that her parents always loved her sister more, she told me she believed that they would rather have Paula than her: "There have been a lot of times when I wish it had been me that died because I thought that's what my parents wanted. I always thought they loved Paula more. And so I always thought they'd be happier if she was here and I wasn't."

ADULTS

Older siblings confronted many of the same issues that younger survivors had to resolve. The year following the death found many siblings struggling to mourn the loss and respond to the developmental pressures they were facing. Distracted by grief and anger and guilt, respondents found it difficult to find energy for the present or hope for the future. One sibling went from being an honors student to being on probation the year following the death of her brother. She stated, "So you tend to say things to yourself like, I'm not going to die a virgin." Another young woman, 19 years old when her older sister died, explained:

> My college years were very mixed up. When I first started, my sister died a month later. I went back and I ended up flunking a few classes. The next semester was even worse. January 'til June was even worse. I think I was going home a lot then, every weekend. It was strange, I should have just dropped out of school, and not even tried, and just spent some time at home.

One young woman remained very angry for a long time following her brother's death when she was 23 years old. Reading about youngsters that would terrorize the neighborhood, she would compare them to her brother, who could have given so much to people, and she would think, "Why couldn't it have been one of them instead?" She married 4 months after her brother's death. Feeling very guilty about separating from her mother, she found herself calling her every day to make sure everything was okay. Angry that all the burden falls on her because she is the sole survivor, she struggles to separate from her mother and to live her own life:

> The first Christmas that I was married was hard. I can remember her calling me. She had been baking cookies and she called up in tears and asked us to

please come over. When I was home things were on a pretty even keel. It wasn't until after I left that I felt that I had to. ... I still feel that way. I'm the only one they have, and if my mother's going to be alone on Sunday I say, "Gee, you know, we can't have that."

Several respondents had accidents, particularly while driving, while pondering the meaning of the event or their guilty feelings over their relationship with the sibling. Some respondents developed illnesses with symptoms very similar to CF, as we see in chapter 10.

Frank

Frank's younger sister died when she was 17, and he was 24 years old. His mother had a nervous breakdown when he was very young. He was extremely close to his little sister and helped out with her respiratory therapy, which brought them closer. Sharing artistic talent and interests, they had been "team players" for painting decorations in store windows at Christmastime. After his sister died, he moved back to his parents' house to give them support and "get some for myself." A couple of months later, while driving to his graphics class, his car was totaled:

> I suddenly saw this white dove flying exactly at the same speed as me right over my car and I slowed down and it kind of fell back. And I thought "Gee, that was really strange. I wonder if that's Gayle, letting me know that she's watching over me." So I said a prayer, and got on the bridge. There was a girl following me too close. I hit the brakes, and I just barely came to a stop before hitting the other car but then she just rammed me and shortened my car by about a foot.

Roland

Roland was 20 years old when his younger sister died at the age of 14. He has childhood memories of visiting the CF clinic and being wrapped in plastic and left alone all day to sweat, and not having the slightest idea of what was going on. He knew something was wrong because of the look of dread on his parents' faces. He felt his father was distant and not the disciplinarian he should have been. Roland's parents had grown apart since he was about 14 years old. About a year before his sister died, he realized her death was a distinct possibility. After she died, the house seemed empty. His mother, previously a nervous woman, frequently locked herself in her room following her daughter's death. The family never talked about the death or its emotional impact. Roland felt that his sister had been the one to keep the family together. When she died, there just did not seem to be anything left for him in the family:

> After she died it was just empty, a big empty house. I thought that we should've sat down and talked about how we felt about it, but we never did. And I wanted to get out. I wanted to get out. I hung around with the wrong group of people. Towards the end it got bad. I was bored, bored, bored growing up, bored older, and I was looking for an escape, some action.

Bored at 17, 18, and 19, he became involved with drugs and was sent to jail several times, for periods lasting as long as 6 months. Now describing himself as being very moody, he has periods of panicking in crowds and stores. Deeply wishing that he had been more informed about CF and that they had been able to talk as a family about the illness and death, Roland regrets the web of secrecy that had enmeshed the family, the mystery and the "hocus pocus."

Chapter 8

Fear

And what I looked for on the road first of all,
was not so much an inn as my hunger.

—André Gide (*Fruits of the Earth*, 1972)

The individuals I interviewed had experienced a psychic trauma in the loss of their siblings, and, as clinicians have documented, traumatized individuals have difficulty controlling their anxious and aggressive feelings (Van der Kolk, 1987). The warding off of unpleasant affect becomes central and avoidance defenses come into play. The hallmarks of posttraumatic stress disorder—amnesia, detachment, restriction of affect, and foreshortening of the future—surfaced in individuals who lost their sibling or siblings.

In the statistical sample, respondents were divided into three groups based on their age at the time of the death of the afflicted sibling: 9 to 12 (preadolescent), 13 to 17 (adolescent), and 18 years old. Those who were adolescent at the time of the loss presented themselves as more anxious, depressed, and guilty than either those who were preadolescent or adult at the time, whereas those who were preadolescent at the time appeared more highly defended. These clinical impressions were confirmed by the standardized measures (Table 1 in the appendix). Although the means on anxiety and depression scores for the sample fall well above those of a random normative sample of community adults (Lieberman & Mullan, 1978; see Table 2 in the appendix), the means of the adolescent group in particular are very high (see Table 3 in the appendix). Through differences both in symptoms and certain social behaviors, group differences emerged that were compelling (see Table 4 in the appendix).

YOUNG CHILDREN

At first glance, the preadolescent group appeared the least disturbed, both through their own report during the interview as well as on the standard measures of anxiety and depression. However, in looking beneath the surface, something did not seem quite right. When I called them to arrange the interview, it was these individuals whose wives or husbands told me how much they hoped that their spouse would talk to me about their feelings concerning what had happened, for they had never confided in them. Interviews tended to be much shorter than were those of the adolescent group, and these individuals demonstrated less affect.

Taken in the aggregate, for this group feelings seemed very frightening, and self-control was highly valued. Janice, 12 years old when her first brother died, reported, "That's not one of my strong suits, talking about my feelings." Another respondent stated: "Nothing gets me real excited. I'm just sort of too cool maybe." Many siblings sensed that they handle things that are unpleasant by using various avoidance strategies. Leslie explained: "Everything that I know is going to get worse, I try just to shut it out. Maybe if I ignore it, it will go away. I've learned that because I've been through a lot in 18 years. I didn't know how to handle it then, so I just ignored it. But there are certain things that you can't ignore." The preadolescent group was not the only group that reported avoidance of commitment as adults, but the reasons differed. The adolescents avoided commitment out of a fear of their potential carrier status. The preadolescents, in contrast, seemed to avoid interpersonal intimacy more out of fear of experiencing painful feelings. Ralph, 10 years old when his older brother died, explained:

> Maybe it's made me so that I don't attach myself to things as much as other people might, because I know that in the end you're going to lose them sometime, and you don't want to feel those feelings that I felt for Russell. They're terrible feelings. And the only way to get around it is to say, this is the way it is, and keep it simple.

Some siblings moved away from investing in human relationships to alternate sources of connectedness. Several siblings acquired literally hundreds of pets, ones that propagated frequently, as a sort of double defense. In other words, they did not have one pet kitten who might die and therefore have to be grieved but rather turned to collecting bees, for example, or hamsters. Andy, 9 years old when his older brother died, told me, "I have a menagerie in the backyard. Now I'm kind of at the point where, God, what am I going to do? I can't go to an apartment. I have 170 animals out back." Several siblings seemed to have moved to a deepened sense of the land. Ralph, 10 years old when his older brother died, spoke eloquently about his farm, explaining that he has never been away from it, nor will he ever leave: "The land is something that is a part of me. I guess it's a part of me that they can't take away. That's what it is. It's something you can't take away." Some siblings commented on their guarded emotional reactions. Ralph explained his detachment, "It's like you grow up too fast and you kinda hold back 'cause you know what can happen, whereas somebody else that hasn't had that experience, they jump right in. I would definitely say that it has had some effect on me in that respect. That's why I say that I'm a loner."

What are the feelings that are so frightening? Raphael (1983), in her work on children who had lost a parent, found anger may be one of these, and it can remain very hidden. Ralph explained that there was definitely a period of time when he was very "unmotivated." His father would admonish him to stop grieving and continue on with his life, and Ralph finally became angry. "I guess you would call it resentment, you just lock up and go on. You know, pick up, and just hold your feelings inside." Anxiety and defenses against fully experiencing it seemed prominent as well. Simon, 10 years old at the time, articulated, "Life is a crap game. Accidents don't happen to other people, they can happen to you." Another sibling told me: "I worry about all the possibilities, the number of illnesses and forms of cancer. It's a battlefield of stuff out there and how the hell are you going to get through that?"

Confusions over their own carrier status also abounded in the interviews. One sibling told me that he was not going to have children because if he had four children, three would have CF. Another respondent, remembering a medical test he had in Boston many years ago, was convinced that he was "the strongest carrier" in the family and decided not to have children. The majority of siblings denied any fears or concerns, however, often engaging in what appeared to be counterphobic behavior. Ben noticed a profound change in his way of being in the world since his sibling died. Stating that he is not afraid of death at all, he was concerned about all the automobile accidents he has been having:

> There are situations where I should be nervous where I'm not, possible situations of danger, let's say. Hiking, skiing. Something that makes me more nervous than it should is driving right now. Just in the past 3 weeks I've gotten into two bad accidents. I'm a thrill seeker, I go parachuting. I would say I've had in my education a little bit of a motivation problem ever since. Education-wise. Kind of in life too. I don't know. I'm motivated for certain things, certain things I'm not motivated for. Pleasure. Hedonism.

Most siblings in the preadolescent group denied having had any worries over the possibility that their children might have cystic fibrosis. Janice, 12 and 23 years old when she lost her brothers, reported that she never had any fears that her son was going to be born with CF. She explained why she decided not to have him tested for CF through a sweat test. She told me,

> I just never believed that both my husband and I would have the recessive gene. My parents were fearful that he would have CF and I refused. I said, "Look, I talked with the pediatrician and he doesn't have the symptoms and he said there's no need to test him." I just believed that he was perfectly healthy.

Other respondents denied any anxiety over their own health. Andy stated that he does not care if he lives to a "ripe old age." However, he sleep walks frequently, has dreams of people chasing him with knives and others in which he is totally out of control of what is happening to him. He reported, "I have one that I've had since I was 6 years old. That's me and my cousin walking down the street and the road turns to mud and soldiers march over us. I get that all the time. I hate that one." In fact, many siblings who vehemently protested that they were ever consciously anxious reported a very active dream life in which they suddenly found themselves in situations beyond their control. Common dreams were of people chasing them with guns or knives, although in the dreams they rarely got caught and rarely died. Ralph told me his dreams were always situations "meeting something around the corner, another force or something that you have no control over." In the cases of these individuals, the dream life may be an attempt to master the trauma of the sudden intrusion of the sibling's death.

Many siblings remarked that losing a sibling has led them to an almost fatalistic view of life. Andy commented: "I think it's changed my way of life. I can't say I'm not scared of dying but if I'm going to die, I'm going to die. I could care less." Modell, Weiss, and Sampson (1983) used the metaphor of the cocoon to describe the state of nonrelatedness as a response to early trauma and an unconscious sense of survivor guilt, with problems of safety and entrustment of the self to another paramount. Lifton (1979) wrote of psychic numbing as a response to trauma. A. Freud (1946) and Vaillant (1977) posited that there exists a developmental line of defenses, where denial and restriction of the ego are seen as less mature styles of defense. Niederland (1981) described a severe guilt complex affecting survivors of the Holocaust in which individuals appeared and felt like living dead. Horney (1950) described individuals who were undisturbed by overt conflicts. Having no particular "symptoms" such as anxiety or depression, they seemed not to suffer from disturbances; rather, they seemed to lack something. Fromm (1944) suggested that this lack reflected conditions of defect rather than of neurosis.

ADOLESCENTS

Those siblings who were adolescents at the time of the death were much more articulate about their concerns. While there was less denial, there was much more conscious pain. The following themes emerged from the interviews and were coded for the statistical sample.

Global Anxiety.   All of the adolescent group expressed a global sense of things always about to go wrong, and concerns ranged from "the nuclear holocaust on down." One sibling mused that he has worried "since the age of 5 months."

Bodily Concerns and Feelings of Vulnerability.   Three fourths of the adolescents expressed various hypochondriacal concerns related to their bodies or to the possibility of getting sick or dying at an early age. Going to the doctor for a routine checkup was an ordeal, eliciting dormant fears that something may be very wrong. Danelle reported, "If I go to the gynecologist, I'm gone. I have a real fear of my body, to tell you the truth. A real fear. An abnormal one, almost. And if anyone tells me there's something wrong, I don't know if I could handle it. That would be the end." Fifty percent feared an early death for themselves. For example, Rick said he worries so much about his own death that he felt "boxed in" by his concerns. Often, the siblings believed they would die when they reached the age the age at which their sibling died, although they frequently did not see the connection. Jenny said she was convinced that she will die at age 20, the age her sister was when she died. She believes that her death will come either from an accident or by her own hand. She reported, "I just have this weird feeling that I'll die in a car accident. I have suicidal tendencies. I know I wouldn't do it now because I wouldn't want to hurt my parents, but someday I just might get carried away." Interestingly, most siblings believed that their death would be sudden, probably by an accident, particularly a car accident. Their conviction that it would not be anything prolonged perhaps reflected the way in which they had experienced their sibling's death, similar to the sudden and traumatic nature of the death experienced by their younger siblings. Other siblings fear that they will live a few years longer than their ill siblings had, but still die at an early age. For example, one young woman, whose sibling was 24 years old when she died, explained, "I always thought I'd die at the age of 30. It was like, by the time I'm 30, I'm gonna be dead. Now, I just thought of this, my husband used to say, 'Oh God,' when I finally got through the year of 30 it was like, 'Geez, I don't have to listen to it anymore.'"

Fear of Intimacy. Nearly all of the adolescents discussed concerns related to the establishment of an intimate relationship. CF carrier issues weighed heavily, and emotional commitment in interpersonal relationships signaled not only the fear of losing another loved one but also the worry of having a sick child themselves. Danelle wondered whether her inability to get close to someone in a relationship is a result of her fear that she might have to make a decision about children. She knows that she has a tremendous fear: "I don't even think I want children, but I do. I mean, I want to want children."

For some siblings, the fear of repetition of loss prevented commitment to new attachments. Jenny articulated the fears of many young people in the sample:

> One thing I wanted to mention is that I always have been scared, I never want to fall in love again. I never want to love. It's hard for me to love people because I loved my sister so much and she died. I'm always the one who gets screwed over. I mean my sister was the one that got screwed over, she's the one that died but ... I don't know. It's weird.

When I commented to her that she had in fact lost someone she loved, she replied, "Yeah, it seems like I always do. That's a lot of the reason I keep far away from my parents. I don't let myself get too close to them." Her solution, at least temporarily, was to displace her feelings of attachment onto her pet, seemingly a safer object of her attachment. Ever since she was a young girl, she became emotionally attached to animals because "they can love you and you can love them, but they can't mentally hurt you." She was quite worried that if something happened to her cat, she would not know what to do. Danelle also worried about her inability to form a close relationship with someone:

> I worry that I'm not gonna be able to settle down with someone and make a life for myself. I really think that's my main worry. I don't know if I could psychoanalyze this, but I'm almost tired of fighting. So instead of going through the mainstream of life, I go another way. I take the easy way out. I think there's still a part of me that's numb and shut off. Because of that I have a lot of difficulty with relationships, anyone getting too close to me. I wonder if I'll ever be able to make a commitment to someone. I don't think so.

Rick reflected on his difficulty in being close to people. Rather than having resolved this issue over the years, he thinks that he has moved farther away from an ability to have an intimate, loving relationship. Instead, he fears that he is "cursed with the wandering foot syndrome for the rest of (his) life." Some survivor siblings were so anxious about the possibility of losing loved ones that their ability to form a strong attachment bond to their own children was compromised, illustrating the disheartening second-generation effects which can result from trauma. One young woman remembered that after her brother and sister died, she was convinced that everybody she would ever love would die. Despite this fear, she married. Unfortunately, and further compounding her fear, her father died during her pregnancy. The effect of her losses was that her bond with her daughter was problematic for a long time, out of fear that something would happen to her as well.

Excessive Concern or Worries for Others.   For 50% of the adolescent group, the heightened sense of vulnerability in life extended to worries over loved ones, with exaggerated concern if they left the house and returned a little late. For example, as one sibling related, "It can happen at any time, you just think at any time, how would I handle it, Mom's coming up to visit me, what if she gets in a wreck. I sometimes play games with myself, to ask how I'd handle it." Danelle, worrying every day about her father, commented that she is to the point where she thinks that everyone is "going to just die in front of her." Some siblings realized with dismay that they inherited a fearful view of the world from their fathers or mothers and cannot resist maintaining a negative view of life:

> I feel I was overprotected and now I've got fear instilled in me, like my mother. I sound just like her when I come up with these things that are negative that might happen. My mother will always tell me to be careful, and not to do this and that. Then I'll go and tell my boyfriend to be careful and not to do that, and he's never had anybody overprotecting him. I sound just like her when I come up with these paranoid things that might happen.

Many siblings also reported that they worry a great deal about the health of their children. Kathy, 13 years old when her sister died, is dismayed by her own overconcern for her children. She feels that her mother worries constantly about her grandchildren because of her own experience with parenting a fatally ill child:

> I worry about their health all the time, not necessarily CF but everything. I check them I don't know how many times a night for breathing, and when they leave the house. My daughter's away right now overnight, and I can't wait to pick her up. I'm very overprotective, very. Maybe because my mother is now towards them too. She's like, if they stub their toe, "What are you going to do about it?" I think she's reliving [my sister] in my daughter, and that's hard to see sometimes. I have to bite my tongue from saying, "She's not your daughter."

Somatic Expressions.   Most of the adolescent group is troubled by various bodily complaints such as severe headaches, ulcers, or chronically tense and painful muscles or joints. For many, the years since the death include a litany of physical complaints that have persisted since their inception immediately following the death or in the first year afterward.

Nightmares. Most of the adolescent group reported they still have severe and persistent nightmares. Themes included people breaking into the house, their children getting hurt, images of death, and ghosts. Rick, 13 years old when his older sister died, told me:

> I've found myself periodically in my life, this is late at night, outside my bedroom. I've woken up to find myself there, in a cold sweat and feeling that death is impending. It's weird. It's a nightmare. My heart's going blomm, and I have the feeling, okay, this is it, you're wrapping it up. And I think no, I'm not ready. It's right there, like he's knocking on the door and saying, "Check out time." So I'll have a beer and hit the rack. It's a feeling of being in a corner and just about to have someone's thumb come down and snuff you out.

Many respondents have dreams of people chasing them, particularly with knives, of cars trying to run them over, or of cars parked outside their window with a man inside watching them. Whether the dreams reflect a basic sense of vulnerability or an almost persecutory anxiety, they are frightening and repetitive:

> I have a lot of recurring dreams about a little red Volkswagen that was trying to run me over a lot. And people are chasing me and trying to get at me, and I'm always locking doors. In my dreams people are always trying to come at me with a knife. It's always dark and windy; I'm always running down the street. They'd kill me. They would.

The intricate relationship between guilt and anxiety is at times suggested by the sibling's own associations. The connection between the sense of being angry and therefore bad and the sense of something horrible about to happen can be seen in the following passage from a sibling who expects to die at any moment, although he cannot predict the way it will take place, only that it will be sudden. Rick predicted:

> Trauma. Something traumatic, something unexpected. It won't be in bed with a blonde, I'll tell you that. In seriousness, I have a feeling, and this is terrible too, but sometimes earlier, not so much anymore, I have the most awful feelings about my family. I'm not a nut or anything. Thanksgiving Day the turkey's in front of me and carving it and feeling like you just want to go run amok among the table and nail everybody with a knife. What does that mean? Your guess is as good as mine.

Many of the dreams contained images of a sudden change occurring in some natural situation, reflecting the impact of the sudden death of the sibling. The dreams of one young man were typical:

> I'll be going on in the middle of something and all of a sudden they'll change to something completely different. I had a dream the other night that we were skiing. It was just the three of us. It was almost like a cliff we were going down. We were kind of jumping from patch to patch of snow and then we got to the bottom and it was like we were at the sand dunes. They're very seldom like a story line or something. The people usually stay the same, but the places and the things that are taking place change a lot. I've woken up in the night doing sit-ups and talking to myself. I've never answered, so I figure I'm not crazy.

Tom

Tom is 29 years old and not married. His two older brothers died when he was 14 and 15 years old. Because there had been no discussion within the family about the illness or the possibility of their dying, their deaths deeply shocked him. On reaching the age of 18, the age his first brother was at the time of his death, Tom feared that he also was going to die and simultaneously developed a central tremor, which he still had at the time of the interview. At this time he also began having panic attacks with great fears of losing control. He developed agoraphobia and began avoiding situations which precipitated his attacks, such as boating with friends and shopping at crowded malls. His panic attacks coincided with his first serious relationship with a young woman. The acute anxiety attacks began when, after initially having ended their relationship, they were getting back together. He felt as though he had no control over the relationship and would wake up in the middle of the night shaking and having racing thoughts. Since then, he has avoided any relationships. The connection between establishing an intimate relationship with someone and the resurrection of fears of producing sick children was to some extent accessible to Tom; as he said, "I'm reluctant to get involved at this point in my life because I don't want to deal with that whole thing. I don't want to have children that are going to die. I don't want to have children that are going to spend 20 years dying, maybe more." He described the following depressive episodes which were intertwined with his panic, and explained his attempt to have some control over his level of distress:

> It was a black hole. It's very scary because you feel very dislocated, very cut off from everything. I could get these inklings of it, and eventually I learned

how not to go all the way into it. It's sort of similar to the anxiety. It's like you become friends with it. I occasionally get a very familiar feeling and realize that it's like I'm right outside the door, and if I want to go to the right pathway I can get there but I know I don't have to and I can avoid it.

Bruce

Bruce is unmarried and in his late 20s. His younger brother died at the age of 15, when Bruce was 16 years old. Bruce can remember very little of his childhood except that his mother was with his brother most of the time and that his father was abusive. He knew his brother was very sick and used to give him his allowance whenever he could. The death of his brother was extremely traumatic. Bruce was not able to remember most of his feelings at the time but it was during this period when he started having seizures.

> I'd be doing something and I'd suddenly be laying on the floor shaking. I went into the hospital for tests when I was in art school. I was on a bus going to Boston, and the last thing I remember I was sitting there on the bus. The next thing I remember, somebody put something in my mouth. The police took me to one hospital and then to another.

This went on for maybe 2 to 3 years, as his brother's condition worsened. When his brother died, Bruce considered suicide. He developed agoraphobia. His anxiety attacks have gotten steadily worse over the years and he thinks they are related to his feeling out of control when he contemplates a serious relationship. He used to drink too much until he got a warning at work. He recalled that he "always wished he would die." He still feels guilty about everything and recalled his mother telling him that he had wished that his brother would die. He also remembered that she told him that if he had any children, they would all have CF.

ADULTS

Those siblings who were 18 years old and older at the time of the loss seemed the most well adjusted now. The year following the death of their siblings had been difficult, but most individuals had then been able to get on with their lives. Although they did not deny concerns voiced by the younger groups, they generally did not find them as compelling. If they did feel guilt toward the deceased sibling, for example, it was discussed thoughtfully but neither dwelled on nor denied. Carrier concerns were voiced in a realistic fashion, with awareness of the statistical chances of having affected offspring, and reasonable decisions as to childbearing were being made. Although residual anxieties remained, they were not extreme, neither obsessional nor totally defended against. The adults' anxieties were focused less frequently on their own fears of death than were their younger counterparts. Unlike younger respondents, adult siblings were fortunate in being able to make the decision to have children before the death of their brother or sister cast doubts. Nevertheless, having their own children sweat tested was a nightmare revisited for some individuals. As one young woman, 19 and 23 years old at the deaths of her younger brothers, described:

> It was just like all over again, sitting in that office at Dr. Shwachman's building waiting for the sweat test results of my son. And what would happen if he had it. My parents had just lost their son 9 months ago. I just lost a brother to it. It's more of a reality of death to me now. Now it was death. It wasn't a sickness, it was a death.

Many women commented that they knew they were more overprotective than most mothers, but they could not do anything about it. Having seen firsthand that death can happen only too easily, they frequently checked on their young children throughout the night. Some parents found it difficult to let older children out of their sight. One young woman, 23 years old when her younger brother died, reported that she does not worry about herself, but she hopes nothing happens to her because she would not want to leave her son Wayne without a mother.

> I worry a lot about Wayne. He had a real, real bad case of the croup this past spring, and I had seen my brother go through all these breathing problems and I knew what to do. I didn't lose my cool about it. But after he was all right, my knees were like jelly. I felt sick to my stomach. I kiss him sometimes, and I taste salt, and I think, "Oh, my God."

Some siblings stated that they too often block out unpleasant realities. Several respondents believed that their tendency toward denial stemmed from their experience with their siblings' illness. The dream life of some individuals reflected anxieties kept at bay during the day. One young woman had dreams of the Mafia coming after her to shoot her, because she "found out something she wasn't supposed to know." Frequent themes were of being unable to forestall disaster to the self. One young man, 19 years old when his 20-year-old brother died, described the themes of his repetitive dreams,

> I guess things where I'm powerless. Being chased, cornered, that kind of thing. Not having any power about whatever's going to happen. Maybe it's sharks swimming in the water, and there's a shark and I get eaten, that kind of thing. There are others of that same scenario of being chased and being caught and shot.

One young man does not have what he calls "scary" nightmares but rather dreams where he is unable to alter the negative course of events. Having felt helpless when his little sister died when he was 21, he now dreams about other situations that he is unable to prevent, played out using the imagery of his farm life. He reported:

> Mine are frustration nightmares. Like you dream about a whole bunch of stuff going wrong at once, and you can't fix it. Every time you try to fix it, it gets worse. The cattle all get out and you can't get them back in, or a piece of machinery breaks down. No matter what you do, it just keeps getting worse.

Chapter 9

Waiting

> *Estragon:* *Let's go.*
> *Vladimir:* *We can't.*
> *Estragon:* *Why not?*
> *Vladimir:* *We're waiting for Godot.*
> —Samuel Beckett (*Waiting for Godot*, 1954)

Eth and Pynoos (1985) stressed that traumatized individuals cannot mourn until the traumatic elements of the event have been resolved. Only a few respondents showed signs of having completed the necessary grief work—or, in many cases, of even having attempted it. Parental inability to grieve the loss of their child and maladaptive responses to this loss created a climate in which siblings were directly admonished not to forget. As one young woman reported, "For years we were always told, if people ask you how many are in your family, you should always say five. Never say four. Don't disclude her from the family, because she's part of the family no matter how you look at it. She might be dead, but she's still a part of the family." Her sister, adolescent at the time of the loss, remembered her father's preventing her from going near her deceased sister's possessions, forbidding her to touch them. Other siblings felt too guilty over the possibility of forgetting their brother or sister to allow themselves to grieve the loss. Some siblings were haunted by dreams in which the individual appeared and begged them to remember. Elin, 11 years old when her older sister died, recounted a dream she had 2 weeks before our interview:

> She came back and was complaining that I wasn't relating to her like I used to. I said, "Well, you've been dead for 10 years now. It doesn't seem fair to expect me to treat you like I did 10 years ago, especially since you're dying again." She was about to die again in the dream. When I was 14 or 15 I used to have a lot of dreams where she was checking on me, and she would say,

"I am dead now but you can still think about me. I hope you're doing okay, but I hope you don't stop thinking about me."

YOUNG CHILDREN

Siblings who were preadolescent at the time of the loss rarely cried during the interview when talking about their sibling. Although sad feelings related to the lost sibling were quickly denied, there was frequent evidence of displacement of intense feelings from the sibling to more neutral situations. Dennie, 10 years old at the death, said: "I get sad about the stupidest things. I'm very sensitive to McDonald commercials and Pepsi commercials, and AT&T commercials kill me." Some individuals are only able to get in touch with their sadness when they are drinking. In fact, much of the alcohol use encountered may be not only an attempt to modulate anxiety states but to shift to a state in which true feelings may be experienced. Unfortunately, this did not allow feelings to be mastered and worked through. Peter, whose sister died from CF when he was 12 years old and whose best friend was killed in an automobile accident, tried to understand his own mood swings:

> Just one thing will set me off. I'm happy, and then the next minute I'll be so sad I'll just come right down. I don't understand it. My sister and my best friend, that brings me down a lot. I just start thinking about it. And I just change. All you do is sit there and think, you know, when you're driving. And drinking affects me a lot.

Some siblings have a strange sense that they are blocked in some way, but they do not know what to do about it. The following example is of a young woman who was 11 years old when her older sister died.

Elin

Elin grew up in a comfortable country house and had what she described as an "idyllic" childhood. Her father was emotionally distant but "a nice guy." She was always very close with her sister who was 4 years older; they did everything together. Because her sister looked so normal and led a very active social life, her death when Elin was 11 years old came as a complete shock to her. At the wake, looking at her sister's body, Elin decided that her sister was "faking." When she learned that her sister had been in the hospital for 3 weeks while she was away with friends, and that her parents had not told her, she became furious with them. Her relationship with her mother became troubled, and her father was not around. Her initial grief "turned into a long-time nausea about the whole thing." In the following weeks, she was surprised each day that this had really happened. She feared that perhaps her sister was in a coma somewhere. She spun an elaborate fantasy that the doctors had deceived her sister, taken her to the hospital, given her ether, and said, "We'll see you tomorrow," and that therefore her sister was never given a chance to prepare for her own death.

Elin stayed out of school for weeks at a time, languishing and not really knowing whether she felt sick or not, but hoping that she had mononucleosis or another condition that could be pinpointed as an illness. She guessed that she was "kind of in shock" and could not put together the actual fact of her sister's dying with any coherent emotional reaction. She just remembered feeling tired, unhappy, and unwilling or unable to exert herself:

> Those weeks on end when I refused to go to school, it was probably that I just hated school. But I have a feeling I was just not destined to be a happy teenager. In high school, I think I liked myself, kind of abstractly. But I thought I was blowing it. I always felt like I was waiting for something. All through high school, I felt like, gee, gotta get through this year and gotta get through that year. I was waiting for college to come, and I figured well, college will come and then I'm going to be waiting to get out of college. I felt like I wasn't performing anything right then, I was kind of waiting for something to happen all the time.

When I asked her if she knew what she was waiting for, she replied:

> No. I still don't. I'm still waiting. I think that her dying shortened my attention span somehow. I was an excellent student up to that time, even at the beginning of sixth grade when she died. That year, my grades just took a complete nose dive, and they never really recovered after that. It was hard for me to pay attention and to exert myself. I felt like it was a waste of time to put in hard work on a project that was going nowhere.
> It's kind of put a damper on my, well, I don't want to say emotions, but I tend to be the opposite of melodramatic. I can't imagine myself going through that again. If anybody that was close to me died now, I would grieve, but I don't think I have the capability of going through that again.

Her dream life painted a vivid portrait of her sense of self: "Being a plant ... ivy, ivy plant ... being a plant or being a rock. A lot of dreams about dead bodies. Graves. But the worst ones are the plant dreams." When asked what she did as a plant, she replied: "Nothing. Just sit on the rock and be more or less dead." In talking with survivor siblings, a clinical impression of a restricted self emerged. This may reflect a blocked mourning process in which energy was bound up with warding off unpleasant feelings.

Self-esteem seemed adversely affected through many different routes:

1. unfavorable comparison to the sick sibling whom they have idealized;
2. unfavorable comparison to the sibling whom the parent has idealized;
3. loss of narcissistic supplies provided by the sibling;
4. direct inheritance of damaged self-esteem of parents;
5. acceptance of projection of parental guilt;
6. negative sense of self, derived from their own guilt and envy.

These many strands and others contribute to the survivor siblings' damaged self-esteem.

John

John lost his younger sister when he was 9 years old and his younger
brother when he was 28. Interestingly, John does not speak of his sister's
death, instead focusing on his brother Jimmy's death. He remembered that
it was difficult growing up because of all the arguments between his mother
and father over the illness. If Jimmy started a fight he would say, "Well,
John did it," and his parents would believe him and punish John. Jimmy
would ask him whether he was going to die, and John would not know
what to say or how to respond. Feeling helpless, he used to buy his brother
presents all the time. After his brother died, his father started drinking and
would not come home for long periods of time; John would have to "pull
his father out of bars." His mother, having become very bitter since the
death of her son and the absence of her husband, was withdrawn and John
found it very difficult to talk with her. Feeling very alone and stressed, John
developed some serious somatic symptoms, losing both sight in one eye
and hearing in one ear from pressure behind the eye. At the time of the
interview, he was still having tremendous headaches, and feeling "lost" a
lot. Feeling guilty that he had not done enough for his siblings, and still
feeling useless to everyone, he began to cut at himself with a razor blade at
work. Extremely depressed and unable to find help from anyone, including
his wife and the local priest, he had tried to kill himself by jumping off the
bridge in his home town about 2 or 3 weeks before I spoke with him.

> I was depressed and felt like I wasn't doing any good. Thought about my
> mother and how we don't communicate. I was having awful headaches,
> couldn't sleep, and couldn't talk to my wife because she didn't have time for
> me. I says, "This is it, I've had it." So I went to the bridge. I was gonna jump
> off. Some guy stopped me as I was just starting to get my clothes off and I
> was going over. And I went to work the next day. If that guy hadn't come 5
> minutes ago it would have been all over, that would have been it. One of the

things I was talking to the priest about, I says, "I wonder if I do enough, I work 7 days a week. Maybe I should get another job." I always think, maybe if I did more for my brother, maybe if I did more for my sister, my father, maybe they'd appreciate me more.

ADOLESCENTS

Siblings who were adolescent at the time of the death cried profusely during the interview and expressed a great deal of longing for the lost relationship. They frequently described years in which they cried themselves to sleep at night or constantly thought about the sibling. Unlike the preadolescent group, the adolescent group seemed to have attempted to complete the work of mourning but been unable to do so. The longing for many was intense throughout their adolescence. Kathy, for example, 13 years old when her younger sister died, reported: "I always used to think if she was around now what would we be doing. I think about it all the time, what we'd be doing right now. I used to go to her grave when I was younger and just sit there and talk." As with the preadolescent group, it was frequently their own parents who did not allow the gradual withdrawing of the attachment relationship with the lost child. Some parents expected the sibling not only to remember key dates like anniversaries of the death but to think of the parent at those times. Donna, 14 years old when her older brother died, explained:

It will be 10 years next year since he died. And she [her mother] got upset with me because I didn't call her this year. It's not that I'm forgetting, there's no way I can, but I don't feel I have to remember it sometimes. I know and she knows, and I know she knows that I know. And she knows.

As with the preadolescent group, there was much evidence in the interview material of dissociation from the actual source of sad feelings when they emerged, and the unproductive experiencing of unpleasant affect severed from its original source. Doris, for example, 15 years old at the time, explained that she does not like to listen to depressing stories like those about missing children. She will either go into another room or turn off the TV. For some individuals, while the original loss continued to cause much pain in adult life because it had not been completely worked through, later losses were additive, increasing the depression. Jenny, 14 years old when her older sister died, stated that she has now partially accepted the death, but she still gets depressed when she has a chance to sit down and think about her sister. The lost sibling still appeared in many individuals' dreams, evidence of the ongoing struggle to accept the finality of the death. Ben, 14 years old when his older brother died, reported a recurring dream he used to have:

I remember seeing him on the shoreway, at the ocean. The waves were going in and out, and he was running back and forth with the waves. As the waves went out he ran out, and then ran back, and ran out, and ran back. For some reason he had a long stick in his hand. When he would come back in, he would put the pole down—you know, how they pole vault. That's one of the main dreams I remember, which was a couple of years ago. Or a year ago.

Erin said she was depressed about her brother's death most of the day, "because every little teeny thing reminds me of him. Anything anybody says, if I heard him say it once in my life, I'll think of him." She described her dreams in which he still drops by so they can spend some time together:

I have dreams where he comes back to visit for a little while, and that's a good dream, because then I get to spend a bit of time with him. I know he's not here to stay, but I'm so thankful for that little bit of time with him. I know that he's going to go away and die again. When I greet him in my dream it's always an awkward thing, because I haven't seen him in so long. But yet it's the best thing in the world, because I get to see him again. And we always try to keep it on the upbeat when we're together. We don't talk about the fact that he's going to leave again.

The link for many between depression and guilty feelings is quite explicit. Some siblings torment themselves with any slight thing they later regretted. Rick, 13 years old when his sister died, is haunted by thinking: "You shouldn't have done that, and I'm gonna think about it and remember it. I dwell, I don't forget." Depression is a problem for some siblings because they feel "worse off" than everyone else, displaying intense envy of friends who have brothers or sisters. Erin feels emotionally distant from her boyfriend, the youngest of 10 children: "Sometimes I get jealous of that and I really envy him. I really envy the good relationships that he has with his sisters." Out of disappointment that her brother was not around, and because of the futile search to find an effective substitute for him, she was never able to develop close friendships in school:

It's really strange. Sometimes I think it's because I was really looking forward to this relationship with my brother Jim and now I'm not going to have it so I don't want anything else instead. On the other hand I think that I look for qualities in Jim in other people, especially guys. I think I'm always looking for a brother to look up to.

Many siblings, anxious to start a family of their own because of their fear of having children who have CF, face the impossibility of repairing what has happened. Unlike concentration camp survivors, who tried to rebuild shattered families by building their own, those who survive a sibling afflicted with a genetic disorder find any attempt at restitution of the loss more difficult. Some siblings described serious bouts with depressive episodes in the past, where some ability to gain control over the depression has come about over the years.

Danelle

Danelle lost her only sibling, an 11-year-old sister, to CF when she was 15 years old. She and her sister had been extremely close and were very similar in many ways. Sensing for some time that something was terribly wrong by the pain in her parents' eyes, she would try to broach the subject with them, only to run up against their inability to talk about it with her. She was staggered by the death. "Numb" for a year, she found everything very difficult. Forcing herself to go through the motions, she received the lead in a musical, and dutifully performed her lines. She reported that right after the play was over, she slowed down, developing migraine headaches for which she took Valium for a year. Because she was a "good actress," her school grades did not suffer.

> I felt sad, I ached inside. I felt such pain I almost couldn't breathe. I remember saying to my mother one day—I was lying on her bed crying—and I just said, "I wish I could die." I remember those words. I meant it. I hyperventilated a lot after that. I couldn't catch my breath. I lost it. All I could think of was this. I didn't care. I didn't care.

She drove like she did not care as well, having at least four accidents because she was distracted. Still very angry, she feels she continues not to care when she is driving. Danelle described her life over the next 8 years in the following manner:

> I lived in a fantasy land. I didn't face the world at all. I took no responsibility for anything. I went with people that there would definitely be no future in, absolutely no question. I went to places that nobody would go, just to dance the night away. And I did that for about 8 years. It's a long time. It scares me because I wonder if part of it is my nature, or I wonder if I just needed to ease the pain. I needed to be diverted. But 8 years of diversion, that's a lot.

When I asked her why she thinks that she led the life she did, she replied, "I think it was more of an annihilation." She just wanted to soften the pain, to have it go away. Although she consciously knew that it was important to have future goals, she would think to herself, "Well, I'm not gonna make any plans for the future. I'm gonna take each day as it comes." Still not looking ahead at all, she feels guilty about everything, particularly in relation to her sister and her parents. Danelle tries hard to please everyone, unable to protect herself from demands of her friends and family. She still feels very guilty about the day when she was angry at her sister when she threw her against a bureau. She also feels bad about a time when she was setting her hair, and her sister was staring at her, and she told her to go away. When she thinks of those two episodes she feels sick. Additionally, she feels extremely guilty that she is not following the direction her parents would like for her. As the only surviving descendant, she reported that she will feel guilty if she should decide not to have children, believing that her choice would deeply trouble her parents. Wanting very badly to please her family and everyone, she has days when she does not even want to answer the telephone. Wanting to "make everything nice," she has a lot of guilt saying "no" to people. Very angry about the loss of her sister, she continues to miss her terribly and can find no answers to her question of why it had to happen. Danelle still struggles with severe depressive attacks, the other end of her manic spectrum:

> Well, I'm sort of an all or nothing person, so when I get down I'm gone, on the floor. I'd say every couple of months I get real depressed. It could be that I'm losing control of my life, just absolutely losing it in all ways. It's like I'm drowning. So to save myself I shut the door and start all over again.
> See when my sister died I tried to forget. I used to make plans with a thousand people. I auditioned for every show in town and I did 80,000 things, and I still do. I couldn't get off the roller coaster. I'm toned down now but I still have that compulsion, that old habit to book five things. It's like I'm on a train, and I get derailed, I'd say every 2 months. It stems from needing to forget so badly.

Even though its been 10 years since her sister died, Danelle still experiences anniversary reactions. Every October, the month her sister died, she feels nauseous and achy. She tries not to think about her sister too much, because she is afraid of what she might do. At the school where she teaches, the children remind her of her sister, and memories flood back, which she tries to block out. If she meets anyone with her sister's name, she is devastated. She has just recently decided to face her feelings and work on these issues in therapy. Danelle stated that had I called her 2 or 3 years earlier, she could not have consented to be interviewed. She remains filled with envy of people who have siblings. Recently, she has become best friends with a young woman who looks just like her sister. She still has dreams at night that doctors have found a cure and her sister is going to be saved. Then she wakes up bewildered, only to experience again the horror that her sister is really dead forever: "I think that I still haven't come to terms with it. In my mind she's still somewhere. "

ADULTS

Those individuals who were adults at the time their siblings died were more able to master the loss. However, parents generally held higher expectations for them to help them with their own mourning, much to the dismay of the adult sibling. Sally, 18 years old when her sister died, explained that if she did not call her mother each year on the anniversary of the death, her mother would phone her and complain. One young woman gets sick every autumn, dreading Christmas and her mother's inevitable depression during the months that lie ahead. Some individuals blocked out their feelings and never really mourned, although they were more likely to be consciously aware of this than younger siblings. One young man, 21 years at the death, mused: "I don't think about it very much, to be honest with you. I just kind of blocked it out. It's an unpleasant emotion so I try not to think about it at all." One young woman explained that she tried to get on with her life, and for her that meant not taking time out to deal with it. When families failed to provide support for mourning, it was easier not to begin the painful process at all. Sally, 18 years old when her younger brother died, explained: "I pushed everything way, way, way, way down. I think I just wanted to push everything out of the way. What usually happens is that if you push it away until everything's all right, you're never going to find the time. Everything had to be so damned intact."

Siblings still have periods of sadness about the irreplaceable loss of a person who grew up with them, an individual who shares the same history. One young woman, 31 years old when her younger brother died, reported:

> I think nobody loves me and then I start thinking I wish I had a brother or sister. Then a few days later I'm okay, but I do think of it every time I get depressed. When you're older, you think your mother's not going to live forever, and then you really won't have anyone else just like you, that was brought up like you.

Some individuals reminisce about the sibling every day. Holidays and birthdays are particularly difficult. One young woman, 19 years old when her sibling died, reported that it is really hard for her family to have a good time when they get together. They had attempted a traditional Christmas at home the year before, but the empty places at the table were extremely depressing, she reported. "You can't think about anything else. It's terrible. So this Christmas we decided we're all going to go to Mexico." Still, those respondents who were adult at the time of the death were more able to grieve the death and experience sadness when they thought of the lost relationship. One young man offered this poignant reflection:

There is a carillon that rings at noontime in my town. My sister used to have the window open so she could hear the carillon bells ringing when she was in her bed in her room. She knew the songs, and liked to listen to them. I go out to the garden and think about all the times that my sister was here at the hospital and how she liked to go out in the garden. I think I see the garden differently than anybody else when I go out there. I look at it through different eyes.

The dream of one young woman, 25 years old when her younger brother died, illustrated how dreams sometimes signaled the end of a mourning process:

I had a dream about 6 months after he died that we were someplace, like a family get-together, and he walked in and was big, strong and healthy looking. Walked in perfectly happy, how he would have looked if he was healthy. Just came in and said, "I came to say that I'm okay." It was a good feeling to me that he was okay. It was kind of like the end of it for me.

Self-esteem issues persisted in this group as well, although less dramatically. Some individuals speculated that their quiet or withdrawn siblings have an "inferiority complex" because the sick child had received so much love and attention throughout the years. Siblings brought patterns learned in childhood to their adult lives. One young woman spent her childhood trying to make everybody in her family happy and always blamed herself when something was wrong in her marriage. Some self-esteem difficulties seemed related to a proneness to feeling guilty. One young woman, 19 years old when her sibling died, said she felt she has no right to be happy if she knew that someone else was sad: "If somebody else is miserable, then how can I be happy?" Others reported depression about their career. The result of being distracted by the illness and death of their sibling during crucial career-building years left many bereft, falling into jobs without actively setting and pursuing goals. Now feeling trapped or stuck, they lamented the lost years.

Relationships for these adults also suffered. Having resolved their anger against parents for having been unavailable to them throughout their childhood, they have accepted with sadness that the injured relationship cannot be repaired. Siblings were concerned about the kinds of choices they have made in their lives. One young man, 27 years old when his younger brother died, worried:

It's funny, I don't ascribe to myself the quality of being a lonely person. Yet I feel I'm a loner in a way. One of my fears is that I'll reach the end of my life and then realize that I am lonely, that I always was lonely, and that I thought I was a loner and could handle it.

Chapter 10

Guilt

We die with the dying:
See, they depart, and we go with them.
                                        —T.S. Eliot (*Four Quartets*, 1962)

Although anxiety can serve as a defense against depression, both anxiety and depression can mask an underlying sense of guilt. Clinicians have reported that a frequent theme expressed by Holocaust survivors was their feeling that they should not be alive and that they should have died instead of the parent or sibling. Based on his clinical work with almost 2,000 survivors of the Holocaust, Niederland (1981) believed that it is not guilt over repressed death wishes but the survival itself that stood at the core of the inner conflict .

For the individuals in this study, guilt was a major concern. Some siblings felt they should have been the one to die because they felt that is what their parents wished. Others felt guilty that survival was so difficult for the afflicted child while everything came so easily to them by comparison. These siblings went out looking for challenges and seemed to drive themselves relentlessly as a test of their endurance. Many of the siblings expressed guilt that they did not love the sibling enough, or do enough for him or her. Jenny was obsessed with the time that her dying sister asked her to bring some pills to her, and she delayed for a few moments. Even though this happened several years before her sister died, Jenny was convinced that somehow her tardiness was responsible for her sister's death. Some guilt seemed to have arisen out of a basic belief that to survive was to do so at another's expense. Modell, Weiss, and Sampson (1983) theorized there is an unconscious bookkeeping system within a nuclear family such that the fate of particular family members determines how much good is left over for others. Several siblings wished that they had been a little sick, so that their brother or sister would not be so sick. Another type

113

of guilt is separation guilt as distinct from separation anxiety (Sampson, 1983). In families with fatally ill children, the mother is often seen as depressed and fragile, and the child may fear that he or she has in some way damaged the mother. Later on, in families in which the father is not emotionally available to his wife, she may turn to her children for support, binding them to her beyond age-appropriate stages.

Sources of guilt appeared to be complex and fed from many streams. Some siblings assumed that, because they have been punished by having a sick sister or brother, they must be "bad." Other siblings, hearing friends and neighbors try to comfort the family by stating the popular myth that "only the good die young," accepted the verdict of their badness and their dubious gift of life. After all, in the days of witch-hunting, it was more honorable to drown than to live a witch. Other respondents, aware of their anger at parents and their resentment of the sibling, feared retribution for their badness. Joan, only 7 years old when her brother died, developed symptoms of anorexia just before going to college. She eloquently attempted to explain her own struggles with guilt:

> Mommy and daddy are upset about losing your sibling, so you feel guilty because maybe you did something wrong. You know what went on, and the whole sequence of events, but for some reason you feel guilty because they hurt. It's a totally abstract and unrelated feeling of guilt that also very much contributes to your feeling of insecurity, and that kinda goes down the line. "If I were a better kid ..." dumb stuff like that.
> And guilty that I survived and he didn't. There's nothing you can do to make your parents feel better. Maybe it should have been me, he's smarter and better. Kids that were at an age where they're old enough to feel like they had to be good little troopers felt responsible to support the family. They'd feel something like "I'm not helping. Why aren't I helping? I should be helping." Then the third part would be feeling, "Well, maybe I should be the one to go, 'cause nothing else is working."

YOUNG CHILDREN

Generally, however, as we see in chapter 8, the preadolescent group expressed less conscious guilt than the adolescent group, both in self-report and on the standardized measures. In a study of children bereaved by the loss of a parent, Raphael (1983) suspected the survivors exhibited excessive guilt, which was well defended. In interviews with the preadolescent group, it is very interesting that a sense of the guilty self did not emerge directly, as it had in the interviews with the adolescent group. It seems possible that, with the likelihood of having had less time to work through their own denial and omnipotent fantasies, the preadolescent group may have felt more need to resort to denial and omnipotent defenses. For example, a reaction could have been that it was not the individual sibling's bad wishes that caused the death of their sibling, it was God's. Indeed it is very intriguing that, unlike the adolescent group, for whom religion was lost, for the preadolescent group, religion was more likely found.

The preadolescent group also demonstrated a compelling relationship between guilt, propensity for accidents, or various somatic expressions. The following case examples illustrate this relationship.

Leslie

Leslie was 5 years old when her younger brother died and 8 years old when another brother was born with CF. She described her mother as having been very overprotective of her. Wondering why her brothers were sick and she was not, she always felt guilty that she did not have their illness. As she became older she heard that some children were not diagnosed until they were 15 or 16 years old and worried that would happen to her. About a month and a half before the interview, her brother was hospitalized, which was very frightening for her. Before this event, he had seemed so healthy that she had been able to deny that anything would happen to him. For the first time, she realized that he too could die. Several weeks following her brother's hospital stay, she woke up one morning with a swollen neck, pain in her chest, and great difficulty breathing. Her mother took her to the emergency room at the hospital, where she was seen by her brother's physician. Her diagnosis, confirmed by x-rays, was bilateral pneumo-thorases and a pneumomediastinum: "I was a sight to see. I was pretty funny looking. This is the first thing that's happened to me. No one around here can seem to believe it, because I'm so healthy, and this normally doesn't happen to healthy people. Just like kids with cystic fibrosis."

Although her doctor gave her a clean bill of health, she reported that her breathing was still at a faster rate and that she found herself always gasping for air and frequently getting sharp pains in her lungs. Leslie said she still has repeated nightmares in which she is running down a street screaming frantically that her mother has died.

Simon

Simon was 10 years old when his 17-year-old brother with CF died. Adopted at 6 months, Simon grew up in a farmhouse in which there were always friends and neighbors over and there was much laughter. Simon never really felt accepted by his father, who was quick to anger; he would go to his mother for comfort rather than his father. Simon always felt left out because his brother received more attention and was given special foods. Simon tried to do things to get attention, and at times wished he was sick like his brother. He even felt jealousy toward a man who had lost his leg because the man was receiving a great deal of attention. When Simon was in third or fourth grade his brother began to require frequent hospitalizations. Following his brother's death, Simon thought that he, too, would die young, not from an illness but from an accident on the farm. When he turned 17, he realized that he was only a few months older than his brother had been when he died. Two weeks before I interviewed him, he graduated from high school, a milestone that his brother had been unable to achieve. At this time, he had just developed what he called a "hole in the lung." Denying that there was any connection in his mind between his pulmonary difficulties and his brother's death, he reported:

> It's really awful to be sick. It was pleurisy in the left lung, that was a viral infection. Then I had fluid around my heart. Then I had white spots all over my throat. I still have two little white spots. This has been a good 2 weeks, and this is as long as I've ever been sick, and it's the sickest I've ever been. That occurred to me, that I was the age he was when he died. I don't think I had a fear of death or anything. I probably said to myself, I wonder if I'm going to die, but I just dismissed that. There's no connection really. I know that it occurred to me, with his being the oldest boy, that now I am the oldest boy, to carry on.

Now Simon realizes that in life, accidents do not happen only to other people, they can happen to anyone. His predominant relief is his religion, which allays his guilt and anxiety to some extent. When he was 12 years old, he became a Born-again Christian and said to himself that he would do "whatever God wanted" him to do. This gave him the assurance that he does not have to worry about his future: "not that I think nothing will happen to me, but uh that God doesn't want to happen."

ADOLESCENTS

A strong sense of guilt was a major problem for siblings who were adolescent at the time of the loss. One young man always felt guilty for not working enough, even though he worked 10 hours a day. He explained that he has "a really big conscience." Some siblings wished they had spent more time with their brother or sister before the death, feeling that they somehow should have realized that the end was near. Many individuals felt guilty that they resented that the sibling was sick. Others felt guilty about their past or present relationship with their parents. Erin looked back with chagrin at her own behavior as a teenager following the death of her brother: "I feel guilty about causing my parents problems at a time when they least needed them." Another young woman feels that her mother tried to substitute her for her sister after the death, and now that she has her own children, feels that her mother views them as substitutes for her own lost child. Her mother sees her and her husband spending time with their children, and she tries to become part of their family unit, but the young woman does not want her mother to be this involved. She reported: "This is my time with my children and I don't want to give it to anybody, I don't want to share it with anyone." Expressed guilt, experienced most consciously by those who were adolescent at the time of the death, fell into the three main categories discussed here.

Global Sense of Guilt.   All of the adolescent group in the statistical sample expressed a strong sense of feeling guilty. Perceiving themselves as bad, they professed a readiness to blame themselves for anything that may go wrong. Feeling a chronic sense of being "bad," some turned to peers who supported their outlook and their anger. Danelle reflected that for the past 9 years since her sister's death, she has surrounded herself with people who are unhappy and bitter toward life, although she feels this outlook does not reflect her true nature: "I really think that if this had never occurred in my life, I wouldn't have taken that cynical road. I think I would have been married with kids. I would have seen more brightness. I don't know if that has anything to do with it. But I almost wanted to hear negative things about life."

Guilt Over Handling of Illness and Death.   All members of the adolescent group expressed guilt over their relationships with their afflicted siblings while they were alive or the way they had handled the death. Rick, only 13 when his sister died, was told by his father that she had died. Rick then went on with his plans for the afternoon, totally shocked and uncomprehending. He still ruminates guiltily over his reaction, wondering, "when you go out and play baseball the day your sister died, what does that tell you?" In fact, it seemed fairly typical for youngsters to continue on with daily activities, and then view their behavior in retrospect as evidence of being "bad."

Survival Guilt.   Fifty percent of the adolescent group in the statistical sample expressed concerns that they did not have CF or that they had lived longer than their sibling. Two very difficult times for many were reaching the age at which the sibling had been when he or she died or achieving a developmental marker that the sibling had just completed before dying or had not had a chance to complete. One sibling, upon reaching the age of 19, the age his brother had been when he died, was very afraid that he "wasn't going to make it," and developed a central tremor, which he still had at the time of the interview. Many were conscious of a sense that it was somehow wrong that their lives were going on.

Nancy

Nancy, who lost her 16-year-old sister to CF when she was 13 years old, is very reluctant to think back to her childhood. She is obsessed with the memory when they were children that she told her sister that she should die. For years she thought that when she would turn 16 she would die, probably in a car accident, and that her death would be prolonged. Pointing out the myriad of dents in her automobile from recent accidents, she still tries unsuccessfully to forgive herself for her one childish angry statement: "One thing I'll never forget is that we used to fight. It's natural, kids fight with each other, and one day I told her, 'I hope you die.' And it still hurts me. I still often say to myself, why wasn't it me instead of her? She was more brilliant, she had more things going for her." She still asks herself why her sister died instead of her. Fearing that she will succumb to cancer, she becomes very anxious when she goes to the doctor for a routine exam, reporting that she "can't make it through a physical."

Her younger sister described her home life growing up as a zoo. She remembered constant fights over trivial incidents. What was most highlighted in her memory was that after the death of her sister, her father would constantly say to her, "You wanted her dead anyway." Her friends would try to intervene and tell her father to stop being mean to her and to stop comparing her unfavorably to her lost sibling. Unlike her older sister, she is not afraid of death at all, figuring "I'm too awful to die."

Ben

Ben, now 22 years old, was 12 when his older sister died and 14 when his older brother died, both from CF. He felt his brother was more "the apple of his parents' eyes," and he resented him for this. After his brother died his parents separated and got back together at various times over the next 4 to 5 years. Following the death of his brother, his parents suddenly shifted their focus of attention to him. He reported that he would like to move away from the area now, and is annoyed with himself that he is taking into consideration his parents' feelings more than he feels he should. He said he believed that had his brother and sister been healthy, he would not have had the "overbearing and protective parents" that he had now. Claiming not to be afraid of death at all, he described himself as a thrill seeker, enjoying recklessly parachuting and skiing. Ben had just turned 22, which was the age his brother had been when he died. He had many automobile accidents over the last several weeks before I met with him, including one on the way to the interview. The recurring automobile accidents had him worried, although the connection with his brother's death is vague in his mind:

> I get this feeling that my time is coming up and I missed it both these times. As I was driving over here I got a green light and started into the intersection. This guy comes flying through and swerves out of the way, and I thought, "Oh god, almost another accident today." It's crazy. I'm almost scared to drive. I'm freaked out right now with these car accidents. Because I'm 22 and my brother was 22 when he died, and this is really scaring me. And you want to know something else? After I got in my second accident, I visited the cemetery. For some reason.

Ben remembered that he had gotten sick right after graduating from college. Recalling that his brother had died only a week after graduating from college, Ben remarked that he never before put the connection together. He feels that he has surpassed him now, and feels guilty about that. "I feel like 'oh oh, maybe I wasn't supposed to go this far. I've outreached him and I'm on my own. This is it, and this is new territory.'" Fatalistic in his outlook on life, he said he feels that he is still alive because it is not yet his time to die. However, he stated that when it is the right time for him, "I'll be gone."

Rick

Rick lost his older sister when he was 13 years old. He described his childhood as happy until then, despite his father's emotional detachment and his mother's tendency toward self-sacrifice. Because he had never realized that his sister's illness might be terminal, her death was a shock to him. Devastated by the news, he went out and played baseball that day, a memory that currently haunts him. His family was torn apart by the death, and for several years his parents' relationship remained shattered. During this period Rick tried to be a peace maker and get his parents back together. Angry and frustrated with himself and his parents, he started having serious behavior problems at school. In his early 20s he was very depressed and felt suicidal. He remembered that period as being the worst time of his life. His parents recently reconciled, and he feels somewhat better now although he still struggles with feelings of fear and guilt; in fact he said he feels he could "write books on guilt." He said he is very afraid he will die young of something unexpected. His relationship with his father, his taking on other people's problems and "assuming their guilts," all contribute to a chronic sense of distress. Feeling that he is not accomplishing as much as he should, he said he regrets that he did not handle the situation at the time better than he did. He described his expectations of himself as never-ending. He reported a sense of not having accomplished what he should have, especially in his father's eyes. "There has to be a link between the whole thing around Jill and the fact that I often feel that I have not fulfilled what my father wants. What the link is, I don't know." He continued:

> I feel guilty a lot. I almost look for it. I do it by nature, and it's not good. It's not healthy. Why do I inflict unnecessary worry and guilt on me? I wish I knew. I do get headaches. I wake up at night with these traumas probably from that [feeling of death] and it's acute and boy, it's really weird. It's real, it's real. I always feel it's going to be a bad way of going. I don't know whether to get back to the thing with Jill again, there's some connection. I just can't think. Part of it is in receiving her death, in handling her death.

At the time of the interview, his nightly battles with his conscience and his memory continue, with no sign of immediate resolution.

Kathy

Kathy lost her younger sister when she was 13. Having very little memory of her early years, she talked about what she could recall, wishing that her mother had been able to communicate with her more openly about the illness. Never understanding the seriousness of the illness, Kathy resented the attention which her sister received. Just when she thought her sister was getting better, her sister went into the hospital and died. Kathy was devastated. Unable to understand the death, she thought that maybe doctors had hidden her sister in the hospital, and kept expecting to run into her. Kathy started smoking marijuana and taking other drugs. Her relationship with her mother, always problematic, further degenerated. She now regrets both her resentment of her sister and the way she treated her mother at the time.

> I still feel guilty to this day, I think I always will. I always resented it, because she always had more attention. I never understood. I was young, I wanted to go out a lot and I couldn't, you had to stay home and do therapy. I used to take it out on her, which wasn't fair. I see that now, but I'll always feel guilty about that. I still don't understand why it had to happen. Why us? Why anybody? It made me take it out on my mother. I took her dying out on my mother, made life miserable for her, blamed it on her. I had to blame it on somebody. I didn't understand.

Committed to a psychiatric hospital at the age of 15, Kathy was "forced" to talk about her sister's death for the first time, so that the staff would let her go home. She was institutionalized again at 18, following an abusive relationship with her boyfriend and difficulties with other parts of her life.

"I did everything I could to destroy myself." Trying to sort out the reason why her sister had died, Kathy finally decided that she "didn't want to be around." Hospitalized for 4 months, her insurance ran out, but, she reported, "luckily I was cured." Still struggling with guilt and many somatic complaints, she said she can now look back and begin to forgive herself for the times when she had been careless with her sister's treatments. "I used to feel it was my fault, like I killed her. Those nights I just wanted to go out with my friends, walking around the streets doing nothing, I would do her therapy half-assed." She still has headaches "like a chain saw." Kathy's younger brother, 11 years old when his sister died, could remember almost nothing of his childhood, except setting fires in his house, which he described as fun. He spent his teenage years involved with drugs and getting into trouble, and basically "screwed everything up." Now in his early 20s, he is beginning to turn his life around, largely inspired by Kathy's example.

Donna

Donna was 14 years old when her 22-year-old brother Matthew died. Family life revolved around her brother's illness; for example, her parents chose not to relocate to another part of the country because they lived near the CF clinic. Her father was in the Navy and at sea much of the time; he left permanently when she was 10 years old. She remembered her mother as always being tense and constantly yelling. Donna idolized her sick brother, who tried to fill in both missing parental roles, helping her with homework nightly and encouraging her to study. She would become very frightened when he had coughing spells during which he would gasp for air.

Although she knew he was sick, she never thought he would die, and was totally shocked when he did succumb to the illness. She vividly remembered the day the phone call came from his doctor with the news. She was shocked and furious, kicked a hole through the kitchen wall, and went on a "stormy rampage" for days. The funeral was "torture" for her, and going to back to school an ordeal. His death left her emotionally bereft. She attempted to replace her lost brother by turning to her other brother, but it just was not the same. To take her mind off things, she turned to extracurricular activities—cheerleading and partying with her friends—and her motivation for school work plummeted. Her mother idealized her brother following his death and would frequently ask Donna why she could not be more like him. At night, thoughts of "if you hadn't done this or that, everything would be okay" raced repetitively through her mind. She began to drink heavily and drove while intoxicated, getting into many accidents. She would spend hours staring at her fingernails trying to decide whether they were curved as her brother's had been. Two years ago, when she turned 21 years old, she came down with a serious respiratory ailment. Her doctors suggested to her that maybe she had a mild case of CF:

> It started out as a cold. The doctors asked if there were any respiratory ailments in the family and I told them. What I had turned into like an asthma bronchitis but they really couldn't detect it. And they said, "Well, you may have a very, very slight case of it." You think about it, 'cause I was really sick. I was short of breath. And this lasted for like 10, 12 months. To this day I if I laugh or cough, I have a little shortness of breath.

At the time of the interview, Donna still carried a little inhaler around with her, which she took out of her purse to show me.

The day of her 23rd birthday, her brother made a comment to her that she told me that she will never forget. He reminded her that she was now older than their brother ever lived to be, and she said she felt that was a very profound statement that "will stick with me for the rest of my life." When I asked Donna what made that statement so profound for her, she replied that all she could think was, "Look at everything I've done right now that he hasn't, and he would kick my butt if he knew." She often wished she had been the one to die instead of him, because he had so much more potential than she had—of the two of them, she viewed him as the clearly superior one.

Donna's older brother was 18 years old and in his second semester of college when Matthew died. He took off the rest of the semester, and the following semester he still did not feel like going back to college. Then he couldn't figure out what he wanted to do; he felt "lost" much of the time. When he turned 22, he "totaled" the car that he had inherited after his brother's death, ending up in the hospital. In reporting the incident, he made an interesting slip of attribution of death: "I remember thinking that it was very warm, this was shortly after *I* died, after *Matthew* died, because I was driving his car. And uh ... the last thing I remember was thinking that it was very warm and taking off my coat and that's the last thing I remember" (italics added).

ADULTS

Siblings who were adult at the time of the loss had not completely resolved their guilt feelings, although they were reported less frequently than they were in the adolescent group, and they seemed less defended against than those of young children.

Some siblings expressed guilt over their responses toward the sibling during the illness period—lack of sensitivity, perhaps, or annoyance over the mist tent—but by the time of the interview, many had talked it over with someone or had been able to resolve their feelings on their own. One sibling felt bad that he had been annoyed when he was awakened in the middle of the night by his brother's coughing, but remembering the good times they spent together helped him to feel better. One young woman had felt very guilty when she was a little girl about asking for time from her parents but now will not feel guilty about anything: "It's like I have to make up for that guilt. Now I refuse to feel guilty under any circumstances." Another young woman had felt guilty for many years that she had celebrated her birthday 3 days before her brother died. She could now be thankful that they had been able to have such an enjoyable day and that he had been able to share her birthday with her. One young woman felt guilty that she had asked her parents to come home from the hospital to go to her high school graduation. They did, and her sister died that night. A young man reported feeling bad that he had gotten married shortly before his brother's death, because he felt that he had been one of his brother's few contacts with the outside world. Several respondents felt guilty that they never really got to know their sibling, and wished they had spent more quality time with them. Some siblings deeply regretted one single episode in which they felt they missed an opportunity for some kind of resolution. One young man recounted the one episode that really bothered him after his sister died. When she was lying in the casket, she was holding a flower, and before they closed the casket, they took the flower out of her hands:

> I was the only person who saw them do that. I thought that she was the type of person it would be appropriate to bury with a flower in her hand. And I didn't say, "Look, put that flower back." I figured a funeral was not the time to start asserting your aggression. But I realized that here was a moment where one action I could have taken would have consequences that would last. And that will bother me forever.

More able to feel compassion for others, some were acutely aware of the devastation the death caused their parents. One young man, who has a healthy brother, wished that he could have died instead of his sister so that his parents would not have had to lose their only daughter. One young woman, 23 years old when her younger brother died, almost hoped that she was a carrier. She tried to explain why she felt that way:

> Maybe so it wouldn't be so unfair for my brother. But then thinking about my parents, and having them know that they produced one child who was free of it, made me feel good. But thinking about my brother I kind of wished that I had been a carrier, and I could maybe take the burden off. Which I really couldn't, of course. But psychologically, I felt that it would have been easier for me to accept everything that he had been through if maybe I could go through a little bit of it myself. I always thought it should have been me

instead of him. I just think he had more to offer people; he was a lot smarter. I just loved him so much. I just wish it could have been me instead of him. I guess that's what it boils down to.

For a long time she felt that she "had to be perfect to make up for all the terrible things that had happened" to her parents. She stated that she frequently takes on too much, and that she is always worrying about somebody else rather than herself.

Another young woman feels guilty for taking a salami sandwich away from her younger brother with CF because it was not good for him. She "carried that around for years," asking herself why she took that sandwich away. She also regretted the way she handled the night before he died. She had gone to the hospital to see him, and she was so upset, she left. "I wish I had stayed. I wanted to hug him so bad, and I'm sorry I didn't hug him." Another woman had moved back home to help out with the chores on the farm as her sister was getting sicker. When her sister died, she remembered feeling, "I've got to be her and me, be the two." Exactly 1 year to the day following the death, she developed a severe cough.

> I sounded just like she did, and I felt awful about bringing back memories. The doctor wanted to put me in the hospital, and I was so against going in the hospital, 'cause I thought I'm going to be on the same floor, probably one of the same rooms she was in. I really fought hard against being admitted, and yet I didn't want to be home coughing away. I wondered if it had anything to do with her dying, especially when I didn't have pneumonia, I didn't have bronchitis, they couldn't find anything, and it lasted 2½ months. When things get to be going too good, you just start to feel guilty about it, and maybe think I should have been the one. She should have had more time or something. And it's less and less, the "Why me?" It does get easier as the years go by. Wherever she is she's healthier and happier, I hope.

Now 29 years old, she feels trapped living with her parents. She resents how much they seem to cling to her, and she wants some distance from them. Considering herself fairly well adjusted in other ways, she still struggles with her right to be happy and alive, feeling that it should have been her instead.

Martin

Martin is 28 years old now and was 22 when his 23-year-old brother died. Growing up, he was very close with his brother and had what he described as a fun childhood. His mother had a nervous breakdown when he was very young, within a year of the diagnosis of CF. He and his brother were raised almost like twins, dressed in identical outfits. He was a typical big brother and Martin always "followed his lead." He adopted his idols and imitated everything he did. His brother wanted to be a fireman but died before he had the chance. When I asked him if he felt guilty about anything, he protested vehemently. He then described a serious illness he had when he was 21:

> I don't like guilt, I don't think that's a very good feeling. I can't think of anything I'm guilty about. I'm drawing a blank there. I had a pretty good illness when I was 21. I got a strep throat that went into a strep infection of the pleural cavity. They had to cut a section of rib out, open me up and drain it out. I was in about 3 weeks.
> [His brother] was going downhill from 18 on, and there was a time, I can't remember the exact age, when he had three lung collapses in a short span. So they put a sealer in to seal the pleural cavity and it was risky, kind of a new thing. It worked. They had to talk it over and all that. I think they sealed both lungs, if I'm not mistaken. They made an incision high in his chest and poured it in to the pleural cavity with a tube. It was probably a couple of years prior to mine. I was training for the fire department test. I used to jog on the beach and then jump in the ocean and swim. It was kind of cold water. They attributed it to that. I don't know what exactly caused it.

At least three to four times a week over the last years, since moving out of the house to live with his wife, he has been troubled by nightmares. At the time of the interview, they were coming almost every night.

> I'll bolt right out of bed and turn on the light and I'm sleepwalking. My poor wife ... I'll jump up and say, "Turn on the light, there's something coming in the window." So she turns on the light and I go back to sleep and I don't even remember it. And the next morning she'll ask me, "Well, did those fuzzy little things get in the window?" and then I'll remember what I had said. But it's almost always weird animals of one kind or another. When I was in construction it was something falling on me like a ceiling, a piece of plywood, a piece of sheet rock, a beam, and I'd jump up in bed and try to stop it from falling.

Chapter 11

Resolution

Imagine, then, by miracle, with me,
(Ambiguous gifts, as what gods give must be)
What could not possibly be there,
And learn a style from a despair.
            —William Empson (*This Last Pain*, 1949)

Tragedy has the capacity to promote growth as well to interfere with development. An early realization of mortality in life may foster increased anxiety, but it also can spur a sober and accurate realization that everyone is vulnerable. Although some siblings found planning for the future difficult because they grew up in a family in which there was a sick child, as discussed in chapter 2, they considered an increased ability to live for the moment as a present strength.

Ralph, 10 years old when his older brother died, stated that his experience has made him grow up faster than other people, by learning that one does not live forever: "It's a major fact of living. 'Cause we're all going to die. And it can be any time." Rick, 13 years old when his sister died, felt that he became more aware of the preciousness of life. Although he struggles with a pervasive sense of anxiety, he makes an effort to live as intensely as he can: "Life is a hardball game. We're not pussyfooting around in any respect. You can take a positive effect from that. People die young, wonderful, intelligent, beautiful people, and it's not harmful for kids to learn it. They might as well learn it. Why cocoon them?" Because his father had been emotionally unavailable to him during his childhood, he has been self-reliant from a very early age. Regretting that he had missed some of the benefits of having a father to give him direction, he explained that the "flip side" of that is that he will not let life be boring: "I never allowed it." One young woman, 13 years old when her older sister died, reported that she

126

has to live her life to the fullest because her sister did not have a chance to do so:

> If I'm going to be bothered, I stay home. If I don't want to stay home, I go out. If I want to go to Rocky Point and ride on the rides all day, I'll go by myself or I'll call my friends. I don't think you should save all your life. I probably have $30 in the bank. I'm going to live my life for today 'cause tomorrow I might not be here. And I've felt like that for a long time.

One young man's philosophy of life was that there is a lot of pain and suffering in the world. It may be an effort to try to enjoy life, but he considered it a worthwhile effort: "You owe it to yourself and society to go out of your way to make life a thoroughly enjoyable experience. Because if you don't, you blew it. There's no second chance. When it's over, there's no instant replay. That's it. Then it's a long, long, cold sleep."

A frequently reported theme was the benefit of being forced to adopt an early independence because parents were not around. Listening to the stories, it appeared that this trait had both adaptive qualities as well as appeared at times rather sadly defensive. Jenny, 14 years old when her sister died, reported the enduring legacy of her lonely childhood years: "I'm very independent. I'm actually more happy sitting by myself and reading or taking a walk. I have a lot of fun by myself, 'cause I always had to when I was little. I just grew up by myself." Some siblings believed that because they were "dealt a hard blow" early in life, they have learned not to be surprised when life is difficult. Danelle reported that she feels she could deal with anything now, which may be a mixed blessing, stating, "If someone told me that my mother just died, God forbid, or my father, I'd say, 'Oh, okay.' I've already given all I have. I think that I've developed a real strength. I have put up with a lot more than other people. I don't quit real easy. I stay in there. I can take a lot of abuse, to tell you the truth."

Living with a person who was physically ill made some siblings more compassionate toward others, more "real" as some respondents described it, and more sensitive to people who have physical problems. Some siblings, who grew up with a person who was physically frail but a wonderful person, mentioned that they learned to take people for what they were inside, not for what they looked like on the outside. Others commented they had learned to be grateful for their own good health or that of their children. Some individuals mentioned that they had learned to appreciate friendships and not take a relationship for granted. Some cited an increased tolerance toward people. Several siblings felt they could be more useful to other grieving individuals because they remembered what had been helpful for them at the time.

Martin reported that he has been grateful when people encourage him to talk about his brother's death:

I'm not hesitant to go up to people who have had a loss and say something about it. Before it was a taboo subject. I realize now that I enjoy talking about him, and I would rather talk about him than not talk about him. So when I deal with other people who have had a loss, I try to bring them into a conversation about that person.

Anna, who lost her older brother when she was 26 years old, cited several positive lessons that emerged from her family's coping with the illness and death of her sibling. First, she reported that they became a very close-knit family and very responsible to each other. When her brother was sick, someone was there with him 24 hours a day. She said she believed that her relationships with her siblings have improved because of the situation. Second, she feels that her attitude toward people who are sick is different from the way it would have been if she had not grown up with someone who was chronically ill. Last, she reported that she thinks that it has helped her to relate to people who are going through what she went through. She found that her ability to understand the paradox of wanting suffering to be over for the loved one and yet wanting to keep them alive as long as possible is helpful to others. Some siblings found ongoing inspiration in watching the sibling cope with such a serious illness and continue to play, work, hope, and love. With this perspective, siblings felt that few difficulties that life might throw in their path can come close to what their sibling had to confront. Dan, for example, watched his sister with CF never take any leaves of absence from work despite receiving intravenous antibiotics, developing a lung abscess, and having three operations. He reported that his achievements are really nothing compared to that. "I consider myself successful, but I'm successful because I really never had that much of a challenge. I went looking for my challenges."

One young man said that he found that when he is faced with a difficult problem in his life, particularly minor health difficulties, he reflects on his brother's experience:

I think this is nothing compared to what my brother had to go through. I used to mope around the house complaining about a cold. It was only temporary. I've had real bad hay fever. I couldn't breathe too much out in the country. I always used that to think how could I even start to feel sorry for myself when this is the way my brother lived for 26 years.

He finds inspiration in having watched how hard his brother fought. Even through the worst of times, his brother had maintained his sense of humor and tried to stay in school as long as he possibly could: "It was his example of fighting what he was faced with that will always be with me. I think it helps you keep things in perspective. Whenever there's days where you think you're getting shortchanged or something, you say, well, nothing matches that."

At the time of the interview, only about one fifth of the sample had any exposure to professional counseling at all. Some individuals remembered that when they were young their families had seen a therapist once or twice but felt that therapy had been not helpful for them. Several siblings who had been adolescent at the time of the loss had received counseling only after they had made suicide attempts and were hospitalized. Only a few had received counseling for a period of time substantial enough for them to feel that it had actually helped them. Several interviewees had just begun therapy, sensing that the issue was a major one for them. Several male respondents mentioned that their wives had helped them develop an emotional range not previously accessible. One young man, 10 years old when his older brother died, stated that he has developed emotionally with his wife's help over the last 15 years: "If something like that happened today, I would have a much better range of reactions. I have better emotional equipment now than I had at age 11 or 12." One young man was inspired to turn his life around by watching his older survivor sister receive help in a psychiatric hospital that enabled her to put her life back in order.

The passing of years had allowed some siblings to begin to resolve their anger at their parents for not having been there for them. Some individuals were not able to forgive their parents until they had children of their own. One young woman realized that she never really looked on her parents as parents who had lost a child until she had her own baby. With growth in compassion, they were able to look back at the situation and realize that their parents were good people caught in a difficult predicament: "If you do 99% right, the 1% might really affect you somehow." As siblings became parents themselves, they were also more able to resolve issues related to survivor guilt as well. One sibling reported that she was able to stop feeling guilty when she realized that it was right that she had survived so that she could be there for her children.

As parents began to relinquish the loss, siblings were increasingly able to have a more balanced environment. One young woman described how her family's home is evolving:

> The house is changing. When Chris first died there were pictures in every single room. You couldn't go into a room without a picture of Chris being in it. We have gotten away from that. There's just a portrait in the living room now, and my parents have a picture in their room, but not the museum/mausoleum thing. Visits to the cemetery are much less than they used to be.

Religious beliefs had been helpful for some siblings in mourning the loss, particularly if their parents found comfort that "it was God's will." One young man, 14 years old when he lost his younger brother to CF, had been brought up in a Mormon family. Their beliefs helped both his parents and himself to give meaning to the experience. He explained that people who have physical or mental handicaps were so good in their life that they did not need to be "tested" here on earth for long. When his sibling died, he thought, "Well, he's with God. He's gone back, he's happy, and a lot better off than when he was here." Erin, able to get in touch with increased compassion for herself, resolved her anger at a God that could have taken away her sister: "I started to believe afterwards that maybe God doesn't always have control over everything, and sometimes he gets himself into things that he can't get himself out of."

The passing of time has also allowed some siblings to work through their fear of commitment. One married woman, 31 years old when her sibling died, explained that it took her a long time before she could allow herself to become seriously involved with someone. She took a vacation by herself each year but had been becoming discontented with this lifestyle. On the last trip before meeting her future husband, she reflected:

> I'm not enjoying this with someone that I can share the memories with afterwards. Then the following year I met Peter. But I had already made plans to take a trip to Europe, and I went. I had the most miserable time on that trip, because I finally realized that I needed somebody. That's when I realized that I fell in love with him and he was really special to me. But it took 10 years to get me to realize that.

For the majority of the sample, resolution of their conflicts had still not come. Van der Kolk (1987) pointed out that theorists since Freud have noted the tendency of trauma victims to re-expose themselves voluntarily to situations reminiscent of the trauma. This voluntary exposure may be an attempt to achieve integration through experiencing and re-experiencing the dissociated traumatized self. Many of the siblings I spoke with had altered their life courses in what would seem to be examples of "addiction to trauma" discussed by Van der Kolk. The stories I heard bore varying levels of awareness of the reasons for their career choices, as well as varying successes in working through the trauma.

Andy

Andy felt that his brothers, both of whom had CF, received all the attention while he was growing up. His older brother, who died when Andy was 9 years old, had been his hero. He had wanted to do whatever his brother did, and when he died, Andy stated in the interview, "it wrecked me." Nightmares began of soldiers marching down a road, walking over him and his brother and trampling them to death. Other dreams plagued him in which he and his brother were camping in the wilderness, and his brother fell off a cliff. The death of one brother made him realize that this turn of events was a distinct possibility for his twin brother Bill as well. Attempting to distance himself emotionally from his twin, he moved away from home: "It made me not hate Bill but I was scared of him. I knew he was next. I knew he was going to be the next one and like when it was going to strike, I didn't know. And I was afraid to get close. And God he was my brother, and I was more distant than if he was a stranger."

Bill died when Andy was 23 years old. Sensing that he had to do something to help people, he immediately went to work in a hospital as a psychiatric assistant. Feeling guilty that he had run away just when his brother needed him most, he had a conversation one day with one of the psychiatrists with whom he worked. With the help of this coworker, he tried to understand that he had done all he could at the time, and to start to forgive himself. Working in the psychiatric ward had given him time to begin to explore his feelings and to allay the full force of his remorse so that at least he felt able to talk about it currently. He commented that had I phoned him 5 years ago, he would not have been able to talk about it at all. He said he still mostly tries to forget it, trying to comfort himself with the belief that "God makes the choice, not me." With no intimate relationship, he devotes himself to a menagerie of pets he has out in his backyard. Although he is unhappy in his present living situation, and would like to change apartments, he cannot face the thought of rebuilding all the pens for his animals. Although his investment in pets has allowed him to avoid facing his difficulties with intimate relationships, the cost in restricting his life is considerable.

Janice

Janice, who was 29 years old at the time of the interview, lost two brothers to CF. Her older brother died when she was 12, and her younger brother died when she was 23. She felt a lot of the love in her family had been expressed by giving material possessions, and she wished that they had been able instead to spend time together talking. She remembered her mother trying to get her brothers to take better care of themselves. Janice helped out with the treatments and was very upset that her brothers were not cooperating as much as they could have been. Perceiving the hospital as a congenial place and enjoying the hustle and bustle, she decided, when she was in third grade, to become a nurse when she grew up. Following her first brother's death, she "clamped down on her emotions." She explained that being a nurse helped her to avoid thinking about herself, to externalize her own pain while helping others. She felt that her continuing emotional "coolness" has helped her professionally as a coronary care nurse, where she has to meet daily crises with detachment and calm. Currently working on the coronary unit, she is increasingly frustrated by the damaging habits and maladaptive lifestyles of her patients. Now married and a mother, Janice is considering taking a job that will allow her to spend much more time with her own young son. Somewhat apologetically, she confessed that her son's life has become more important to her than the lives of people who can be helped only in a limited way. Her increased ability to enjoy her own life and her family could be interpreted as indicative of a partial resolution of her guilty feelings.

Doris

Doris, who at the time of the interview was a homemaker with three children, lost her younger sister to CF when she was 15. Although she knew that her sister was quite ill, Doris never thought that she would die. Discussing the death was taboo in her parents' home, because any attempt to talk about what had happened further upset her mother. Receiving no help with her own mourning, Doris was deeply depressed for a long time. She believed that her sibling might have lived longer if only restrictions had been placed on her diet. Wanting to make a difference in the lives of other sick people, she went on to become a nurse. Her parents had interpreted the death as a punishment from God, and Doris accepted this interpretation as well. Doris always thought that she and her family would be the ones to be on the receiving end of unlucky odds, no matter how low the chances were of something going wrong. Having recently become involved with a religious group, she no longer saw God as evil and bent on punishing her and her family but rather as one who did not want it to happen either and who was grieving with her.

Her younger sister had grown up wanting to become a doctor and to find the cure for CF. She was 12 years old at the time of the death and even less prepared than Doris for its possibility. She was devastated by the death, and preoccupied by a fear of dying. She married a man who has had an "inflammation of the intestine" since he was 9 years old and who was still chronically ill and requiring frequent hospitalizations. She believed that some of her reason for seeking him out was that she thought she could really help him.

Sally

Sally had grown up in an abusive home and lost her younger brother to CF when she was 18 and a freshman in college. There had been no discussion about her brother's illness during the time she was growing up, and she worried throughout her childhood and adolescence that she too might have CF. Once she found a lump in her neck and was convinced that she was dying, but to her relief it turned out to be only a swollen gland. Following her brother's death, she decided that she wanted to become a nurse. In fact, she realized at that point that she had always wanted to be a nurse. She applied for jobs in different hospitals in her area, including the very one in which her brother had died:

> I had this idea in the back of my mind that someday if I got good enough, I could work with children with cystic fibrosis. And maybe by that time I would be able to handle it better, because obviously at that time I knew I couldn't. And I was accepted at Children's Hospital.

Sally had 3 days to make up her mind whether or not to accept the position. On the third day, she decided to turn down the offer. She did not know the reason but just felt that it was not what she wanted at that time. However, then she did not know what she wanted to do with her life.

The year before she got married she started having panic attacks. Afraid to be on an airplane, she once made the pilot stop the engines just before takeoff so that she could get off the plane. Several years later, she joined the ambulance association in town. She maintained this job for 4 years and then went on to college. Strongly believing that her family should have been helped throughout the illness by some kind of counseling, she decided to major in psychology. It was difficult for me to assess her level of awareness of using psychology as a way of getting help with her own issues.

Chuck

Chuck grew up in what he described a happy family. When he was about 9 years old, his sister was born and diagnosed with CF. Although he understood what was happening with the illness much of the time, her death when Chuck was only 18 years old was very difficult for him to process. The next few years were filled with Chuck's "digging himself down":

> It was kind of an emptiness inside me and I was trying to fill it. When I was out doing something, like going to school or working, I could throw myself into that and really do good. I've always done supergood. But when I was off work I devoted myself to doing that. I guess I devoted myself to being the best drinker, the best doper, that I could be.

Chuck's situation improved when he fell in love and married a young woman. The daughter of an alcoholic, she "kept up with" his drinking quite well, until she became a Born-again Christian. Impressed by the change in her, Chuck also converted 5 years ago. He reported that over the next few weeks he would be starting a new job as a life insurance salesman. He enjoys helping families plan their financial futures in the event of a death. He feels that his early experience has helped him come to grips with the inevitability of death for everyone: "A lot of people have the feeling that they're not going to die for a long time, and that death's kind of an unrealistic idea. Really, nothing can be farther from the truth. You can die at any time." His job selling life insurance has allowed him to attempt to master his experience through repeated re-exposure to dealing with realities of death and its financial consequences.

Dan

Dan is a 38-year-old physician who lost his younger brother to CF when the latter was 16 and he was 19. His earliest memory is of falling into a fish pond when he was 3 years old. At the age of 8, he developed severe allergies and asthma, which necessitated his getting shots two to three times a week. He described this competitively with his brother, who "only got to visit the doctor once a month." Even though he was first in his class throughout his school years, and brought home trophy after trophy for his considerable prowess in sports, he was unable to capture his parents' attention; he was "second in a two-horse race."

He always knew his brother was very sick, and from the age of 9 exhaustively read medical books on CF. Watching his mother turn not to his father but to the doctor for advice, he fantasized about becoming a famous physician and discovering the cure for CF. His brother's death made him feel very cheated, because by then childhood rivalries had dissipated, and he had felt that now finally he and his brother could be friends. After his brother died he was involved in three nearly fatal car accidents within 6 months, one of which occurred on his way to a medical school interview. He drank too much at parties for the first time and got behind in his schoolwork, receiving "incompletes" in many of his classes. "I was really screwed up would be a good description," he told me.

Pulling himself together, he went on to medical school. During his residency, a girl with CF died in his arms, and he was so shaken that he changed residencies and went into another specialty. On Sunday nights he works in an emergency room, however, where he gets the chance "to be heroic." His consuming passion is weightlifting, and he bench presses weights every night for several hours before falling asleep. Despite the fact that he is a highly successful physician, he appeared to have much energy bound up in assuaging issues of survivor guilt.

Anna

Anna lost her older brother when she was 26 years old. Her father was an alcoholic all her life. Because she was more comfortable than her mother with the respiratory therapy equipment, she was the designated caregiver in the family. As an undergraduate she was pre-med, because she wanted to discover a cure for CF. It was clear to her that she did not want to be just any kind of doctor, but rather "a doctor in research, in a medical research area."

When she did not get accepted into medical school, she went back to school and completed a year's internship in medical technology. She became fascinated with immunology. She has been working on her master's degree in immunology for some time and has been having trouble completing it. Ever since the death of her brother, she has been terrified that she will make a serious mistake. She finds this puzzling. She obsessionally checks and rechecks the labels on bottles of substances she is combining, convinced she has made an error. She also obsesses that she wished she had been more willing to do her brother's therapy, and more fastidious in her efforts:

> I remember the last time I did his physical therapy, he went into the hospital the next day. It was Easter day and we had been entertaining people all morning long. We had a [gin] fizz breakfast and I had a couple of fizzes before I went up to do his physical therapy. For some reason that sticks out in my mind.

She hopes someday to finish her thesis. Unfortunately for this young woman, her unresolved guilty feelings may have been contributing to her obsessional concerns at work.

Chapter 12

Recommendations

*Twenty years gone, and here I've come again
to my own land!*

—Homer (*The Odyssey*)

The clearest message from nearly all survivor siblings was that they wished they had been prepared for the possibility that their sibling might die. Many siblings lamented that it would have been so helpful if only their parents had been able to discuss the illness with them. Aware that there are many ways for distressed parents to communicate the news inappropriately, they regretted that no professional had been available to tell them the truth and help them process their emotional reactions.

One young man stated that he feels that, in his experience, there is a tremendous need for someone to interact with the siblings and be very straightforward about the situation. Having spent his own childhood basically in the dark about the disease, he stated that talking about it would have made a tremendous difference in his life: "I think it's important to present it as an opportunity for the whole family and to actively zero in on how it's an opportunity, and how everyone can participate in it."

Communication patterns set within the family during childhood frequently continued, as each family member tried to protect the other. Even at the time of the interview, many individuals still found it impossible to talk about the study with their parents. When I asked if my interview had generated any family discussion, often the answer was one of frustration. As one young man reported, his parents had come by just after he had talked with me, and "six times I tried to tell them, but they changed the subject." It was the rare sibling who found his or her family able to talk about the loss, even many years later, in an open and supportive manner. Rick's report of what had happened recently in his family, years following the loss, was gratifying but unfortunately all too rare:

Somehow we're all coming around now. Whatever brittle cocoon individual noncommunication was going on between us, we've come around the curve. Whether it's because of our interests, or we're fed up with holding shields up, or we have a natural tendency toward that, I don't know.

Many siblings felt strongly that immediately after the death something should have been provided for them to help with grieving the loss and normalizing their feelings. When I reassured Tom that many people experience a sense of strangeness on reaching the same age as the individual with CF, he said: "Even if you're just told it happens to everyone else, you suspect something like that, but you don't realize it. When you said that, that made sense to me." Repeatedly, siblings reported that they should have had counseling all along. Many individuals felt strongly that some kind of psychotherapeutic help should have been provided by the hospital as part of the treatment plan. One young woman, 19 years old when her older sister died, explained that counseling would have been helpful both following the diagnosis as well as the death of her sister:

When my sister was diagnosed had we been referred to a chronically ill counseling project, and had counseling before she died as a family. ... no need to make a big deal out of it, especially for the kids, but a lot of it would have been good. After she died, I went right back to school, and my parents stayed home, and there should have been something in between there to help us accept the fact that she had died and then to go on.

Many siblings wished that they had been able to speak directly to one of the doctors and ask questions. Siblings are onlookers to the unfolding medical drama but rarely have access to its players. One young man felt that doctors could do more toward teaching families to communicate with each other about serious illnesses, and that would be more valuable than medicines. He thinks that the family might become more upset for awhile, but he feels that in the long run, relationships would be much more open and healthy for everybody. He concluded: "It's going to hurt when you have to talk about it, but you've got to talk about it."

The experience of having their own children has allowed some siblings to realize how common it is for children to fantasize about a concern if no one talks to them. One young woman finally understood her own childhood fantasies about CF when she observed her children's mental life:

I'm thinking of just relating it to my own kids. One thing we've learned is that if you don't discuss things, they will build up a fantasy in their mind. It may be totally untrue, and they won't ask about it, and if you don't mention it, they can go on believing something quite bizarre and inappropriate. It probably would have been very good if I could have said to my mother, my

father, the doctor, *somebody*, "What's wrong with my brother?" Someone who
would have taken the lead off me. I shouldn't have had to take the lead with
anybody.

Another sibling wished that she had known other families who had a
child with CF, so that she could have talked to someone about her feeling
that there was something wrong: "It was a question of putting it on the back
burner and trying not to look at it, but it was still there and it still bothered
me." Another young woman has always been angry about the fact that,
from the time of the diagnosis, the hospital failed to provide her parents
with therapy to help them deal with the guilt they felt about the genetic
transmission of CF to their child.

> I guess I was always angry. When I first got your card, I thought, what the
> hell are they doing this now for? It should have been from the moment he
> was diagnosed, for him, and ma, and pop. And then when I finally sent the
> card in and you called me and everything I got angry all over again. 'Cause
> I felt that would have helped them so much and they missed out on so much
> because of it.

Sally, 18 years old when she lost her younger brother, believed that her
mother should have been in counseling, and that her brother with CF
should have had counseling to help him prepare for his death.

> How the hell did he learn to deal with death? I'm sure there was a point where
> he knew he was going to die. And it's like we all walked around with that
> terrible secret. It's the family secret. People shouldn't go through what we
> went through without some kind of emotional support. I see a key person a
> counselor, who would have been assigned to the family, once the history was
> established. Who would have sat down and counseled my mother for a
> certain amount of time, and then sat down with us to watch how we deal with
> each other and to help us to talk about this with someone else present.

The survivor siblings generally had strong defenses against viewing
their psychological problems as stemming from growing up with a fatally
ill child in the family. Holding the illness and death of their sibling as
responsible for their own difficulties is somehow seen as an aggressive
thought on their part. With so many taboos against expressing aggression
toward their sick sibling, it took years for the siblings to realize that there
might be a connection between that experience and their current life. One
individual stated, "I don't want to blame anything on her, my own. ..."

The sibling's internal resistance to discovery of the link is helped along
by the failure of the medical establishment to erect preventive lines of
defense.

THE ROLE OF THE HEALTH PROFESSIONAL

Why does the medical system fail siblings? The explanation is complex and involves several areas in which the sibling "falls through the cracks" of the medical establishment.

The Pediatrician

The death of a child represents a failure for the doctor. This difficulty is expressed in differing ways by the pediatricians themselves. One doctor, for example, told me that after spending all of his life in private practice, he can still remember vividly every one of the children with CF who died under his care. On the other hand, another pediatrician who had cared for many patients with CF had almost no recall of any of them. He confused facts about patients with whom, according to the families and his nurses, he had been extremely involved over a number of years. Many pediatricians chose to work with children because it seemed to them to be less depressing than working with patients who for many years habitually engaged in behavior that damaged their health, such as cigarette smoking or alcohol abuse. Children are, after all, generally farther from death than the rest of us. Many pulmonologists who treat patients with CF have come into the specialty through a fascination with disorders of the lung, bringing them both into the laboratory and to patients who have more serious and there-fore more "interesting" disorders. This does not mean, however, that they are any more comfortable with death than their counterparts in private practice who encounter it less frequently. Because death claiming one of their patients represents a personal failure, denial as a defense against their own guilt is prominent, and feeds into the parents' own propensity for denial. The team rationalizes that denial within the family is good, because it allows for attachment relationships to develop between members of the family and the afflicted child, and it is good for the patient to maintain hope. Although both rationales may be correct, they are patient centered. The question that is raised is this: Is what is good for the patient (and the doctor) necessarily good for the sibling?

The doctor has a formal relationship with the patient and the parents of the patient, but not the sibling. Additionally, for the doctor to become aware of the impact of the illness and death on survivor siblings is to force him or her to confront yet another failure. Not only will the child die but the siblings may be adversely affected. Defenses against believing that the illness experience can disrupt family life and frustration over inability to help families struggling with the illness is expressed in such statements overheard by CF caregivers that "the CF gene is located next to the crazy

gene." At any rate, the pediatrician typically has little training in psychological counseling, may not be not inclined in that direction, and is too busy.
He or she may cast a harried glance at the sibling fidgeting in the waiting
room, but that may be as close as he gets to assessing the sibling's functioning. Preferring to handle his or her own grief and failure by working harder
to try to save the next patient, the CF specialist intuits correctly that to
ruminate over the lost one is to risk being viewed by staff as being "dys-
functional."

The Nurse

The pulmonary nurse builds a long-term relationship with the patient with
CF and often with the mother as well. Sensing the unmet need for psychosocial support on the part of most families, the nurse tends to fill in as much
as he or she can, time permitting. Again, nurses tend not be trained in
counseling, and although well meaning, may fall into some of the traps that
experienced counselors might avert. Nurses are more likely to become
enmeshed with the concerns and views of the most vocal family member,
generally the mother, who has the most access to the nurse. The nurse may
ask about how the other children in the family are doing but primarily
depends on the report from the mother. Any complaint about the sibling's
coping style or behavior may not be interpreted as a cry for help but rather
as another problem for an already overwhelmed mother. Sympathy for the
mother too is conditional; if demands become too intense, and the mother
gets defined as "needy," and the family becomes defined as "dysfunc-
tional," less help may be forthcoming. Needs beyond the usual time allotted
per patient threaten to overburden a system generally already overbur-
dened and could overwhelm preferred defenses on the part of medical
team. There are therefore quick and sturdy controls exerted, even among
the most caring staff.

The Respiratory Therapist

The respiratory therapist also has a long-standing relationship with the
patient and the primary caretaker, again usually the mother. Several times
a day, for 45 to 60 minutes per session, the patient's body is pounded on to
dislodge mucus from the lungs. This treatment, postural drainage, requires
close physical contact with the patient; it also requires close contact with
the caregiver who is trained by the therapist to do the procedure at home.
The intensity of the relationship between the therapist and the sick child
increases considerably toward the end, when the patient is hospitalized.
The respiratory therapist is often deeply saddened, feeling the loss as that

of a close friend. However, there is no institutional support for a mourning period, no time off to attend the funeral, and always new patients to help. Turning to coworkers who are also grieving does not help because they are grieving, too. As one respiratory therapist put it, "caring is not seen as part of the job description." If a worker is moping about depressed, the supervisor is likely to remind him or her of other tasks to be done. The work continues and there are always other patients waiting. If the therapist tries to go outside the system for support, he or she generally finds it is a rare friend who can tolerate hearing about the death of a child. Burnout is not unusual and may stem from repetitive blocked mourning, where there is no time to process one loss before the next one occurs. With staff in so much difficulty themselves, it is hardly likely that they can help out a grieving sibling who may stray into their path.

The Social Worker

CF centers generally have one or two social workers on staff. Although there is a prevailing myth that the social worker is there for the psychosocial needs of the family, the reality is quite different. The ratio maintained by most hospitals, and often mandated by funding sources, is generally one or two social workers for anywhere from 100 to 400 affected families. The social worker therefore usually sees only the patients who are hospitalized, which is often only during the last few months before the death. Family members who come to the hospital might be noticed but there is little time to deal with most psychological problems even if they were observed. The role of the social worker is to steer families toward agencies that will help them meet financial obligations.

Social workers who have time and energy left over try to run support groups for families, which meet about once a month. However, support groups for CF do not work well. The reasons are complex. First, they often provide more "education" than support, presenting the latest advances in genetic technologies. The medical staff unwittingly colludes with parents by neglecting to handle feelings of anger and guilt. Second, because families have often been allowed to use denial as a coping strategy, it is difficult to convince them to join a group in which they sense they might have to face reality. Third, although support groups are considered a necessary part of the package of treatment by state agencies that provide funds for centers, they are given reluctant support in some centers because they all too often turn into "bitch sessions" with parents listing complaints they have stored up against staff. On the other hand, if medical personnel are present, parents rarely dare to express their true feelings about the staff, for fear of jeopardizing the child's ongoing treatment. Fourth, with families at such different points of the process, homogeneity of issues is difficult to achieve. Families who have a child doing well do not want to see a child wearing oxygen and gasping for breath. Families with a very sick child do not want to confront their envy of those who have a healthier one. Finally, the support groups tend not to separate family members from each other, incorporating any siblings who might want to come into the group. But sibling issues are so different from parental issues and at times so at odds with them that one single group will not work. Siblings need their own group, where they can express honestly feelings such as anger, guilt, and sadness without fear of reprisal from parents or fear of hurting the feelings of the sick child.

The Psychologist or Psychiatrist

The psychologist is called in only in situations judged to be beyond the skills or abilities of the social worker. For example, if the family is visibly devastated at painful news from the physician, the physician may refer to his or her psychological colleague. The psychologist often has to establish an immediate relationship with a family in the midst of dire crisis. It is rare for a sibling to be referred to a mental health professional earlier in the process. It is extremely rare for a sibling to continue to be seen by any medical professional.

The Genetic Counselor

The genetic counselor has access to the family usually only at the time of diagnosis of the child with CF. What this means is that the genetic counselor speaks with the parents of the child, and the parent is left to transmit the information to the well siblings. The sibling rarely participates in this conversation. Even if a sibling is present, that may be the only time in which the child or adolescent has easy access to the counselor. There is little provision for communicating genetic information as developmental increases in cognitive functioning would allow. Even though the genetic counselor may communicate his or her continuing availability to the growing sibling as questions may arise, it is the rare parent who takes advantage of this offer (Hadley, personal communication, May 2, 1995). Medical genetics departments are set up to deal with identification and counseling for individuals, usually adults, who request such information. Somehow, genetic information must be made accessible directly to siblings, perhaps by closer integration with CF clinics. Recently, some CF clinics have tried to utilize these services by integrating a genetic counselor into the clinic once a week (Valverde & Denning, 1991), but this does not solve the problem of access for the siblings.

Hospital Administration

Psychosocial needs of families have very low priority for support by hospital administrators. What often happens is that a sensitive caregiver, untrained in psychology, will sense that the needs of the family are not being met by the system and try to fill in, spending his or her time talking to the family and battling exhaustion and burnout. Preventive psychological services are not directly reimbursable; they cost money and the benefits may not be seen for many years. Hopefully, as the pressure for comprehensive family care in tertiary settings mounts in the United States, these needs will be more appropriately addressed.

Organizations

CF organizations tend to confine their activities largely to raising funds for biomedical research—specifically, to find a cure for CF. Active members are often parents who have a child with CF and who are, understandably, most invested in finding a cure. They are less eager to allocate resources, even meager ones, to psychological research on the family, particularly on siblings. The reluctance to allow funds to help siblings is another expression of the difficulty in managing guilt over the possibility of losing a child.

IMPLICATIONS

There are many clinical implications of this study. First, it seems overly optimistic to assume that parents will be able to help their children work through the loss. Although a lucky few eventually married people who were able to teach them to develop an emotional range not previously accessible, most siblings were on their own, with parents overwhelmed with their own grief or actively imposing their preferred coping style on their children. Further compounding their sense of isolation, siblings seemed unable to help each other. We must recognize that the siblings—or, as Spinetta (1981) pointed out, those who will live longest with this loss—have very real needs too. Critical times should be taken seriously by caregivers, including the period immediately following the loss, marker times such as passing the age at which the sibling was at the time of the death, and milestones such as graduations.

Second, siblings need help with the issue of their deviation from normal experience, their feeling "different" and their feeling "bad." Feelings of anger, hostility and resentment must be fully acknowledged and integrated with the "good" self; compassion for the self and for the parents as victims themselves must be developed. I would strongly suggest that it would be quite helpful to provide a setting in which survivor siblings could meet and share feelings with others who have experienced the loss of a sibling, too. If survivorship, like aging, represents a devalued position with ambiguous norms (Rosow, 1974) and with weak socialization processes operating, assistance could be given on this level. Although self-help groups proliferate for parents, their offspring are left to fend for themselves.

Finally, physicians should be alert to recommending therapy as soon as possible if there is any indication of disturbance in the siblings, not just as a response to the acting out reported by parents. They could take a much more active role in inquiring about the siblings, or bring them into view through the social worker or clinical psychologist. Those siblings in this sample who were in therapy at the time of the interview wasted years avoiding issues that could have been confronted earlier. As Andy stated, "For a long time, I was so guilty about running away. Then I talked to one of the doctors one day about it and he said, 'You did what you had to do at the time, that's what you had to do.' The minute he said that, it was like bricks fell off my shoulder."

Even the interview was at times of enormous help. With many years mercifully behind them, family members began to make initial efforts to talk with each other about what had gone on, stimulated to do so by the letter contact or phone call to make arrangements for the interview. There was something about a person outside the family system actively violating the long taboo that somehow gave permission to bring the topic out into the open, and, with the discovery that talking about the experience proved helpful, courage was found to continue exploration on their own. As Rick resolved:

> If you could draw a correlation psychologically, they packed everything my sister had in this trunk and put it in the attic and it sits there today. I sometimes think that's basically what we did as a family in that God damn trunk up in the attic. It hasn't been opened since, and I told Judy that I think we're gonna pull it out the next few weekends and see what's in it.

Appendix: Methods

THE SAMPLE

A total of 241 families drawn from the CF clinics at two west coast hospitals and one east coast hospital were contacted. Of these, 83 undelivered letters came back from the post office, and 87 families actively refused or did not respond. This provided a pool of 71 families. One hundred forty siblings were contacted from 65 of these families, the remaining residing too far away geographically. Of these, 24 refused to participate or did not respond. This provided a pool of 116 siblings who were willing to participate. Because of the geographic distance involved, 75 siblings were interviewed.

Children's Hospital, Oakland

Names of all children who died from CF between 1963 and 1982 were obtained from medical records. There were 68 in all. The files were drawn and the final hospital admission record was searched for the most recent address of the parents. The parents were then sent a letter explaining the nature of the study and requesting the names and addresses of any adult children still living in the area.

The adult children were then sent a letter and asked to return a postcard stating whether or not they would mind being contacted about the study. Out of the 68 mailed letters, 34 were returned by the post office; out of the 34 who actually received them, only 8 families responded positively. From the 18 siblings contacted, 11 agreed to participate.

University of California, San Francisco

Names and addresses of parents of children who had died from CF from 1963 to 1982 were provided directly by the physician who had been director of the CF clinic during this period. This clinic has seen very few families over the years and the physician was therefore able to provide the names of 7 families in the area. Three families were located, providing the names of 5 adult children in all. All contacted siblings agreed to participate.

Children's Hospital, Boston

Names of all children who died from CF from 1963 to 1973 were obtained from medical records. There were 166 in all. Names and addresses of the parents were obtained from the physician's records, which contained more current information than medical records. Forty-five envelopes were returned from the post office, and 60 parents responded positively. Of the 117 siblings contacted, an overwhelming 100 responded positively.

Comparison of Response Versus Nonresponse Siblings

From available information regarding the characteristics of the siblings who refused to respond, the size of the nuclear family does not appear to be particularly relevant in differences between those who responded and those who did not, while gender differences did emerge; males were less likely to respond than females.

Description of the Sample

Seventy-five individuals were interviewed. They ranged in age from 18 to 45 years (mean = 30 years). There were 35 males and 40 females in the sample. Thirty-nine percent were single, 57% were married, and 4% were divorced at the time of the interview. Forty-three percent have at least one child, whereas 57% had no children. The median educational level was some college. About 33% were employed in a managerial or office occupation; 19% were professionals. Thirty percent were firstborn children, 49% were middle-born children, and 21% last born. The age of the participants at the time of the death of the first individual with CF ranged from 4 to 36 years old (mean = 17 years).

THE INTERVIEW

Individuals were asked where they would like to be interviewed. Some chose to come into the physician's office at the CF clinic, many chose their own home, and others chose a neutral place such as a hotel lounge in the neighborhood or their office. The interviewer always followed the lead of the individual as to time and place so they would be most comfortable; at times this meant talking to the subject by a lake or on favorite bleachers in a nearby schoolyard. The average interview lasted slightly more than 90 minutes and ranged anywhere from 45 minutes to 2 hours. The interview began with open-ended questions and moved to more specific probes if material was not forthcoming. The interviewer followed the subject's lead whenever possible and went back at the end to areas that had not been sufficiently covered. The following is a rough outline of the type of questions asked of the respondents.

Family Relationships

What is your earliest memory when you think back to when you were a young child? Can you tell me a little about your childhood? Can you tell me a little about your father when you were growing up? Can you tell me a little about each of your siblings when you were growing up? Were there other family members you could rely on for support? Did your parents have friends over much? Was there much discussion when you were growing up of your future plans? How was your relationship with your parents as a teenager? How did your parents react when you left home/got married?

Illness Experience

Can you tell me a little about your understanding as a child of your sibling's illness? If you had questions about it, was there anyone you could bring them to? Did you attend the CF clinic with your family? Could you tell me a little about this experience? How did you feel about the doctors? Were you aware of the time when your sibling was diagnosed? Did your understanding change as you grew older? How did this come about? Did you ever talk about it with your sibling? Healthy siblings? Would you tell me a little about your experience when your sibling died? What were your feelings at that time? Did you discuss concerns with anyone? How did your parents react? Do you feel your relationship with your parents changed in any way following the death?

Possible Current Difficulties

Do you worry about anything? How do you feel when you go to the doctor for a checkup? Visit a friend in the hospital? Do you ever get depressed? How often? About what? How long does it last? How much do you think about your brother/sister now? Can you tell me a little about your work? Can you tell me a little about your friends? Hobbies? Do you feel guilty about anything? Is there anything you still wish you had done differently with your sibling?

Possible Current Strengths

Now I'd like to ask if there are any ways this experience might have had a positive effect on your life. Was there any one person that helped you resolve this experience? Have you ever seen a therapist? What was your first reaction when you heard of this study?

ASSESSMENT OF DEPENDENT VARIABLES

Anxiety and depression scales derived from the Hopkins checklist (Derogatis, Lipman, Covi, & Rickles, 1971) were used. A large background of research in the literature demonstrates the stability of the anxiety and depression scales for various types of populations. These measures were developed for use in normal community settings (Pearlin, Lieberman, Menaghan, & Mullan, 1981). Recent developments in psychiatric epidemiology indicate that symptom scales can identify individuals who will more likely seek medical and psychiatric care (Mellinger & Balter, 1982).

No suitable standardized measure for the kind of guilt under examination exists. Therefore, a 3-point scale (*none, moderate, high*) was developed from the interview material to address this construct. Questions in the interview were raised to elicit information around these dimensions: general sense of being guilty; ruminations over what should have or should not have been done in relation to the ill sibling; readiness to accept blame when bad things happen to self or others; and current difficulty in separating from parents.

Quantitative Analyses

The sample for the statistical analyses was drawn from this group in the following manner. Seventy-five siblings from 43 families were interviewed from the three clinics. Five families were eliminated because there was a child afflicted with CF still alive; one sibling from another family, a sole survivor, was eliminated because he himself had CF. Thus, 8 siblings from 6 families were not included, leaving 67 siblings from 37 families. Then, out of 18 families in which only one sibling survived or was able to be interviewed, 8 families were eliminated because all survivors were over 18 at the time of the death, leaving 10 families (and therefore 10 siblings).

Nineteen multiple survivor families (46 families in all) were reduced to 15 families because 4 families included siblings who had all been over 18 at the time of the death. Only one survivor sibling was randomly drawn from each of these 15 families in order to avoid confounding of variables for statistical analyses.

The sample for quantitative analysis included 13 males and 12 females. About two thirds of their mothers had worked outside the home for at least part of the time the subject was growing up; about three fourths of their parents had kept their marriages intact; three sets of parents had divorced, one set had separated, and one set had separated immediately following the death of the child but had since gotten back together. About one third of the families were Catholic. The age of the participants at the time of the interview ranged from 18 to 38; age at the time of the death of the sibling ranged from 9 to 18 (mean = 13 years). About one half of the sample had had some college education; about 40% were married; about one third of the sample had at least one child. Three in the sample had been the oldest child, 7 were the youngest, and 15 were middle children; about half had been the same gender as the affected child.

Derivation of Rating Scales

All protocols were tape recorded and later transcribed. Transcribed interviews were read and the material sorted into categories capturing the specific areas of concern. All protocols were then divided into material pertaining to the independent variables and the dependent variable guilt and placed in separate sections. Protocols were rated separately on each scale capturing independent variables to avoid a halo effect.

Interrater Reliability

Seven "training" protocols were selected at random from the sample and all material pertaining to dependent variables was removed, and the remainder was given to an outside rater for calibration. When a suitable level of reliability had been attained, 12 additional protocols were selected at random, and material containing only subject matter relevant to independent variables was given to the rater. Reliability was established using the kappa coefficient at .96 and ranged from .74 to 1, with 8 of the 10 scales yielding a kappa of 1.

All interviews were then rated for guilt. Seven "training" protocols were drawn at random, all material containing reference to independent variables was removed, and the remainder was given to the rater. Twelve randomly selected protocols were rated by the outside rater and reliability on the guilt scale was established at .88 using the kappa coefficient. The scales that were developed in this manner follow.

PREDEATH AVAILABILITY OF PARENTS

(Rate separately for Father/Mother)
Content of responses rated for subject's conception of parents as available.

1. *Good availability*
"He was always there for me."
"She was the one to always put us in our place when we did wrong, and uhm very caring. She was always, you know, made sure that everything was okay with us. I wonder whether I would be able to do the same thing that she's done in the past. You know, she's a good person, and we are very close with her."
2. *Unpredictable or undependable availability*
"He was sort of a moody type, I never knew what kind of mood he'd be in. If he was in a good mood, we were real happy, if he was in a bad mood we were like real tense, and just didn't want to be near each other. And you know sometimes I was afraid if he was in a bad mood, because I didn't like that."
3. *Unavailable*
"I love my father and did then, he was good to us I suppose, but he was very much involved in his existence in his career, he had his own world and remained within it. He was not a family man, and he never was meant to be."
"I don't think he really cared."

K (Mother availability) = 1
K (Father availability) = .74

SIBLING RELATIONSHIP—ATTACHMENT

Relates to extent of preexisting attachment of ill sibling with survivor.

1. *Idealization*
Great warmth or closeness expressed, with idealization present.
"L was a very important link. L was gorgeous. She was just wonderful, really wonderful. She was something, she was very much of a trooper, strong, never a complainer."
"He was my hero. Whatever he did, I wanted to do."

2. *Warmth*

Moderate warmth expressed, but seen in realistic light; warmth and caring expressed, but absence of idealization; seen as human, equal to self.

"I remember one time it was Christmas Eve and I woke up for some reason and I went out into the living room, and B was sitting on the couch all curled up and he was looking at the Christmas tree. It was dark, the lights were on the tree. I sat down on the couch with him and we were all curled up together under a blanket, and we were guessing what Santa had brought everybody—we were close. We had the best, nice times like that."

3. *Slight*

Not that close a relationship. Subject expresses lack of relationship—may mention teasing or whatever but doesn't convey much warmth.

"I didn't get to know him that much."

K = 1

PRIOR SIBLING RELATIONSHIP—RESENTMENT

1. *None*

Expresses no resentment toward amount of time or attention or love given to dying sibling.

2. *Slight*

Expresses some resentment that dying child received more than his share of time or attention but understood reason, no feeling of deceased child having been given more love by parents. May express something about competition.

"I don't think it's true to say that I went through a situation like that completely without resentment or feeling that it was unfair or why did they have to spend so much time with him, there must have been feelings of that, I'm sure I had feelings of that, but there were no lingering feelings of it, and it was obvious even then that the situation demanded it."

3. *High*

"I loved my brothers. I mean, you know, of course I did. But I felt they were getting all the attention and it was like I had to give negative attention to get attention. You know, I was the little hellion. You know, I would do things to aggravate them and get slapped, but, you know, at least I got attention. It wasn't that my mother and father weren't giving me attention. They were, but it was all being projected toward the sick children. And I think they probably thought I should've understood that, but I didn't."

K = 1

FAMILY COMMUNICATION AROUND
ILLNESS/DEATH

1. *Good*

"I knew my parents were very, very honest with us, so that I knew ... I had no fear that they knew something that I didn't."

"I think mom and dad explained it, you know, that her respiratory system and her digestive system weren't right and that she required therapy, and they gave her therapy at home and stuff, and also that she didn't have a normal life expectancy, you know, they let us know that. I think they pretty well laid it out for us right at the beginning."

2. *Veiled*

Parents may have dropped a hint; or person reports parents may have tried, but the child couldn't grasp it; or remembered some attempt but suspected own denial.

"They never really sat down and said, you know, this is what the problem is and this is what we're doing about it or trying to do about it, it was just little things that I picked up in conversation with grandma and grandpa or between themselves. It was just things I'd pick up now and again."

3. *Family secret*

Remember no discussion: for example, thinks they weren't the type parents who would have told their kids something like that.

"My parents didn't discuss it with us. Nowhere was it mentioned that this is a life-threatening disease or that the average life expectancy of a cystic is *x* years. It was never mentioned. Right up to the end they never mentioned it. I didn't know my brother was going to die until after he died. I had no idea it was coming. That's kind of naive, but kids are allowed to be. But I also wasn't prepared."

K = .85

AWARENESS OF DEATH

1. *Good*

Some understanding all along that death was a possibility at an early age.

"I knew he was going to die, I mean it was always explained to us that eventually they're all going to die. And the boys knew that too."

2. *Suspicion*

Siblings suspected something was wrong but it was not made explicit. Contradictory statements or psychological conflict.

"I was always very optimistic and bubbly and energetic, and then I didn't really understand the disease my sister had. I didn't really understand that it was fatal. So I kind of lived a happy life. My parents tried to do it that way. They didn't tell me that. But, I think I'm pretty sensitive and I was attuned to what was going on, because I can see, you know, sad faces. But to tell you the truth—you said what was it like. The one word I can just think of when you said that to me spontaneously I would say, 'hell.' A living hell. For everyone."

3. *Shock*

No awareness until death itself occurred or until the declining phase made it obvious (include last several years). No evidence in interview material that subject sensed possibility of death.

"I never really thought of him as being sick, because he seemed normal, you know, he played with us and the only time was when he was in the hospital, and then he would come home and he was fine."

K = 1

PARENTAL AVAILABILITY TO HELP
CHILD MOURN

(Rate separately for Father/Mother)

1. *Available*

Indication that the parents were not just there while child cried, but the reader got some sense that the parents made some attempt to help with work of mourning. Evidence of focus on help with loss, discounting reports brought back of actual death in hospital.

"My mother would more or less talk to us and I think tried to comfort us. She would say things like, 'she rode off to heaven on a white horse.' Somehow it was quite comforting to have those images, I don't know whose they were, or whether they were made up, or whether she actually said those things. I don't know if she [her sister] gave it to my mother and my mother in turn gave it to us, but it was a big help."

2. *Unavailable*

"I kind of felt left out I think. I remember S saying something about it at one time: 'Well, you weren't very, uh, you don't understand it, or you weren't very close to him anyway,' or something like that, and I felt really left out that nobody cared about what I thought about the whole thing. And I don't remember exactly what she said, but it was, uh, you know, you don't have any feelings because you're too little. And, you know, 'we don't have time for this, we're all too sad.' You know, that sort of thing. And I always thought, you know, well, geez, I feel bad too, you know."

K = 1

POSTDEATH PATERNAL AVAILABILITY

(Rate separately for Father/Mother)
Content of responses rated for subject's conception of parents as available following the loss.

1. *Withdrew further*
"My father really got withdrawn. As a matter of fact, he really kind of faded out of the picture. He would be down in the workshop all the time. And he really went crazy building things, he was constantly building things."
2. *Refocused*
"The problems started after my sister's death when my mother then wanted me to come in and make up for the difference of the loss of the two kids. And emotionally it wasn't there for me, the relationship had never developed. It was like you know, I needed you 10 years ago, not now. And by that time I had built up some very strong emotional ties with other people in my life and she wanted them to stop, and that's our problem now too."
3. *No change*
"My parents were the same afterward as they were before."

K = 1

GUILT

Content rated for the extent to which guilt plays a part in the subject's affective life; proneness to feeling guilty or "bad."

1. *None*
None expressed by subject.
2. *Moderate*
"I was graduating high school then, and she got sick just then. My parents were up here the day before I graduated. Unfortunately it was the night that she died. I didn't know that it was to that point, and of course they came home, and that made me feel even worse. I feel guilty about taking my parents away that night."

3. *High*

"I could write books about it, if anybody could. I feel guilty a lot. I feel self-inflicted. I almost look for it, so I do it by nature, and it's not good. It's not healthy."

"I don't know. I always feel guilty about everything. Even at work like taking a break when I'm supposed to or taking lunch. Maybe it had something to do with my younger years, the way I was brought up. I was always doing something wrong when I was growing up."

K = .88

RESULTS

Intercorrelations of Dependent Measures

The Kolmogorov–Smirnov Goodness of Fit test indicated that the scores on the anxiety and depression scales were normally distributed throughout the sample. Scores on the anxiety, depression, and guilt scales were strongly correlated with each other and in the expected direction. There were no significant gender differences on the dependent measures. It was decided that no further exploration of gender differences would be made since the small sample size did not permit analyses of sufficient statistical power.

Reliability analyses of the anxiety and depression scales were performed. The full anxiety scale demonstrated a standardized item alpha of .78 that improved to .81 with the removal of one item. The interitem correlation on depression as measured by the standardized item alpha for the full scale was .67, with removal of the four items with the lowest correlations yielding an improved standardized alpha of .72.

Contingency Tables of Independent Variables

The relationship of the rated independent measures of family functioning was assessed through the chi-square procedure. Out of 45 combinations, only 5 were significantly related to each other (awareness of death and family communication, sibling attachment and postdeath availability of father, sibling resentment and predeath availability of mother, availability of father to help mourn and availability of mother to help mourn, and postdeath availability of father and postdeath availability of mother). There was a trend for only 4 additional combinations (awareness of death and availability of mother to help mourn, family communication and availability of father to help mourn, family communication and availability of mother to help mourn, and sibling resentment and predeath availability of father). Therefore, specific hypotheses were tested, because the independent measures are not measuring the same variables.

The Analyses

T tests and one-way analysis of variance (ANOVA) were used to explore the relationship between the nature of family functioning and anxiety, depression and guilt. Nonparametric analyses were used when heteroscedasticity precluded use of ANOVA. Due to the small cell sizes, gender differences were not analyzed.

Predeath Availability of Mother for Survivor Sibling. Only two mothers had been rated as "unavailable" by respondents, thus this category was not included in the statistical analysis. These two cases were dropped in this analysis because there was no clear statistical rationale for their inclusion in either of the two remaining categories. One-tailed t tests yielded strong and consistent differences on anxiety, $t(21)= 5.28, p < .001$, between subjects whose mothers were rated "unpredictable" and those whose mothers were rated "available." That is, those who viewed their mothers as having been available to them have less anxiety, depression, and guilt than those who described their mothers as having been unpredictable.

Predeath Availability of Father for Survivor Sibling. The perceived predeath availability of fathers was examined by one-way ANOVAs. Significant differences between groups were found for guilt, $F (2,22) = 5.18, p < .05$ and a trend for depression, $F (2,22) = 2.67, p < .10$. There were no significant differences on anxiety between groups, $F (2,22) = 1.49$.

The Scheffé procedure of post hoc contrasts yielded significant differences for guilt between those fathers who were rated as available and those who were rated as unavailable.

Significant differences were also found between those who were rated as unpredictable and those who were rated as unavailable. That is, those siblings who reported their fathers as unavailable reported feeling the most guilty; those who saw their fathers as unpredictable reported feeling less guilty; and those who viewed their fathers as available reported feeling the least guilty.

Sibling Attachment. The quality of the preexisting attachment relationship between the sibling and the afflicted child was examined through one-way ANOVAs. Significant differences between groups were found for anxiety, $F(2,22) = 4.97$, $p < .05$, depression, $F(2,22) = 5.77$, $p < .01$, and guilt, $F(2,22) = 3.67$, $p < .05$.

For anxiety and depression, the Scheffé procedure of post hoc contrasts yielded significant differences between those who indicated only a slight degree of attachment and those who idealized the lost sibling, as well as between those who indicated a warm relationship and those who idealized the sibling. That is, the most anxious and depressed are those who idealized the sibling, less so are those who expressed a slight or warm attachment.

The three groups were next collapsed by whether the sibling was "idealized" or "not idealized," and one-tailed t tests were performed. Significant differences between the two groups were found for anxiety, $t(23) = 3.22$, $p < .01$, depression, $t(23) = 3.47$, $p < .01$, and a trend for guilt, $t(23) = 2.77$, $p < .10$. In other words, those who idealized the lost sibling were more anxious, depressed, and guilty than those who did not.

Resentment Scale. One-way ANOVAs were employed to assess the differences associated with the resentment expressed by the subject toward the deceased sibling. Significant differences were found between groups for anxiety, $F(2,22) = 3.77$, $p < .05$, and guilt, $F(2,22) = 7.31$, $p < .01$. There were no significant differences between groups on depression, $F(2,22) = 1.26$. Pair-wise comparisons through the Scheffé procedure indicated a significant difference between those who expressed slight resentment and those who expressed high resentment for both anxiety and guilt; that is, those who expressed strong resentment were more anxious and guilty than those who expressed only slight resentment.

A curvilinear relationship between expressed resentment and anxiety and guilt was explored. A trend analysis for both was performed and yielded a significant quadratic term for anxiety, $F(1,22) = 2.81$, $p < .05$, and guilt, $F(1,22) = 7.31$, $p < .01$.

Communication Variables. The Awareness of Death and Family Communication scales were examined using one-way analysis of variance on the dependent variables. Results were not significant on Awareness of Death for anxiety, $F(2,22) = .58$, depression, $F(2,22) = .48$, or guilt, $F(2,22) = .12$. There were no significant differences for Family Communication between groups on anxiety, $F(2,22) = .35$, depression, $F(2,22) = .76$, or guilt, $F(2,22) = .38$. The interrater reliability on both of the scales were also highly correlated with each other $\chi^2(4)$, $p < .001$. Thus, scaling problems would not account for the lack of findings. It was thought that perhaps the interaction of the two scales together predicts later anxiety, depression or guilt. Two-way ANOVA was used to explore interaction effects and no significant differences were found for anxiety, $F(2,24) = 1.63$, depression, $F(2,24) = .26$, or guilt, $F(2,24) = .66$.

Availability of Parents to Help Survivor Sibling Mourn. The impact of parental assistance with mourning on outcome was assessed using t tests. T tests indicated no significant differences between groups for fathers on anxiety, $t(23) = .61$, depression, $t(23) = .79$, or guilt, $t(23) = .53$. There were no significant differences between groups for mothers on anxiety, $t(23) = .05$, depression, $t(23) = .95$, or guilt, $t(23) = 1.24$.

Postdeath Parental Availability. The availability of the mother and father for the well sibling in relation to adaptation was not statistically explored as a change in the prior relationship was infrequent. That is, only one mother was rated as having withdrawn further, and only four parents were reported as having refocused following the death; interestingly enough, only one father was perceived as having refocused, while five withdrew further. Obviously, however, the majority of siblings reported no long-term change in the relationship after the death.

Structural Variables

Differences in Age Groupings

Participants were divided into three groups based on their age at the time of the death of the afflicted sibling: 9 to 12 (preadolescent), 13 to 17 (adolescent), and 18 years old (those already out of the home). One-way ANOVA was used to examine the differences of the three age groups outcome measures (see Table 1). Highly significant differences were found on all measures: anxiety, $F(2,22) = 6.34, p < .01$, depression, $F(2,22) = 4.72, p < .05$, and guilt, $F(2,22) = 10.33, p < .001$.

A curvilinear relationship (inverted u) between outcome and age was indicated for all dependent variables. A trend analysis was performed, and it yielded a highly significant quadratic term for each dependent variable: anxiety, $F(1,22) = 12.58, p < .01$, depression, $F(1,22) = 9.36, p < .01$, and guilt, $F(1,22) = 17.23, p < .001$.

TABLE 1
Age of Participant at Death of Sibling

Age	n	Anxiety		Depression		Guilt	
		Mean	SD	Mean	SD	Mean	SD
9–12	12	16.6	3.7	11.7	2.4	1.8	.9
13–17	8	21.3	2.8	14.1	2.2	3.0	.0
18	5	15.6	2.9	10.4	2.3	2.0	.0

Pairwise comparisons through the Scheffé procedure indicated the following significant differences:

1. For anxiety, between the preadolescents and adolescents, as well as between adolescents and 18-year-olds (the most anxious group are those who lost the sibling during adolescence, the next most anxious those who were preadolescent at the time, the least anxious were the 18-year-olds).
2. For depression, between adolescents and 18-year-olds (i.e., the most depressed were the adolescent group).
3. For guilt, between the preadolescents and adolescents, and adolescents and 18-year-olds (i.e., the most guilty were the adolescent group, the next most guilty were the 18 year olds, the least guilty were the preadolescent group).

The means for anxiety and depression are well above those of a random normative sample of community adults (see Table 2), and the adolescent group means are very high (see Table 3). Group differences are presented in Table 4.

TABLE 2
Comparison of Community Sample Symptom Levels

Symptoms	Community Sample*		Dissertation Sample	
	n	%	n	%
LIS Anxiety				
None	353	32	0	0
Some	685	62	11	44
High	64	6	14	56
LIS Depression				
None	278	25	0	0
Some	708	65	13	59
High	107	10	9	41

*Random sample ages 18 to 70 years old; from Lieberman and Mullan (1978).

TABLE 3
LISREL Group Means for Anxiety and Depression

Age	LIS Anxiety Means	LIS Depression Means
9–12	1.7	1.7
13–17	2.1	2.1
18	1.5	1.6

LIS Anxiety Levels: None = 1.0; Some = 1.0–1.7; High = 1.7
LIS Depression Levels: None = .9; Some = .9–1.8; High = 1.8

TABLE 4
Age-Differential Reactions

	Latency (%)	Adolescents (%)	18 Year Olds (%)
Symptoms			
Global guilt	25	100	0
Guilt over handling of illness and death	25	100	40
Survival guilt	17	50	0
Global anxiety	17	100	0
Bodily concerns	8	62	20
Carrier worries, with fear of intimacy	8	75	0
Excessive concern for others	0	50	20
Somatic expressions	33	88	0
Sleeping difficulties	25	88	40
Social Behaviors			
Married	50	13	80
Ever in therapy	25	75	20

Exploration of Possible Confounding Variables for Age Differences on Dependent Variables

The question that arises concerns whether contaminating factors could account for these apparent age differences. That is, it may be that what appear to be age-differential responses are actually reflective of other processes. For example, it seems possible that those siblings who were adolescent at the time of the loss experienced the loss more recently than those who were preadolescent, and therefore they may have had less time to recover. Or, perhaps those who lost a sibling during adolescence were more likely to have lost an older sibling, and presumably the afflicted child had lived longer and had developed more of a unique personality. Or, the adolescent group simply may have been exposed for a longer time to the potentially damaging effects of the chronic illness. That is, perhaps the chronicity of the illness depleted parental emotional resources more than exposure to a shorter duration of stress would have. And last, it is possible that family structural variables such as family size and birth order are implicated.

Number of Siblings Lost. Differences on outcome variables between those who had lost one sibling and those who lost two were assessed through t tests and were not significant on anxiety, $t(23) = .65$, depression, $t(23) = .26$ or guilt, $t(23) = .83$.

Birth Order.   Differences on outcome variables between survivor siblings who were first born, middle born or last born were assessed through ANOVAs and there were no significant differences on anxiety, $F(2,22) = 1.92$, depression, $F(2,22) =1.44$, or guilt, $F(2,22) = 1.02$.

Following the death, status changes in terms of birth order were assessed in relation to outcome measures (i.e., the survivor sibling became the oldest in the family, or a middle child became the youngest or the sole offspring), and there were no significant differences for anxiety, $F(3,21) = .64$, depression, $F(3,21)= .61$, or guilt , $F (3,21) = 1.31$.

Birth Order and Gender.   Two-way ANOVAs were used to explore the interaction of birth order and gender in relation to outcome. There were no significant differences in adaptation for age relationship on anxiety, $F(1,21) = 2.80$, depression, $F(1,21) = 1.72$, or guilt, $F (1,21) = .16$; nor gender relationship for anxiety, $F(1, 21) = 1.06$, depression, $F(1,21) = .30$, or guilt, $F(1,21) = 1.67$; nor the interaction for anxiety, $F(1,21) = 1.21$, depression, $F(1,21) = .09$, or guilt, $F(1,21) = .22$.

Family Size.   The relationship between the size of the family and sibling adaptation was explored through Pearson's correlation and no significance was found for family size before the death on anxiety, $r = .13$, depression, $r = -.04$), or guilt, $r = -.25$, or after the death on anxiety, $r = -.14$, depression, $r = -.02$), or guilt $r = -.16$.

Distance From Death for Sibling.   It was possible that those who had lost their sibling during their adolescence had experienced the death more recently than those who had experienced the death during preadolescence and were therefore more disturbed. Pearson's correlation was used to examine the relationship between the distance from death and outcome measures and it was not significant for anxiety, $r = .17$, depression, $r = .01$, or guilt, $r = .06$.

Age of Sibling Who Died.   It was thought possible that it was harder to lose a sibling who had lived longer than one who might have died earlier. The relationship between age of the afflicted child at death and sibling adaptation was explored through Pearson's correlation and the relationship was significant for anxiety only, $r = .39, p < .05$, and a trend for guilt, $r = .31$, $p < .1$. The relationship was not significant for depression, $r = .17$. Since it was thought possible that the adolescent group of subjects had been more likely to have lost a sibling who was older than the preadolescent group, age of afflicted child at death was assessed in relation to the three age groupings and there were no significant differences between groups, $F(2,22) = 1.32$.

Duration of the Process for the Sibling.   It was thought possible that the length of time that the sibling lived with a dying child may be related to adaptation later on. Length of time that the sibling was directly exposed to this process was operationalized as lthe date of last death minus the date of the first birth of the child with CF and the relationship was explored through Pearson's correlation. Findings were not significant for anxiety, $r = -.21$, or depression, $r = -.21$; an association for guilt only was found, $r = -.31$, but in the opposite direction one might expect.

Duration of Stress Process for Parents.   It was thought possible that the length of time that the parents had had to cope with a dying child might be related to sibling adaptation. Duration of the stress process for the parents was operationalized as the date of the last death minus the date of diagnosis for the first child with CF and the relationship was examined through Pearson's correlation. Findings were not significant for anxiety, $r = -.19$; associations were found for guilt, $r = -.41$, and depression, $r = -.28$, but, as with duration of the process for the sibling, results are in the opposite direction one might expect.

References

Abraham, K. (1924). A short study of the development of the libido viewed in the light of the mental disorders. In E. Jones (Ed.), *Selected papers of Karl Abraham M.D.* (Vol. 13, pp. 418–501). London: Hogarth Press.

Ainsworth, M. D. S., Blehar, M. C., Waters, E., & Wall, S. (1978). *Patterns of attachment.* New York: Wiley.

Altschul, S. (1968). Denial and ego arrest. *Journal of the American Psychoanalytic Association, 16,* 301–318.

American Psychiatric Association. (1994). *Diagnostic and statistical manual of mental disorders* (4th ed.). Washington, DC: Author.

Aries, P. (1975). The reversal of death: Changes in attitudes toward death in western societies. In D. Stannard (Ed.), *Death in America* (pp. 134–158). Philadelphia: University of Pennsylvania Press.

Armstrong-Dailey, A., & Goltzer, S. Z. (1993). *Hospice care for children.* Oxford: Oxford University Press.

Balk, D. E. (1983). Effects of sibling death on teenagers. *Journal of School Health, 53,* 14–18.

Balk, D. E. (1990). The self-concepts of bereaved adolescents: Sibling death and its aftermath. *Journal of Adolescent Research, 5,* 112–132.

Balk, D. E. (1991). Death and adolescent bereavement: Current research and future directions. *Journal of Adolescent Research, 6,* 7–27.

Bank, S., & Kahn, M. (1982). *The sibling bond.* New York: Basic Books.

Barnard, C., in collaboration with Bill Pepper. (1970). *One life.* New York: Macmillan.

Barocas, H. A., & Barocas, C. B. (1979). Wounds of the fathers: The next generation of Holocaust victims. *International Review of Psychoanalysis, 6,* 331–343.

Bearison, D. J., & Mulhern, R. K. (1994). *Pediatric psychooncology: Psychological research on children with cancer.* Oxford: Oxford University Press.

Becker, E. (1973). *The denial of death.* New York: The Free Press.

Benedek, T. (1959). Parenthood as a developmental phase: A contribution to the libido theory. *Journal of the American Psychoanalytic Association, 7,* 389–417.

Benner, P., Roskies, E., & Lazarus, R. (1980). Stress and coping under extreme conditions. In J. E. Dimsdale (Ed.), *Survivors, victims and perpetrators: Essays on the Nazi holocaust* (pp. 219–258). Washington, DC: Hemisphere.

Bergler, E. (1948). Psychopathology and duration of mourning in neurotics. *Journal of Clinical Psychopathology, 9,* 478–482.

Berlinsky, E. B., & Biller, H. B. (1982). *Parental death and psychological development.* Lexington, MA: DC Heath.

Berman, L. E. (1978). Sibling loss as an organizer of unconscious guilt: A case study. *Psychoanalytic Quarterly, 47*(4), 568–587.

Binger, C. M., Ablin, A. R., Feuerstein, R. C., Kushner, J. H., Zoger, S., & Mikkelsen, C. (1969). Childhood leukemia. Emotional impact on patient and family. *New England Journal of Medicine, 280,* 414–418.

Birenbaum, A. (1970). On managing a courtesy stigma. *Journal of Health and Social Behavior, 11,* 196–206.

Birenbaum, A. (1971). The mentally retarded child in the home and the family cycle. *Journal of Health and Social Behavior, 12,* 55–65.

Birenbaum, L. K., Robinson, M. A., Phillips, D. S., Stewart, B. S., & McCown, D. E. (1989). The response of children to the dying and death of a sibling. *Omega, 20,* 213–228.

Black, D., & Urbanowicz, M. A. (1987). Family intervention with bereaved children. *Journal of Child Psychology and Psychiatry and Allied Disciplines, 28,* 467–476.

Blos, P. (1962). *On adolescence.* New York: The Free Press.

Bluebond-Langner, M. (1991a). Living with cystic fibrosis: A family affair. In J. Morgan (Ed.), *Young people and death* (pp. 46–62). Philadelphia: Charles Press.

Bluebond-Langner, M. (1991b). Living with cystic fibrosis: The well sibling's perspective. *Medical Anthropology Quarterly, 5,* 133–152.

Blum, G., & Rosenzweig, S. (1944). The incidence of sibling and parental deaths in the anamnesis of female schizophrenics. *Journal of General Psychology, 31,* 3–13.

Boer, F., & Dunn, J. (Eds.). (1992). *Sibling relationships: Developmental and clinical issues.* Hillsdale, NJ: Lawrence Erlbaum Associates.

Bowlby, J. (1961a). Childhood mourning and its implications for psychiatry. *American Journal of Psychiatry, 118,* 481–498.

Bowlby, J. (1961b). Processes of mourning. *International Journal of Psycho-Analysis, 42,* 317–340.

Bowlby, J. (1969). *Attachment and loss (Vol. 1): Attachment.* New York: Basic Books.

Bowlby, J. (1973). *Attachment and loss (Vol. 2): Separation: Anxiety and anger.* New York: Basic Books.

Bowlby, J. (1979). *The making and breaking of affectional bonds.* London: Tavistock.

Bowlby, J. (1980). *Attachment and loss (Vol. 3): Loss: Sadness and depression.* New York: Basic Books.

Bozeman, M. F., Orbach, C. E., & Sutherland, A. M. (1955). Psychological impact of cancer and its treatment: The adaptation of mothers to the threatened loss of their children through leukemia: Part l. *Cancer, 8,* 1–19.

Breslau, N. (1982). Siblings of disabled children: Birth order and age-spacing effects. *Journal of Abnormal Child Psychology, 10,* 85–96.

Breslau, N., & Prabucki, K. (1987). Siblings of disabled children. Effects of chronic stress in the family. *Archives of General Psychiatry, 44,* 1040–1046.

Breslau, N., Wietzman, M., & Messenger, K. (1981). Psychological functioning of siblings of disabled children. *Pediatrics, 67,* 344–353.

Cain, A. C., Fast, I., & Erikson, M. E. (1964). Children's disturbed reactions to the death of a sibling. *American Journal of Orthopsychiatry, 34,* 741–752.

Caudman, D., Boyle, M., & Offord, D. R. (1988). The Ontario Child Health Study: Social adjustment and mental health of siblings of children with chronic health problems. *Journal of Developmental and Behavioral Pediatrics, 9,* 117–121.

Chodorow, N. (1978). *The reproduction of mothering: Psychoanalysis and the sociology of gender.* Berkeley: University of California Press.

Cowen, L., Mok, J., Corey, M., MacMillan, H., Simmons, R., & Levison, H. (1986). Psychological adjustment of the family with a member who has cystic fibrosis. *Pediatrics, 77,* 743–753.

Crain, A. J., Sussman, M. B., & Weil, W. B. (1966). Effects of a diabetic child on marital integration and related measures of family functioning. *Journal of Health and Human Behavior, 7,* 122–127.

Cystic Fibrosis Foundation. (1995). *Facts about CF.* Bethesda, MD: Author.

Davies, E. B. (1983). *Behavioral responses to the death of a sibling.* Unpublished doctoral dissertation, University of Washington, Seattle.

Davies, E. B. (1988). The family environment in bereaved families and its relationship to surviving sibling behavior. *Children's Health Care, 17,* 22–30.

Davis, F. (1963). *Passage through crisis: Polio victims and their families.* Indianapolis, IN: Bobbs-Merrill.

Derogatis, L. R., Lipman, R. S., Covi, L., & Rickles, K. (1971). Neurotic symptom dimensions. *Archives of General Psychiatry, 24,* 454–464.

Deutsch, H. (1937). The absence of grief. *Neuroses and character types* (pp. 226–236). New York: International Universities Press.

Drotar, D., Doershuk, C. F., Stern, R. C., Boat, T. F., Boer, W., & Matthews, L. (1981). Psychosocial functioning of children with cystic fibrosis. *Pediatrics, 67,* 338–343.

Dunn, J. (1985). *Sisters and brothers.* Cambridge, MA: Harvard University Press.

Durkheim, E. (1961). *The elementary forms of the religious life.* New York: Collier Books.

Dyson, L. L. (1989). Adjustment of siblings of handicapped children: A comparison. *Journal of Pediatric Psychology, 14,* 215–229.

Engel, G. (1961). Is grief a disease? A challenge for medical research. *Psychosomatic Medicine, 23,* 18–22.

Eth, S., & Pynoos, R. S. (Eds.). (1985). Post-traumatic stress disorder in children. In D. Spiegel (Ed.), *Progress in psychiatry series.* Washington, DC: American Psychiatric Press.

Fanos, J. H. (1987). *Developmental consequences for adulthood of early sibling loss, Dissertations Abstracts International, 48*–08B, #8723871

Fanos, J. H., & Johnson, J. P. (1992). Still living with cystic fibrosis: The well sibling revisited. *Pediatric Pulmonology, 8* (Suppl.), 228–229.

Fanos, J. H., & Johnson, J. P. (1993). Barriers to carrier testing for CF siblings (Abstract). *American Journal of Human Genetics, 53,* 51.

Fanos, J. H., & Johnson, J. P. (1994). CF carrier status: The importance of not knowing (Abstract). *American Journal of Human Genetics, 55*, 1711.

Fanos, J. H., & Johnson, J. P. (1995a). Perception of carrier status by cystic fibrosis siblings. *American Journal of Human Genetics, 57*, 431–438.

Fanos, J. H., & Johnson, J. P. (1995b). Barriers to carrier testing for adult cystic fibrosis sibs: The importance of not knowing. *American Journal of Medical Genetics, 59*, 85–91.

Fanos, J. H., & Nickerson, B. G. (1991). Long-term effects of sibling death during adolescence. In D. Balk (Ed.), Death and adolescent bereavement [Special issue]. *Journal of Adolescent Research, 6*, 70–82.

Fanos, J. H., & Wiener, L. (1994). Tomorrow's survivors: Siblings of human immunodeficiency virus-infected children. *Developmental and Behavioral Pediatrics, 15*(Suppl. 3), S43–S48.

Farkas, A. (1974). Adaptation of patients, siblings, and mothers to cystic fibrosis (Doctoral dissertation, Michigan State University, 1973). *Dissertations Abstracts International, 34B*, 4659–4660.

Ferrari, M. (1984). Chronic illness: Psychosocial effects on siblings—I. Chronically ill boys. *Journal of Child Psychology and Psychiatry and Allied Disciplines, 25*, 459–476.

Ferrari, M. (1987). The diabetic child and well sibling: Risks to the well child's self-concept. *Children's Health Care, 15*, 141–148.

Fleming, J. (1963). Evaluation of a research project in psychoanalysis. In H. S. Gaskill (Ed.), *Counterpoint: Libidinal object and subject* (pp. 75–105). New York: International Universities Press.

Fleming, J., & Altschul, S. (1963). Activation of mourning and growth by psychoanalysis. *International Journal of Psycho-Analysis, 44*, 419–431.

Freud, A. (1946). *The ego and mechanisms of defense.* New York: International Universities Press.

Freud, S. (1917). Mourning and melancholia. *Standard Edition, XIV*, 243–272.

Freud, S. (1918). From the history of an infantile neurosis. *Standard Edition, XVII*, 7–122.

Freud, S. (1926). Inhibitions, symptoms and anxiety. *Standard Edition, XX*, 77–175.

Freud, S. (1927). Fetishism. *Standard Edition, XXI*, 149–157.

Friedman, S. B., Chodoff, P., Mason, J. W., & Hamburg, D. A. (1963). Behavioral observations of parents anticipating the death of a child. *Pediatrics, 32*, 610–625.

Fromm, E. (1944). *The individual and social origins of neurosis.* New York: American Sociological Review.

Futterman, E., & Hoffman, I. (1973). Crisis and adaptation in the families of fatally ill children. The child in his family, II. In J. Anthony & C. Koupernik (Eds.), *The child in his family* (pp. 37–47). New York: Wiley-Interscience.

Gayton, W. F., Friedman, S. B., Tavormena, J. F., & Tucker, F. (1977). Children with cystic fibrosis: I. Psychological test findings of patients, siblings and parents. *Pediatrics, 59*, 888–894.

Geertz, C. (1957). Ritual and social change: A Javanese example. *American Anthropologist, 59*, 32–54.

Goody, J. (1975). Death and the interpretation of culture: A bibliographic overview. In D. Stannard (Ed.), *Death in America* (pp. 1–8). Philadelphia: University of Pennsylvania Press.

Gordon, N., & Kutner, B. (1965). Long term and fatal illness and the family. *Journal of Health and Human Behavior, 6,* 190–196.

Gorer, G. (1965). *Death, grief and mourning.* London: Cresset Press.

Gray, R. E. (1987). Adolescent response to the death of a parent. *Journal of Youth and Adolescence, 16,* 511–525.

Greenacre, P. (1957). The childhood of the artist: Libidinal phase development and giftedness. *Psychoanalytic Study of the Child, 12,* 47–72.

Gruszk, M. A. (1988). *Family functioning and sibling adjustment in families with a handicapped child.* Unpublished doctoral dissertation, University of Rhode Island, Kingston.

Hardy, M. S., Armstrong, F. D., Routh, D. K., Albrecht, J., & Davis, J. (1994). Coping and communication among parents and children with human immunodeficiency virus and cancer. *Developmental and Behavioral Pediatrics, 15* (Suppl. 3), S49–S53.

Hetherington, E. M., Reiss, D., & Plomin, R. (1993). *The separate social worlds of siblings: The impact of nonshared environment on development.* Hillsdale, NJ: Lawrence Erlbaum Associates.

Hoare, P. (1984). Does illness foster dependency? A study of epileptic and diabetic children. *Developmental Medicine and Child Neurology, 26,* 20–24.

Horney, K. (1950). *Neurosis and human growth.* New York: Norton.

Horowitz, M. J. (1986). *Stress response syndromes.* Northvale, NJ: Aronson.

Howe, G. W. (1993). The effects of mental retardation, disabilities and illness on sibling relationships: Research issues and challenges. In Z. Stoneman & P. W. Berman (Eds.), *Research on siblings of children with mental retardation, physical disabilities and chronic illness* (pp. 185–213). Baltimore, MD: Paul H. Brookes.

Kazak, A. E., & Clark, M. W. (1986). Stress in families of children with myelomeningocele. *Developmental Medicine and Child Neurology, 28,* 220–228.

Kestenberg, J. S. (1980). Psychoanalyses of children of survivors from the Holocaust: Case presentations and assessment. *Journal of the American Psychoanalytic Association, 28,* 775–804.

Klass, D. (1988). *Parental grief: Solace and resolution.* New York: Springer.

Klein, M. (1940). Mourning and its relation to manic-depressive states. *Contributions to psychoanalysis, 1921–1945* (pp. 311–338). New York: McGraw Hill.

Klein, M. (1957). *Envy and gratitude: A study of unconscious sources.* New York: Basic Books.

Kliman, G. (1973). Facilitation of mourning during childhood. In I. Gerber, A. Weiner, & A. H. Kutscher (Eds.), *Perspectives on bereavement* (pp. 76–100). New York: Arno Press.

Koch, A. (1985). If only it could be me: The families of pediatric cancer patients. *Family Relations, 34,* 63–70.

Koch-Hattem, A. (1986). Siblings' experience of pediatric cancer: Interviews with children. *Health and Social Work, 11,* 107–117.

Kohut, H. (1971). The analysis of the self: A systematic approach to the psychoanalytic treatment of narcissistic personality disorders. *Psychoanalytic study of the child,
Monograph no. 4.* New York: International Universities Press.

Kohut, H. (1977). *The restoration of the self.* New York: International Universities
Press.

Koocher, G. P., & O'Malley, J. E. (1981). *The Damocles syndrome: Psychosocial consequences of surviving childhood cancer.* New York: McGraw Hill.

Kramer, R. F. (1984). Living with childhood cancer: Impact on healthy siblings.
Oncology Nursing Forum, 11, 44–51.

Krell, R. (1979). Holocaust families: The survivors and their children. *Comprehensive
Psychiatry, 20,* 560–568.

Krell, R., & Rabkin, L. (1979). The effects of sibling death on the surviving child: A
family perspective. *Family Processes, 18,* 471–477.

Kris, E. (1952). *Psychoanalytic explorations in art.* New York: International Universities Press.

Kushner, H. S. (1981). *When bad things happen to good people.* New York: Shocken.

Lamb, M., & Sutton-Smith, B. (1982). *Sibling relationships: Their nature and significance
across the lifespan.* Hillsdale, NJ: Lawrence Erlbaum Associates.

Laufer, M. (1973). The analysis of a child of survivors. In J. E. Anthony & C.
Koupernik (Eds.), *The child in his family, II: The impact of disease and death* (pp.
363–73). New York: Wiley.

Lavigne, J. V., & Ryan, M. (1979). Psychological adjustment of siblings of children
with chronic illness. *Pediatrics, 63,* 616–624.

Lavigne, J. V., Traisman, H. S., Marr, T. J., & Chasnoff, I. J. (1982). Parental
perceptions of the psychological adjustment of children with diabetes and their
siblings. *Diabetes Care, 5,* 420–426.

Lawler, R. H., Nakiekny, W., & Wright, M. A. (1966). Psychological implications of
cystic fibrosis. *Canadian Medical Association Journal, 94,* 1043–1046.

Leiken, S., & Hassakis, P. (1973). Psychological study of parents of children with
cystic fibrosis. In J. Anthony & C. Koupernik (Eds.), *The child in his family, II, The
impact of disease and death* (pp. 49–57). New York: Wiley.

Levine, H. B. (1982). Toward a psychoanalytic understanding of children of survivors of the holocaust. *Psychoanalytic Quarterly, 51,* 70–92.

Lieberman, M. A., & Mullan, J. T. (1978). Does help help? The adaptive consequences
of obtaining help from professionals and social networks. *American Journal of
Community Psychology, 6,* 499–517.

Lifton, R. (1979). *The broken connection: On death and the continuity of life.* New York:
Simon & Schuster.

Lindemann, E. (1944). Symptomatology and management of acute grief. *American
Journal of Psychiatry, 101,* 141–148.

Lipkowitz, M. (1973). The child of two survivors: A report of an unsuccessful
therapy. *Israeli Annals of Psychiatry, 11,* 141–155.

Lobato, D. (1990). *Brothers, sisters, and special needs: Information and activities for
helping young siblings of children with chronic illnesses and developmental disabilities.*
Baltimore, MD: Paul H. Brookes.

Loewald, H. W. (1962). Internalization, separation, mourning and the superego. *Psychoanalytic Quarterly, 31,* 483–504.

Lowenthal, M. F., Thurnher, M., Chiriboga, D., & Associates (1975). *Four stages of life: A comparative study of women and men facing transitions.* San Francisco: Jossey-Bass.

Mahler, M. S., Pine, F., & Bergman, A. (1975). *The psychological birth of the human infant: Symbiosis and individuation.* New York: Basic Books.

Malinowski, B. L. (1948). *Magic, science and religion and other essays.* Boston: Beacon Press.

Mandelbaum, D. G. (1976). Social uses of funeral rites. In R. L. Fulton (Ed.), *Death and identity* (pp. 343–363). Bowie: Charles Press Publishers.

Martinson, I. M., & Campos, R. G. (1991). Adolescent bereavement: Long-term responses to a sibling's death from cancer. *Journal of Adolescent Research, 6,* 54–69.

Mellinger, G., & Balter, M. (1982). *Collaborative Project. GMIRSB Report.* Washington, DC: National Institute of Mental Health.

Mellins, C., & Ehrhardt, A. (1993). Families affected by pediatric AIDS: Sources of stress and coping. *International Conference of AIDS, 9,* 120.

Miller, J. B. (1971). Children's reactions to the death of a parent: A review of the psychoanalytic literature. *Journal of the American Psychoanalytic Association, 19,* 697–719.

Mitford, J. (1978). *The American way of death.* New York: Simon & Schuster.

Modell, A., Weiss, J., & Sampson, H. (1983). Narcissism, masochism and the sense of guilt in relation to the therapeutic process (Bulletin No. 6 of the Psychotherapy Research Group). Department of Psychiatry, Mt. Zion Hospital, San Francisco, CA.

Moriarty, D. M. (1967). *The loss of loved ones: The effects of a death in the family on personality development.* Springfield, IL: Charles C. Thomas.

Murphy, P. A. (1986–1987). Parental death in childhood and loneliness in young adults. *Omega, 17,* 219–228.

Nagy, M. H. (1948). The child's view of death. In H. Feifel (Ed.), *The meaning of death* (pp. 79–98). New York: McGraw-Hill.

Natterson, J. M., & Knudson, A. G. (1960). Observations concerning fear of death in fatally ill children and their mothers. *Psychosomatic Medicine, 22,* 456–465.

Niederland, W. (1981). The survivor syndrome: Further observations and dimensions. *Journal of the American Psychoanalytic Association, 29,* 413–425.

Oltjenbruns, K. A. (1991). Positive outcomes of adolescents' experience with grief. *Journal of Adolescent Research, 6,* 43–53.

Oremland, J. D. (1989). *Michelangelo's Sistine ceiling: A psychoanalytic study of creativity.* Madison, CT: International Universities Press.

Parkes, C. (1982). Attachment and the prevention of mental disorders. In C.M. Parkes & J. S. Hinde (Eds.), *The place of attachment in human behavior* (pp. 295–310). New York: Basic Books.

Parsons, T. (1951). *The social system.* Glencoe, IL: The Free Press.

Parsons, T., & Fox, T. (1952). Illness, therapy and the modern urban American family. *Journal of Social Issues, 8,* 31–44.

Patterson, J. M., Budd, J., Goetz, D., & Warwick, W. J. (1993). Family correlates of a 10-year pulmonary health trend in cystic fibrosis. *Pediatrics, 91*, 383–389.

Pearlin, L. I. (1980). Life strains and psychological distress among adults. In N. Smelser & E. H. Erikson (Eds.), *Themes of work and love in adulthood* (pp. 174–192). Cambridge, MA: Harvard University Press.

Pearlin, L. I., Lieberman, M. A., Menaghan, E. G., & Mullan, J. T. (1981). The stress process. *Journal of Health and Social Behavior, 22*, 337–356.

Pearlin, L. I., & Schooler, C. (1978). The structure of coping. *Journal of Health and Social Behavior, 19*, 2–21.

Phillips, R. E. (1978). Impact of Nazi holocaust on children of survivors. *American Journal of Psychotherapy, 32*, 370–378.

Phillips, S., Bohannon, W. E., Gayton, W. F., & Friedman, S. B. (1985). Parent interview findings regarding the impact of cystic fibrosis on families. *Journal of Developmental and Behavioral Pediatrics, 6*, 122–127.

Pollock, G. H. (1961). Mourning and adaptation. *International Journal of Psycho-Analysis, 42*, 341–361.

Pollock, G. H. (1972). Bertha Pappenheim's pathological mourning: Possible effects of childhood sibling loss. *Journal of the American Psychoanalytic Association, 20*, 476–493.

Pollock, G. H. (1977). The mourning process and creative organizational change. *Journal of the American Psychoanalytic Association, 25*, 3–34.

Pollock, G. H. (1978). On siblings, childhood sibling loss, and creativity. *Annual of Psychoanalysis, 6*, 443–481.

Pollock, G. H. (1986). Childhood sibling loss: A family tragedy. *Annals of Psycho-analysis, 14*, 5–34.

Pollock, G. H. (1989). *The mourning liberation process* (Vols. 1–2). Madison, CT: International Universities Press.

Pound, A. (1982). Attachment and maternal depression. In C. M. Parkes & J. Stevenson-Hinde (Eds.), *The place of attachment in human behavior* (pp. 118–130). New York: Basic Books.

Quittner, A. L., Di Girolamo, A. M., Michel, M., & Eigen, H. (1992). Parental response to cystic fibrosis: A contextual analysis of the diagnosis phase. *Journal of Pediatric Psychology, 17*, 683–704.

Raphael, B. (1983). *The anatomy of bereavement*. New York: Basic Books.

Rochlin, G. (1965). *Griefs and discontents, the forces of change*. Boston: Little, Brown.

Rommens, J. M., Iannuzzi, M. C., Kerem, B-S., Drumm, M. L., Melmer, G., Dean, M., Rozmahel, R., Close, J. L., Kennedy, D., Hidaka, N., Zsigan, M., Buchwald, M., Riordan, J. R., Tsui, L-C., & Collins, F. S. (1989). Identification of the cystic fibrosis gene: Chromosome walking and jumping. *Science, 245*, 1059–1080.

Root, N. N. (1957). A neurosis in adolescence. *Psychoanalytic Study of the Child, 12*, 320–334.

Rosen, H. (1985). *Unspoken grief: Coping with childhood sibling loss*. Lexington, MA: Lexington.

Rosenblatt, P. C., Walsh, R. P., & Jackson, D. A. (1976). *Grief and mourning in cross-cultural perspective*. New Haven, CT: Human Relations Areas Files Press.

Rosenzweig, S. (1943). Sibling death as a psychological experience with special reference to schizophrenia. *Psychoanalytic Review, 30*, 177–186.

Rosow, I. (1974). *Socialization to old age.* Berkeley: University of California Press.

Rubin, S. S. (1985). The resolution of bereavement: A clinical focus on the relationship to the deceased. *Psychotherapy: Theory, Research, Training and Practice, 22*, 231–235.

Russell, A. (1974). Late psychosocial consequences in concentration camp survivor families. *American Journal of Pathology, 44*, 611–619.

Sampson, H. (1983). *Pathogenic beliefs and unconscious guilt in the therapeutic process: Clinical observation and research evidence.* (Bulletin No. 6 of the Psychotherapy Research Group, pp. 32–33). Department of Psychiatry, Mt. Zion Hospital, San Francisco, CA.

Searles, H. F. (1960). *The non-human environment, in normal development and in schizophrenia.* New York: International Universities Press.

Siegel, K., & Gorey, E. (1994). Childhood bereavement due to parental death from acquired immunodeficiency syndrome. *Developmental and Behavioral Pediatrics, 15* (Suppl. 3), S66–S70.

Sigal, J. J. (1971). Second generation effects of massive psychic trauma. In H. Krystal & W. Niederland (Eds.), *Psychic traumatization: After-effects in individuals and communities* (pp. 55–65). Boston: Little, Brown.

Silverman, P. R., Nickman, S., & Worden, J. W. (1992). Detachment revisited: The child's reconstruction of a dead parent. *American Journal of Orthopsychiatry, 62*, 494–503.

Silverman, P. R., & Worden, J. W. (1992). Children's reactions in the early months after the death of a parent. *American Journal of Orthopsychiatry, 62*, 93–104.

Sims, A. (1986). *Am I still a sister?* Albuquerque, NM: Big A.

Spinetta, J. J. (1981). The sibling of the child with cancer. In J. J. Spinetta & P. Deasy-Spinetta (Eds.), *Living with childhood cancer* (pp. 133–142). St. Louis, MO: Mosby.

Spinetta, J. J., & Maloney, L. J. (1978). The child with cancer: Patterns of communication and denial. *Journal of Consulting Clinical Psychology, 46*, 1540–1541.

Spitz, R., & Woolff, K. (1946). Anaclitic depression: An inquiry into the genesis of psychiatric conditions in early childhood, II. *Psychoanalytic study of the child, 4*, 313–342.

Tasker, M. (1992). *How can I tell you?* Bethesda, MD: Association for Care of Children's Heath.

Terr, L. (1991). *Too scared to cry.* New York: Harper Row.

Tritt, S. G., & Esses, L. M. (1988). Psychosocial adaptation of siblings of children with chronic medical illnesses. *American Journal of Orthopsychiatry, 58*, 211–220.

Tropauer, A., Franz, M. N., & Dilgard, V. W. (1970). Psychological aspects of the care of children with cystic fibrosis. *American Journal of Diseases of Children, 119*, 424–432.

Trossman, B. (1968). Adolescent children of concentration camp survivors. *Canadian Psychiatric Association Journal, 13*, 121–123.

Turk, J. (1964). Impact of cystic fibrosis on family functioning. *Pediatrics, 34*, 67–71.

Vaillant, G. E. (1977). *Adaptation to life.* Boston: Little, Brown.

Valverde, K. & Denning, C. (1991). *American Journal of Human Genetics, 49* (Suppl.), Abstract 1769.

Van der Kolk, B. A. (1987). *Psychological trauma.* Washington DC: American Psychiatric Press.

Vance, J. C., Fazan, L. E., Satterwhite, B., & Pless, I. B. (1980). Effects of nephrotic syndrome on the family: A controlled study. *Pediatrics, 65,* 948–955.

Volkart, E. H., & Michael, S. T. (1976). Bereavement and mental health. In R. L. Fulton (Ed.), *Death and identity* (pp. 239–257). Philadelphia: Charles Press.

Wahl, C. (1976). The fear of death. In R. L. Fulton (Ed.), *Death and identity* (pp. 56–66). Philadelphia: Charles Press.

Wallace, F. C. (1966). *Religion: An anthropological view.* New York: Random House.

Wallerstein, J. S., & Blakeslee, S. (1989). *Second chances: Men, women and children a decade after divorce.* New York: Ticknor & Fields.

Wallerstein, J. S., & Kelly, J. B. (1980). *Surviving the breakup: How children and parents cope with divorce.* New York: Basic Books.

Warner, W. L. (1976). The city of the dead. In R. L. Fulton (Ed.), *Death and identity* (pp. 363–381). Philadelphia: Charles Press.

Wertz, D. C., Fanos, J. H., & Reilly, P. R. (1994). Genetic testing for children and adolescents: Who decides? *Journal of the American Medical Association, 272,* 875–881.

Winnicott, D. W. (1953). Transitional objects and transitional phenomenon. *International Journal of Psychoanalysis, 34,* 89–97.

Wolf, E., & Wolf, I. (1979). We perished, each alone: A psychoanalytic commentary on Virginia Woolf's "To the Lighthouse." *International Review of Psycho-Analysis, 6,* 37–47.

Wolfenstein, M. (1966). How is mourning possible? *Psychoanalytic Study of the Child, 21,* 93–123.

Wolfenstein, M. (1969). Loss, rage and repetition. *Psychoanalytic Study of the Child, 24,* 432–460.

Wortman, C. B., & Silver, R. C. (1989). The myths of coping with loss. *Journal of Consulting and Clinical Psychology, 57,* 349–357.

Author Index

Subject Index

A

Accident-prone behavior, 19, 37, 85, 89, 93, 109, 118–121
Adolescents
  accepting the truth and, 51
  alcohol and, 85
  anger and, 64, 65
  anxiety and, 95
  denial of death and, 65
  fear of being carriers and, 92–94
  guilt and, 64, 116, 117
  handling of death and, 117
  hypochondriac concerns and, 95
  individuation and, 76
  isolation and, 66
  losing religious faith and, 65–68
  mourning and, 107
  reaction of peers and, 65
  shock of death and, 63, 64
  siblings and, 49–52
  see Intimacy, Siblings
Adults
  anger at parents denial of death, 68, 69
  awareness of impact of death, 123, 124
  defenses and, 122
  expressions of love, 66, 67
  fear of being carrier, 100
  final hours with sibling, 67, 68
  guilt and, 122
  helping with life/death decisions, 67
  memories of death, 67
  mourning by, 111
  overconcern for others, 97
  overprotection of children, 101
  self-esteem and, 112
  spousal support, 60

  supporting parents, 68
  see Memory of siblings
Alcohol
  adolescents, 85
  as aid, 104
  mothers and, 30, 32
  siblings and, xiii
Amnesia
  about childhood, 25, 91
Anger, 88
  parental, xiv
  see Parental anger
Anxiety, 98, 100, 105, 113, 114
  adolescents and, 95
  death and, 126
  siblings and, xiv
Attachment, 38–43
  creativity, 22
  insecure attachment, 16, 18, 21
  to sibling, xiii
  to surviving child, 114
  see Substitution
Attention
  parental, 86
  refocusing by parents, 86
  refocusing on sibling, 75, 76
  sibling need for, 74, 75, 115
  see Substitution

B

Bedwetting, 37
Birth order
  sibling death and, 43, 44
Blame, 32, 87, 88
  dealing with, 138
  parental feelings of, 71–73